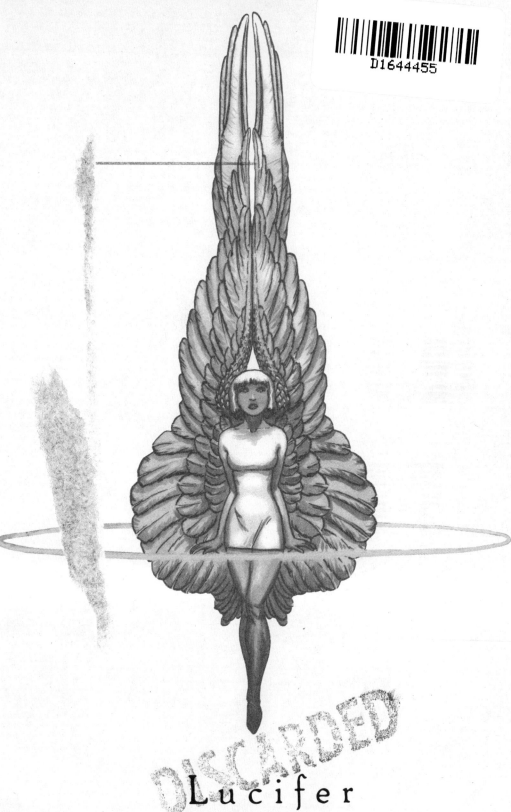

Lucifer

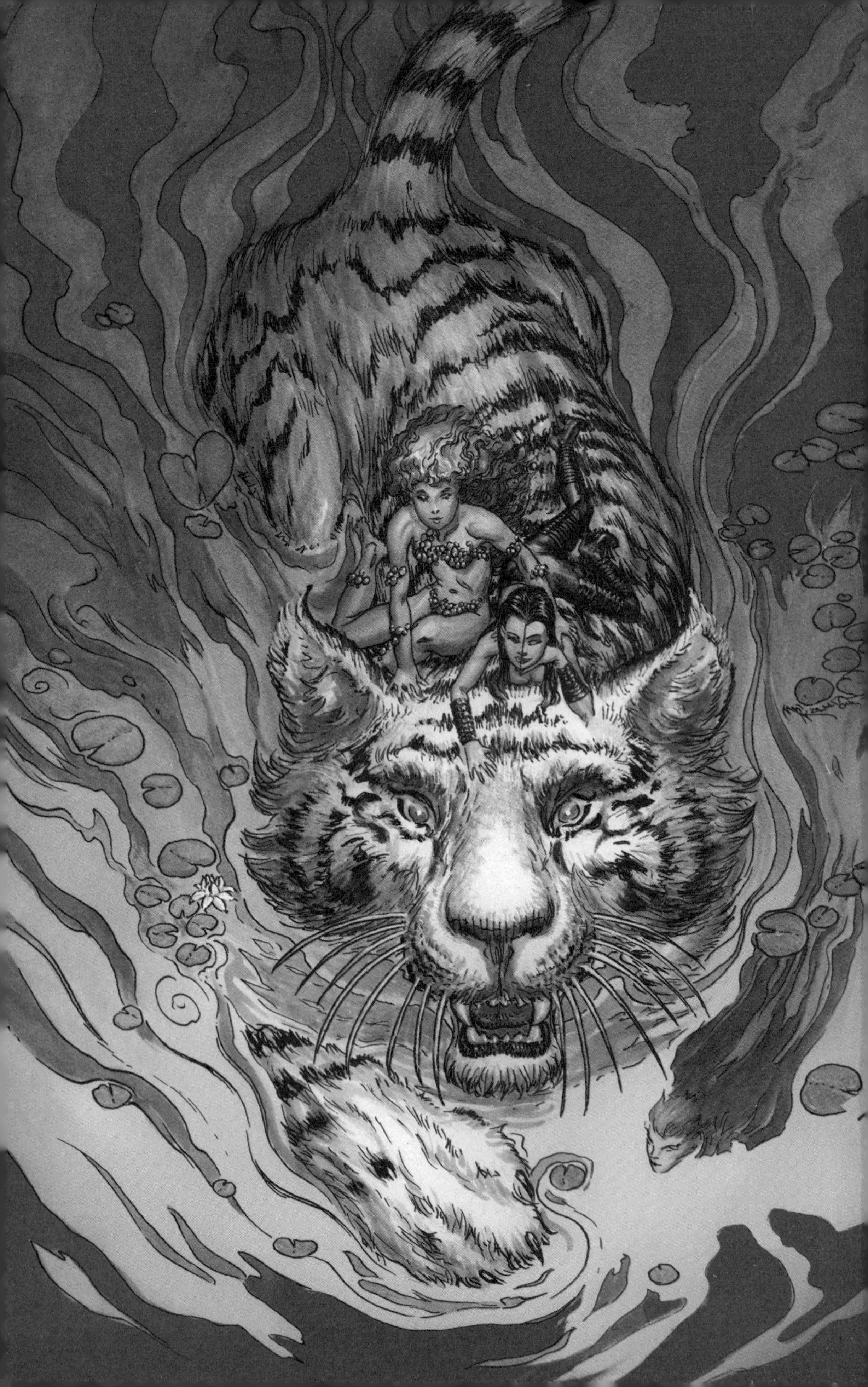

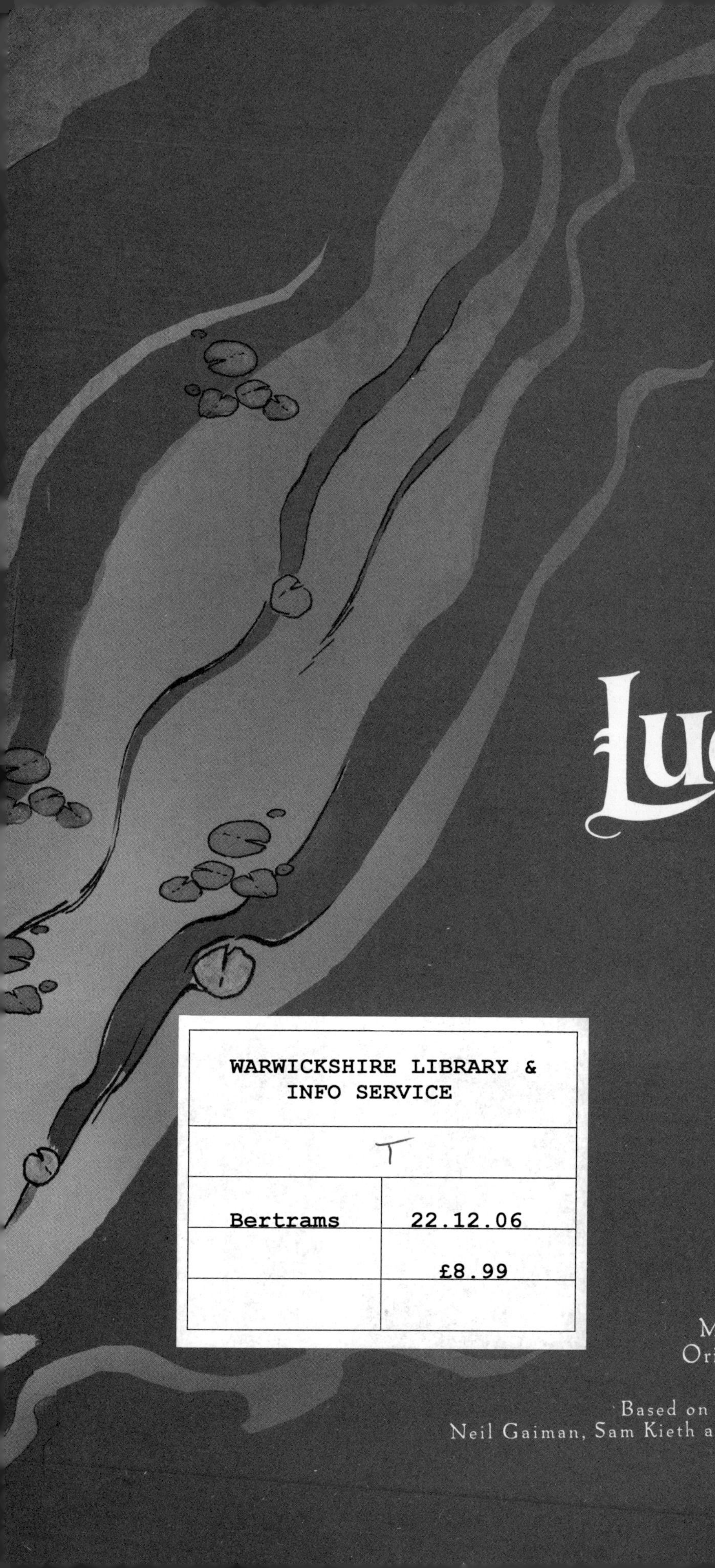

Lucifer

Crux

Mike Carey
Writer

Peter Gross
Ryan Kelly
Marc Hempel
Ronald Wimberly
Artists

Daniel Vozzo
Colorist

Jared K. Fletcher
Letterer

Michael Wm. Kaluta
Original Series Covers

Based on characters created by
Neil Gaiman, Sam Kieth and Mike Dringenberg

LUCIFER: CRUX

*Published by DC Comics. Cover and compilation copyright
© 2006 DC Comics. All Rights Reserved.*

*Originally published in single magazine form as LUCIFER 55-61.
Copyright © 2004, 2005 DC Comics. All Rights Reserved.
All characters, their distinctive likenesses and related elements
featured in this publication are trademarks of DC Comics.
The stories, characters and incidents featured in this publication
are entirely fictional. DC Comics does not read or accept
unsolicited submissions of ideas, stories or artwork.*

*DC Comics, 1700 Broadway, New York, NY 10019
A Warner Bros. Entertainment Company
Printed in Canada. First Printing.
ISBN: 1-4012-1005-8
ISBN 13: 978-1-4012-1005-2
Cover illustration by Christopher Moeller.
Logo design by Alex Jay.*

Table of Contents

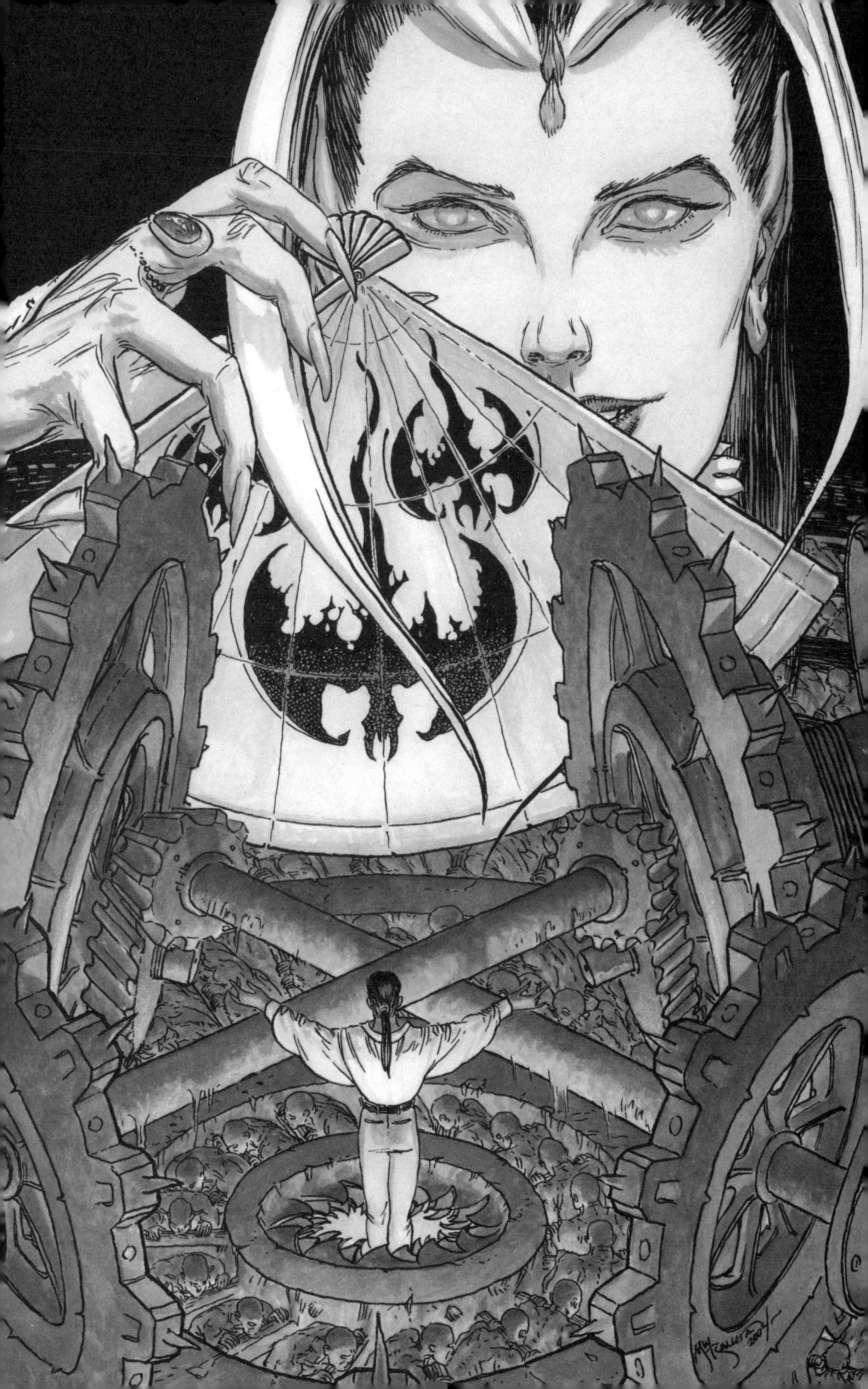

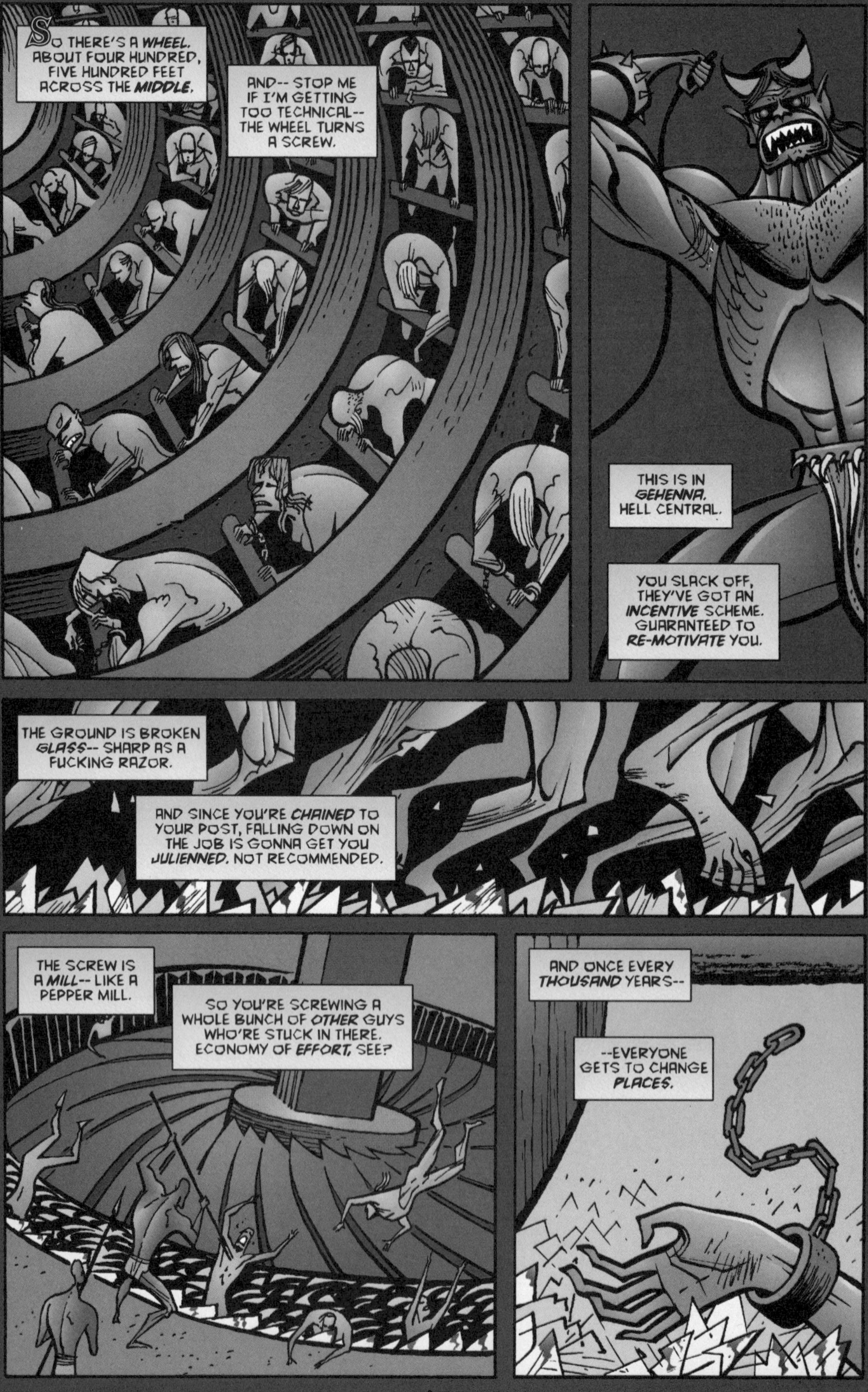
SO THERE'S A WHEEL. ABOUT FOUR HUNDRED, FIVE HUNDRED FEET ACROSS THE MIDDLE.
AND-- STOP ME IF I'M GETTING TOO TECHNICAL-- THE WHEEL TURNS A SCREW.
THIS IS IN GEHENNA. HELL CENTRAL.
YOU SLACK OFF, THEY'VE GOT AN INCENTIVE SCHEME. GUARANTEED TO RE-MOTIVATE YOU.
THE GROUND IS BROKEN GLASS-- SHARP AS A FUCKING RAZOR.
AND SINCE YOU'RE CHAINED TO YOUR POST, FALLING DOWN ON THE JOB IS GONNA GET YOU JULIENNED. NOT RECOMMENDED.
THE SCREW IS A MILL-- LIKE A PEPPER MILL.
SO YOU'RE SCREWING A WHOLE BUNCH OF OTHER GUYS WHO'RE STUCK IN THERE. ECONOMY OF EFFORT, SEE?
AND ONCE EVERY THOUSAND YEARS--
--EVERYONE GETS TO CHANGE PLACES.

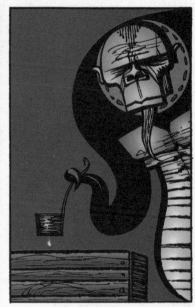

HERE. DRINK.

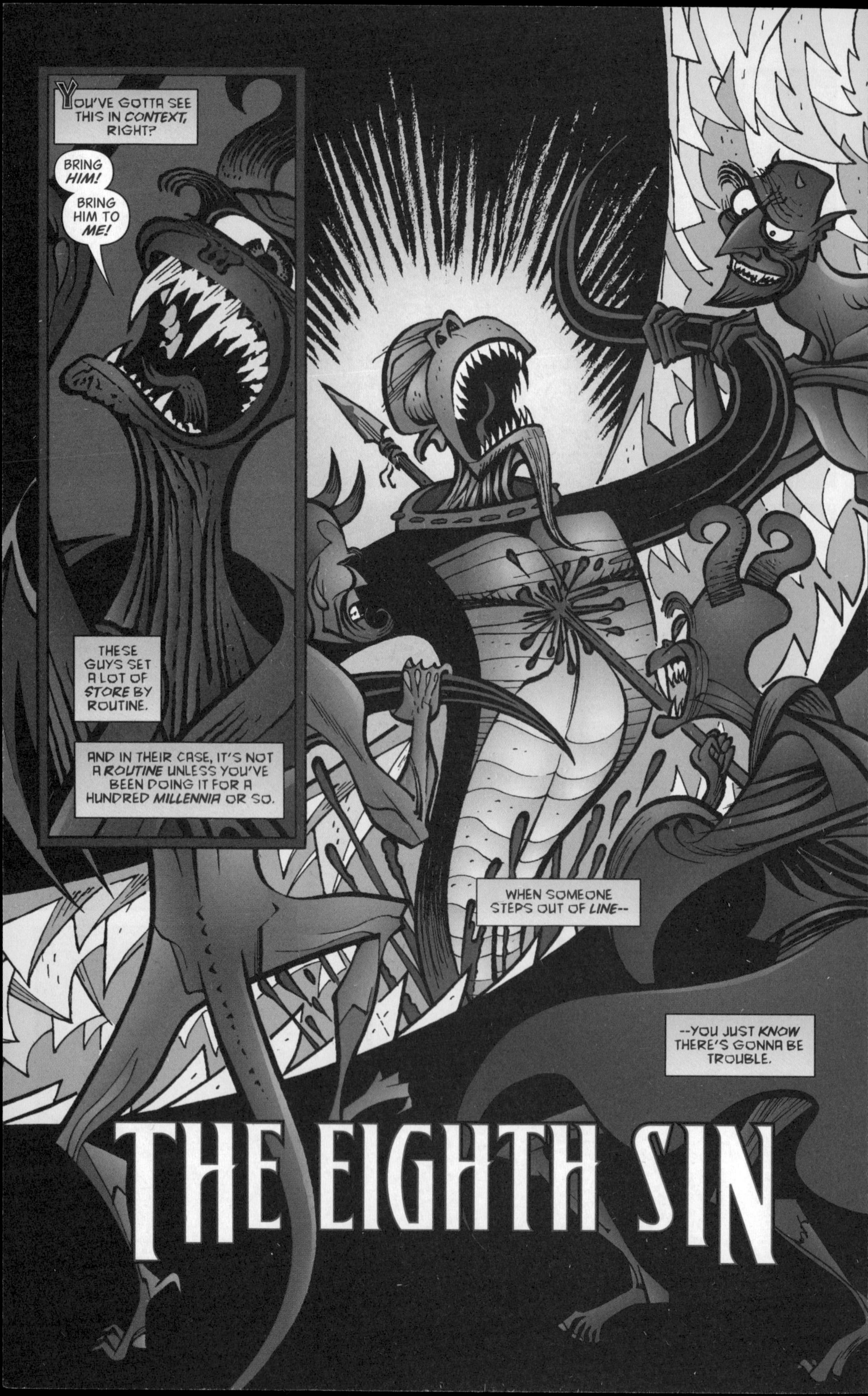

YOU'VE GOTTA SEE THIS IN CONTEXT, RIGHT?
BRING HIM!
BRING HIM TO ME!
THESE GUYS SET A LOT OF STORE BY ROUTINE.
AND IN THEIR CASE, IT'S NOT A ROUTINE UNLESS YOU'VE BEEN DOING IT FOR A HUNDRED MILLENNIA OR SO.
WHEN SOMEONE STEPS OUT OF LINE--
--YOU JUST KNOW THERE'S GONNA BE TROUBLE.
THE EIGHTH SIN

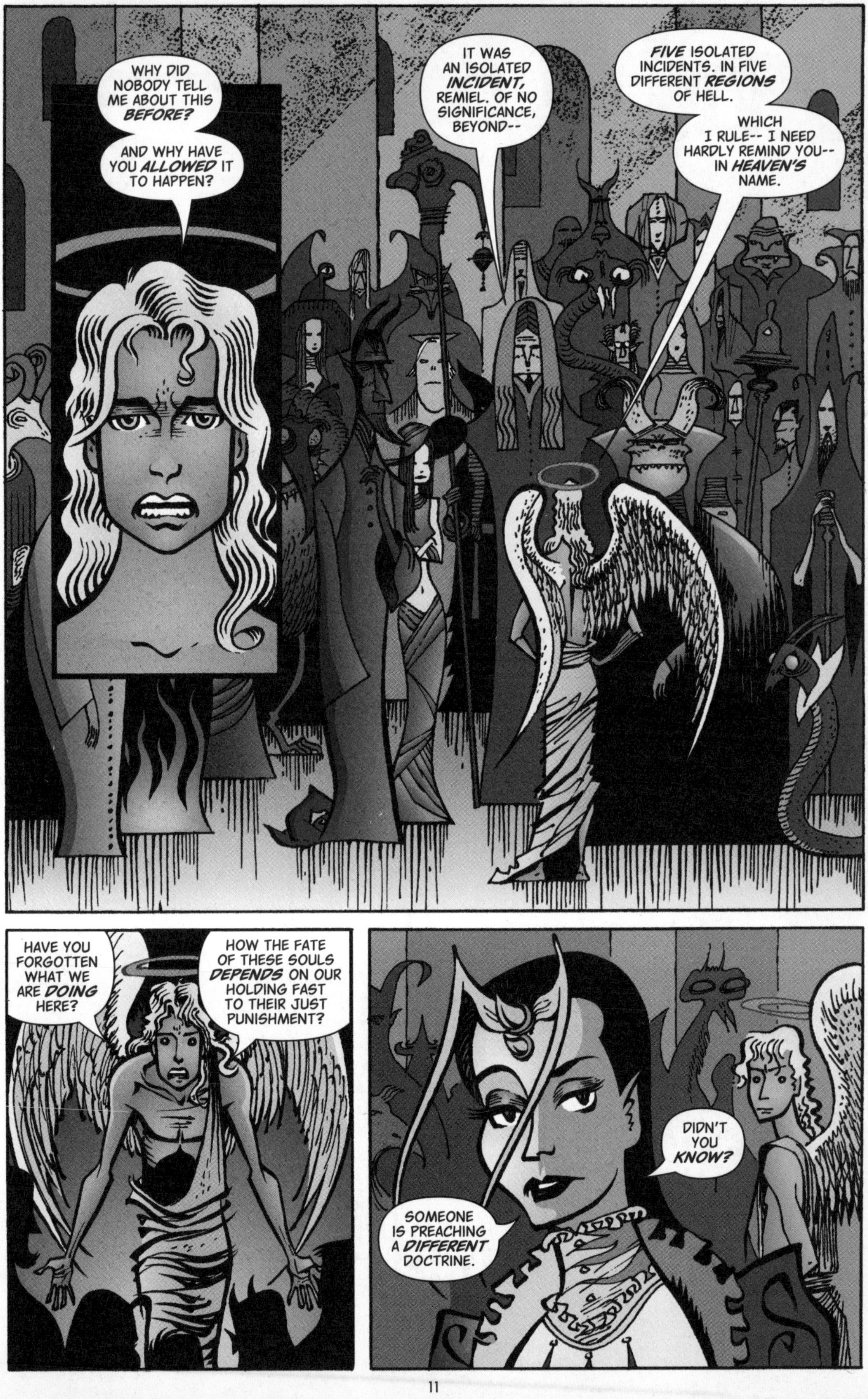
WHY DID NOBODY TELL ME ABOUT THIS BEFORE?
AND WHY HAVE YOU ALLOWED IT TO HAPPEN?
IT WAS AN ISOLATED INCIDENT, REMIEL. OF NO SIGNIFICANCE, BEYOND--
FIVE ISOLATED INCIDENTS. IN FIVE DIFFERENT REGIONS OF HELL.
WHICH I RULE-- I NEED HARDLY REMIND YOU-- IN HEAVEN'S NAME.
HAVE YOU FORGOTTEN WHAT WE ARE DOING HERE?
HOW THE FATE OF THESE SOULS DEPENDS ON OUR HOLDING FAST TO THEIR JUST PUNISHMENT?
DIDN'T YOU KNOW?
SOMEONE IS PREACHING A DIFFERENT DOCTRINE.

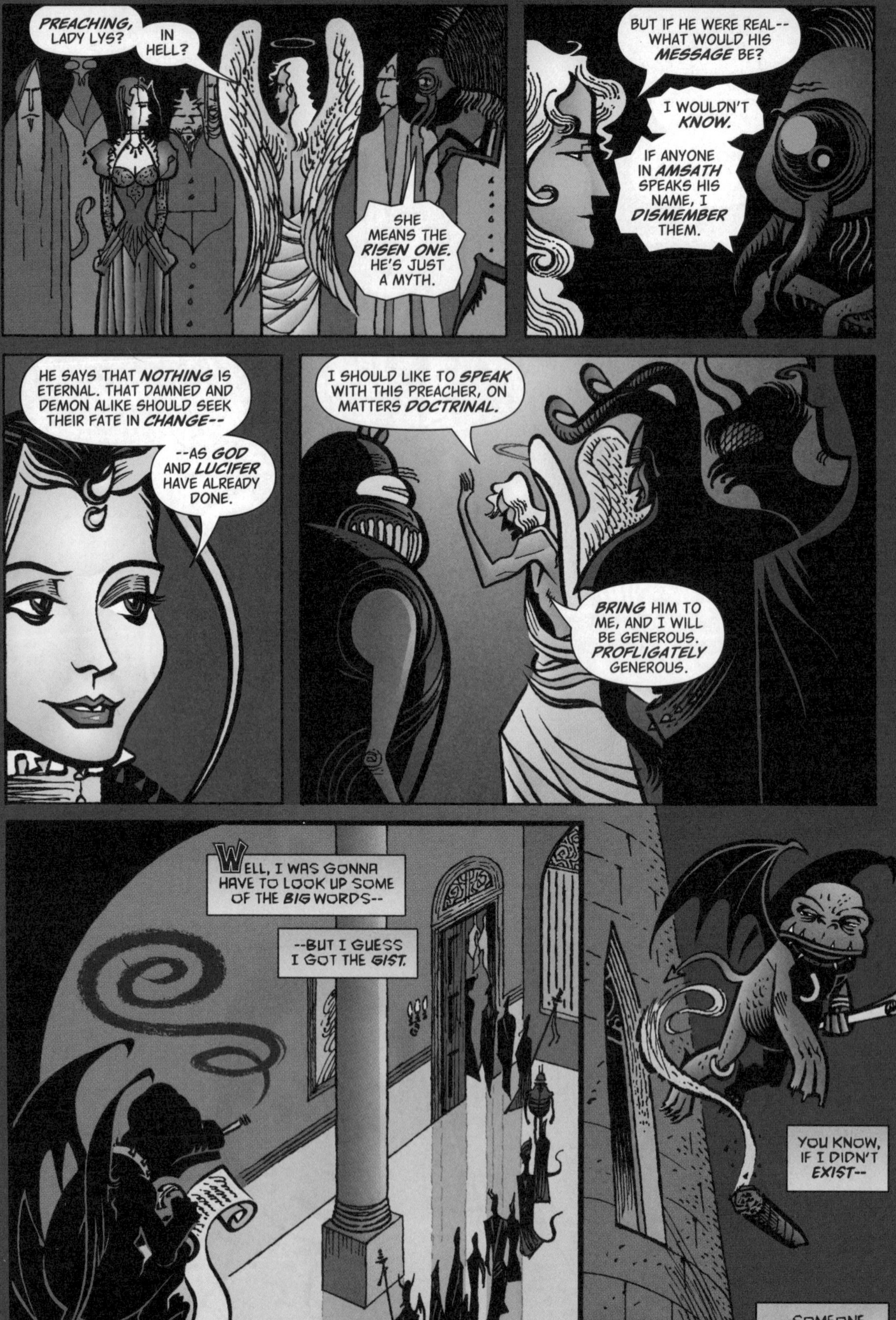
PREACHING, LADY LYS?
IN HELL?
SHE MEANS THE RISEN ONE. HE'S JUST A MYTH.
BUT IF HE WERE REAL-- WHAT WOULD HIS MESSAGE BE?
I WOULDN'T KNOW.
IF ANYONE IN AMSATH SPEAKS HIS NAME, I DISMEMBER THEM.
HE SAYS THAT NOTHING IS ETERNAL. THAT DAMNED AND DEMON ALIKE SHOULD SEEK THEIR FATE IN CHANGE--
--AS GOD AND LUCIFER HAVE ALREADY DONE.
I SHOULD LIKE TO SPEAK WITH THIS PREACHER, ON MATTERS DOCTRINAL.
BRING HIM TO ME, AND I WILL BE GENEROUS. PROFLIGATELY GENEROUS.
WELL, I WAS GONNA HAVE TO LOOK UP SOME OF THE BIG WORDS--
--BUT I GUESS I GOT THE GIST.
YOU KNOW, IF I DIDN'T EXIST--
--SOMEONE WOULD HAVE TO INVENT ME.

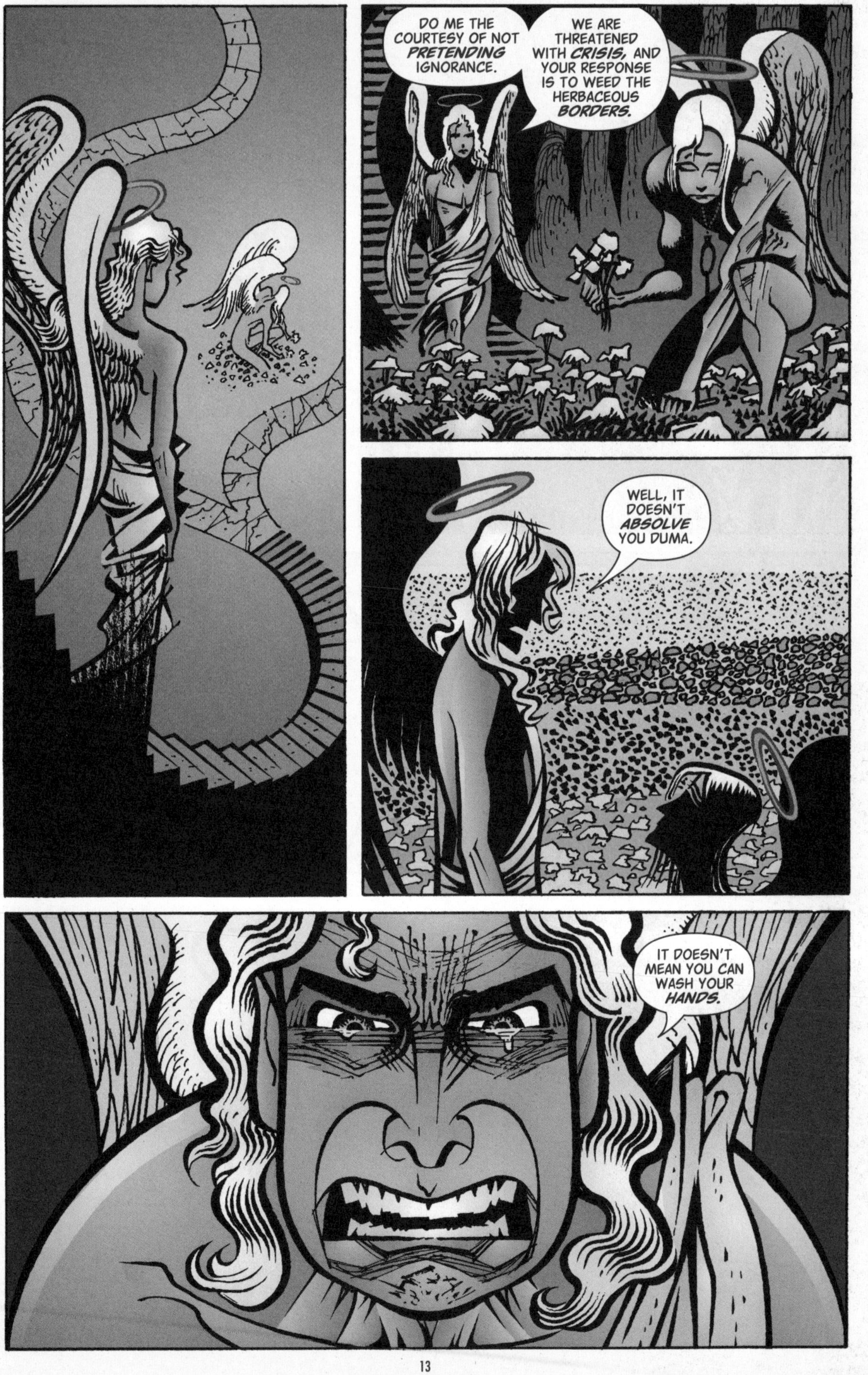
DO ME THE COURTESY OF NOT PRETENDING IGNORANCE.
WE ARE THREATENED WITH CRISIS, AND YOUR RESPONSE IS TO WEED THE HERBACEOUS BORDERS.
WELL, IT DOESN'T ABSOLVE YOU DUMA.
IT DOESN'T MEAN YOU CAN WASH YOUR HANDS.

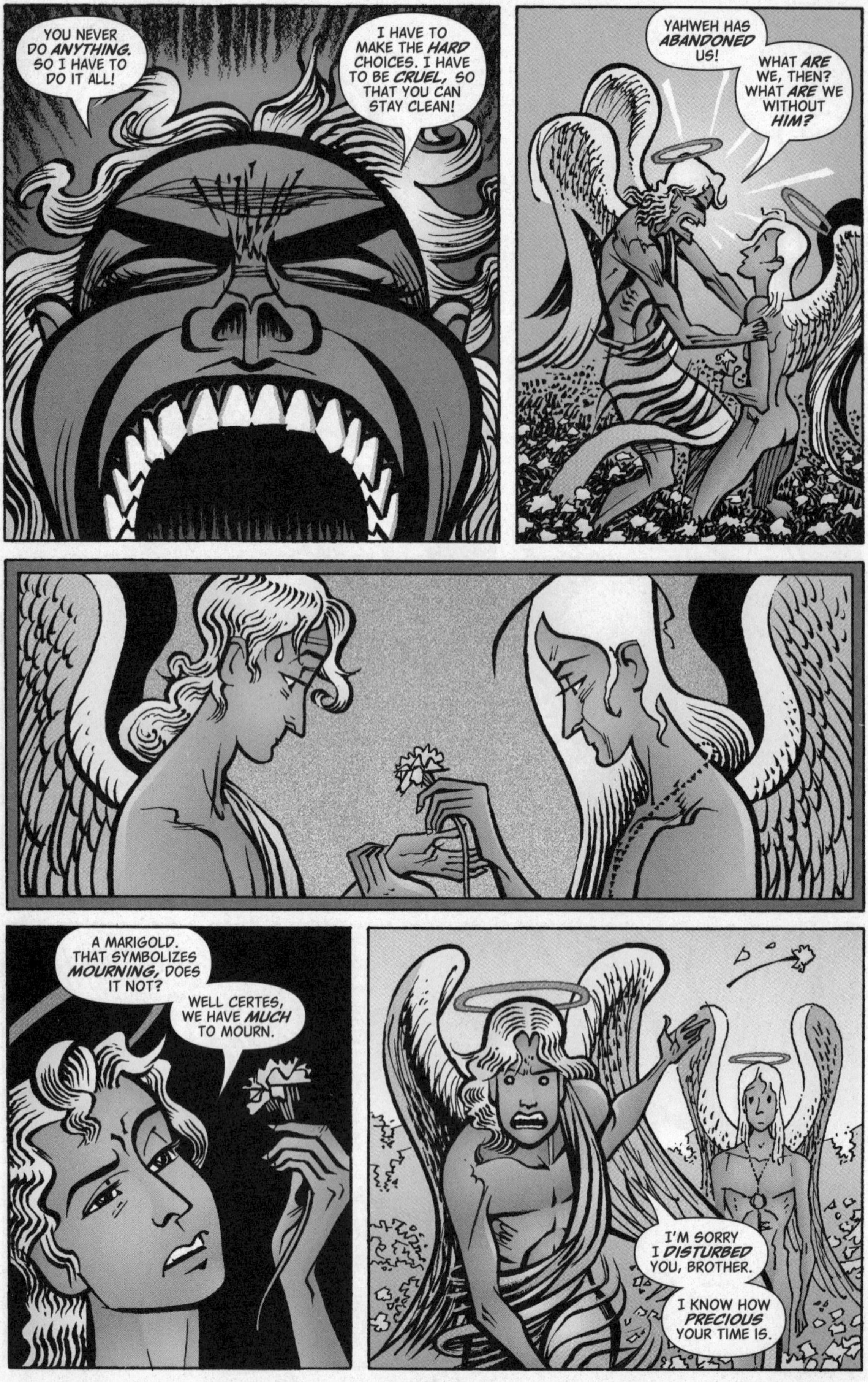
YOU NEVER DO ANYTHING. SO I HAVE TO DO IT ALL!
I HAVE TO MAKE THE HARD CHOICES. I HAVE TO BE CRUEL, SO THAT YOU CAN STAY CLEAN!
YAHWEH HAS ABANDONED US!
WHAT ARE WE, THEN? WHAT ARE WE WITHOUT HIM?
A MARIGOLD. THAT SYMBOLIZES MOURNING, DOES IT NOT?
WELL CERTES, WE HAVE MUCH TO MOURN.
I'M SORRY I DISTURBED YOU, BROTHER.
I KNOW HOW PRECIOUS YOUR TIME IS.

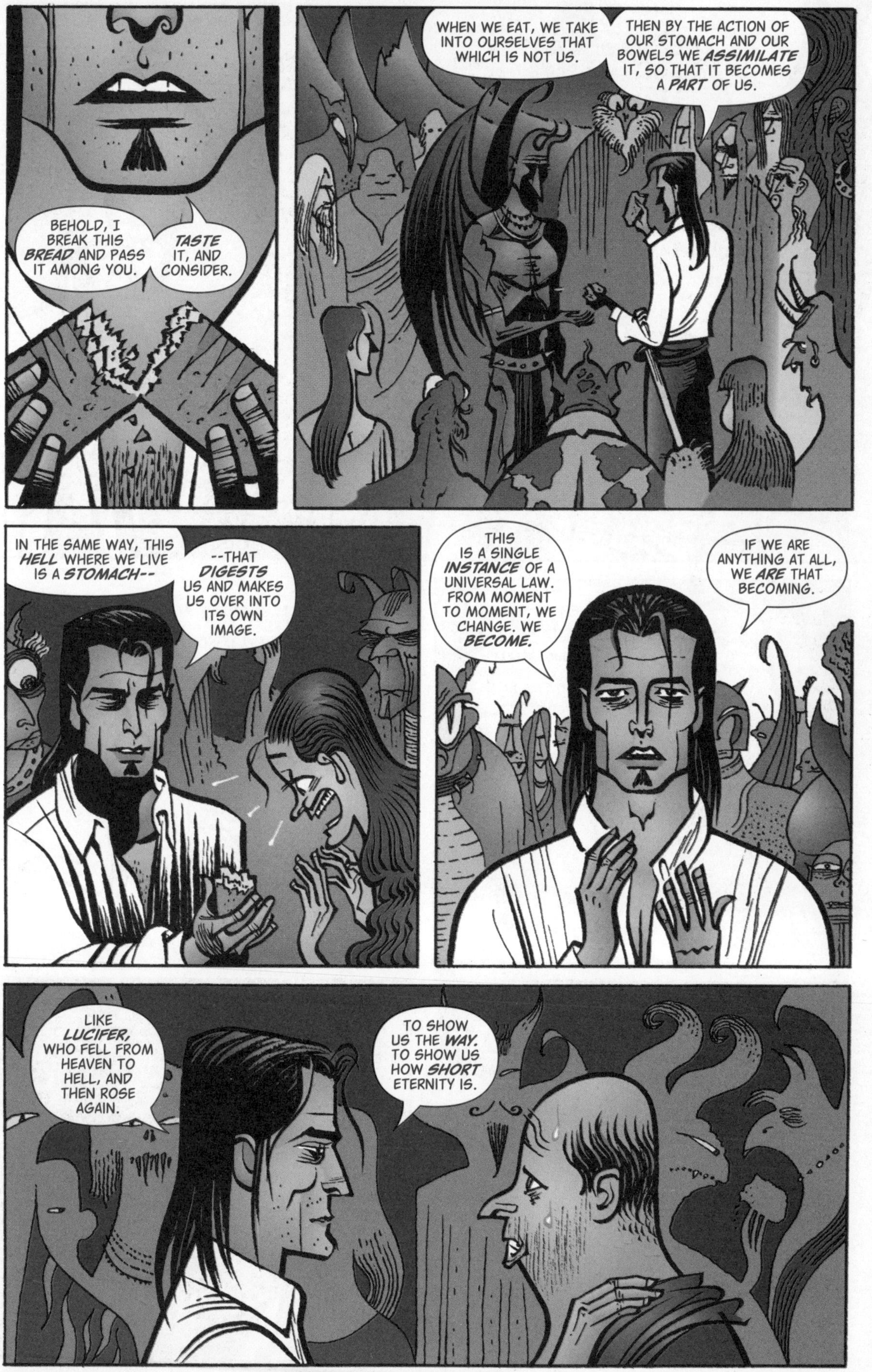
BEHOLD, I BREAK THIS BREAD AND PASS IT AMONG YOU.
TASTE IT, AND CONSIDER.
WHEN WE EAT, WE TAKE INTO OURSELVES THAT WHICH IS NOT US.
THEN BY THE ACTION OF OUR STOMACH AND OUR BOWELS WE ASSIMILATE IT, SO THAT IT BECOMES A PART OF US.
IN THE SAME WAY, THIS HELL WHERE WE LIVE IS A STOMACH--
--THAT DIGESTS US AND MAKES US OVER INTO ITS OWN IMAGE.
THIS IS A SINGLE INSTANCE OF A UNIVERSAL LAW. FROM MOMENT TO MOMENT, WE CHANGE. WE BECOME.
IF WE ARE ANYTHING AT ALL, WE ARE THAT BECOMING.
LIKE LUCIFER, WHO FELL FROM HEAVEN TO HELL, AND THEN ROSE AGAIN.
TO SHOW US THE WAY. TO SHOW US HOW SHORT ETERNITY IS.

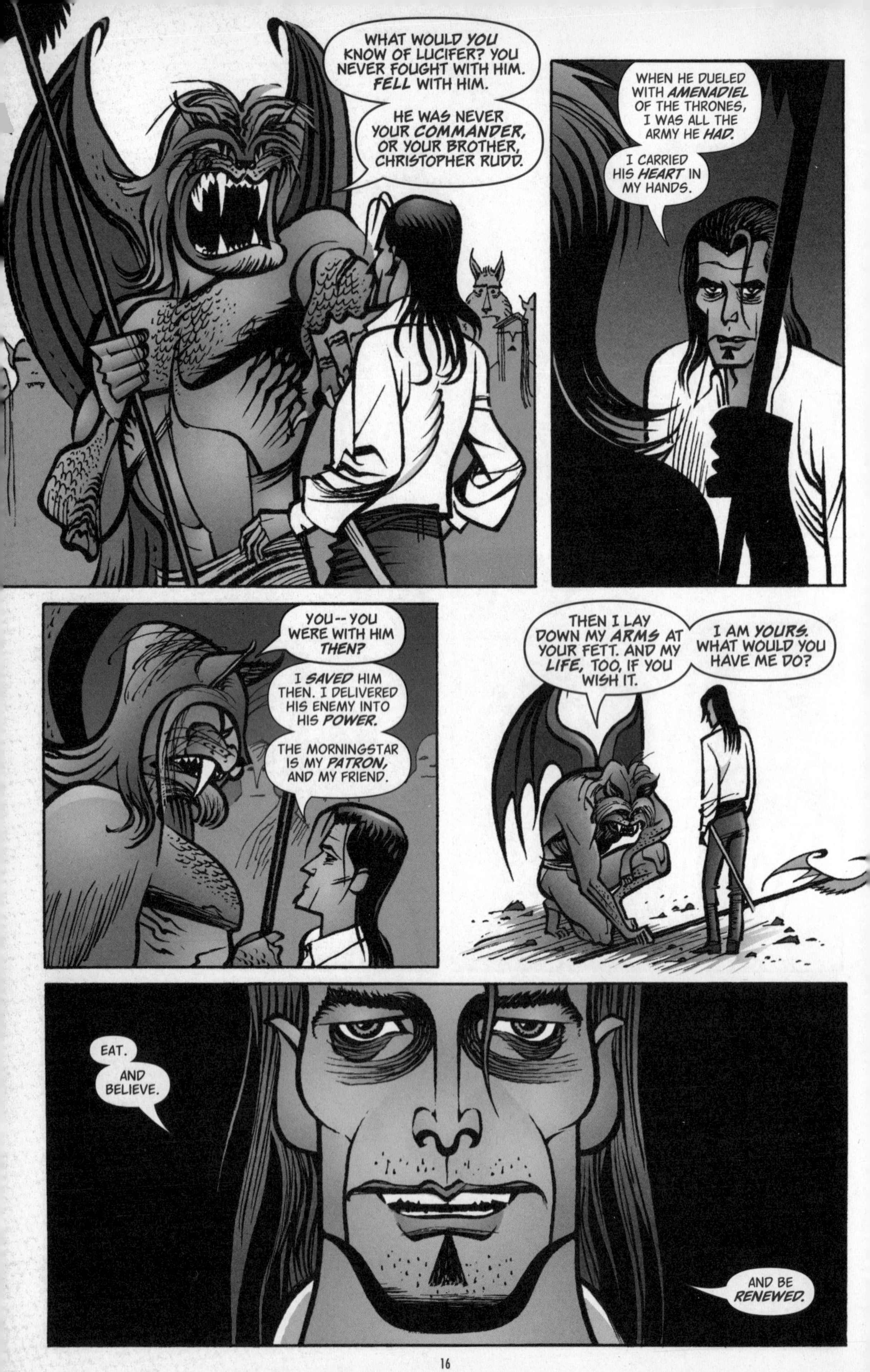
WHAT WOULD YOU KNOW OF LUCIFER? YOU NEVER FOUGHT WITH HIM. FELL WITH HIM.
HE WAS NEVER YOUR COMMANDER, OR YOUR BROTHER, CHRISTOPHER RUDD.
WHEN HE DUELED WITH AMENADIEL OF THE THRONES, I WAS ALL THE ARMY HE HAD.
I CARRIED HIS HEART IN MY HANDS.
YOU-- YOU WERE WITH HIM THEN?
I SAVED HIM THEN. I DELIVERED HIS ENEMY INTO HIS POWER.
THE MORNINGSTAR IS MY PATRON, AND MY FRIEND.
THEN I LAY DOWN MY ARMS AT YOUR FETT. AND MY LIFE, TOO, IF YOU WISH IT.
I AM YOURS. WHAT WOULD YOU HAVE ME DO?
EAT.
AND BELIEVE.
AND BE RENEWED.

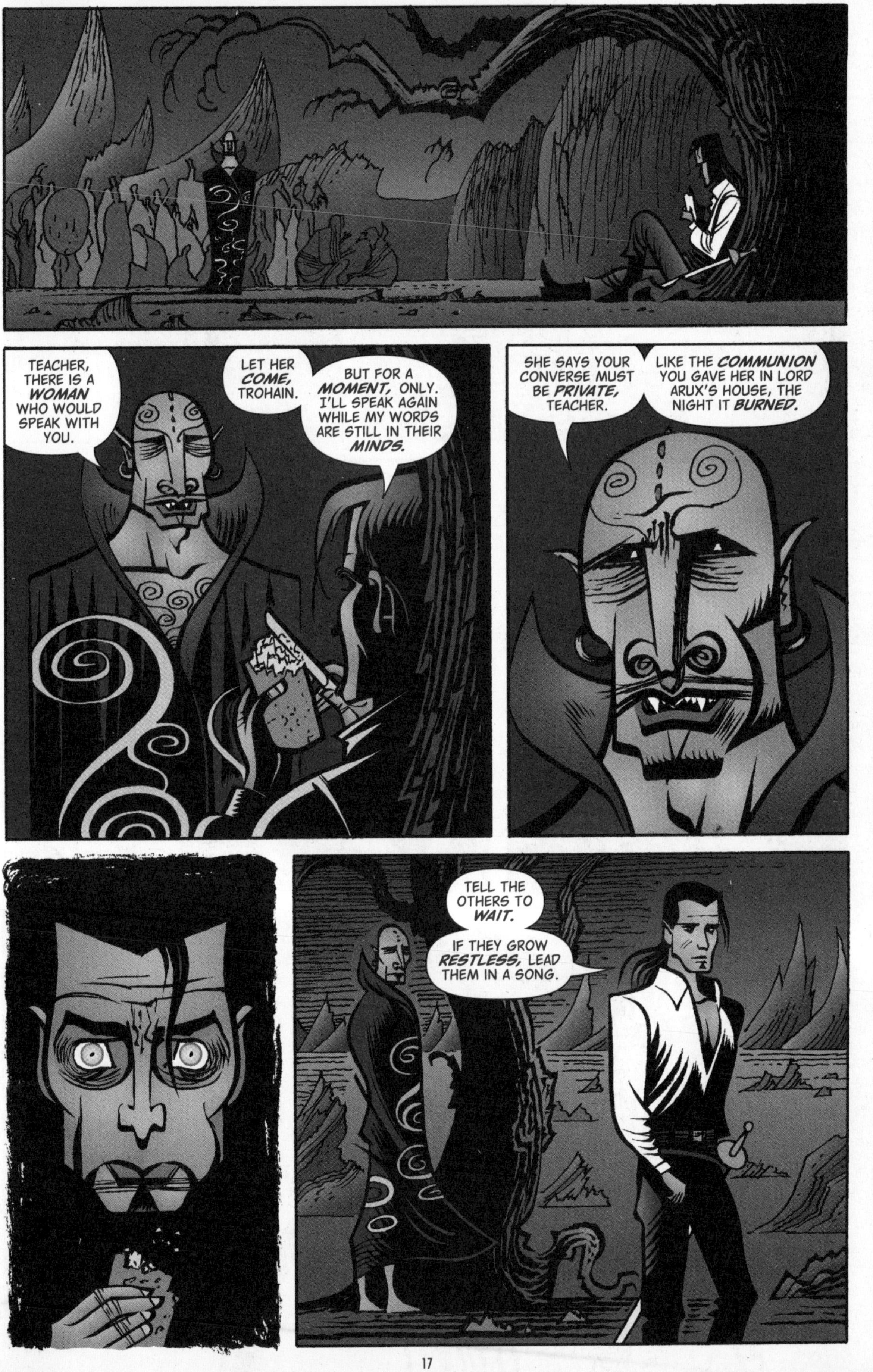
TEACHER, THERE IS A WOMAN WHO WOULD SPEAK WITH YOU.
LET HER COME, TROHAIN.
BUT FOR A MOMENT, ONLY. I'LL SPEAK AGAIN WHILE MY WORDS ARE STILL IN THEIR MINDS.
SHE SAYS YOUR CONVERSE MUST BE PRIVATE, TEACHER.
LIKE THE COMMUNION YOU GAVE HER IN LORD ARUX'S HOUSE, THE NIGHT IT BURNED.
TELL THE OTHERS TO WAIT.
IF THEY GROW RESTLESS, LEAD THEM IN A SONG.

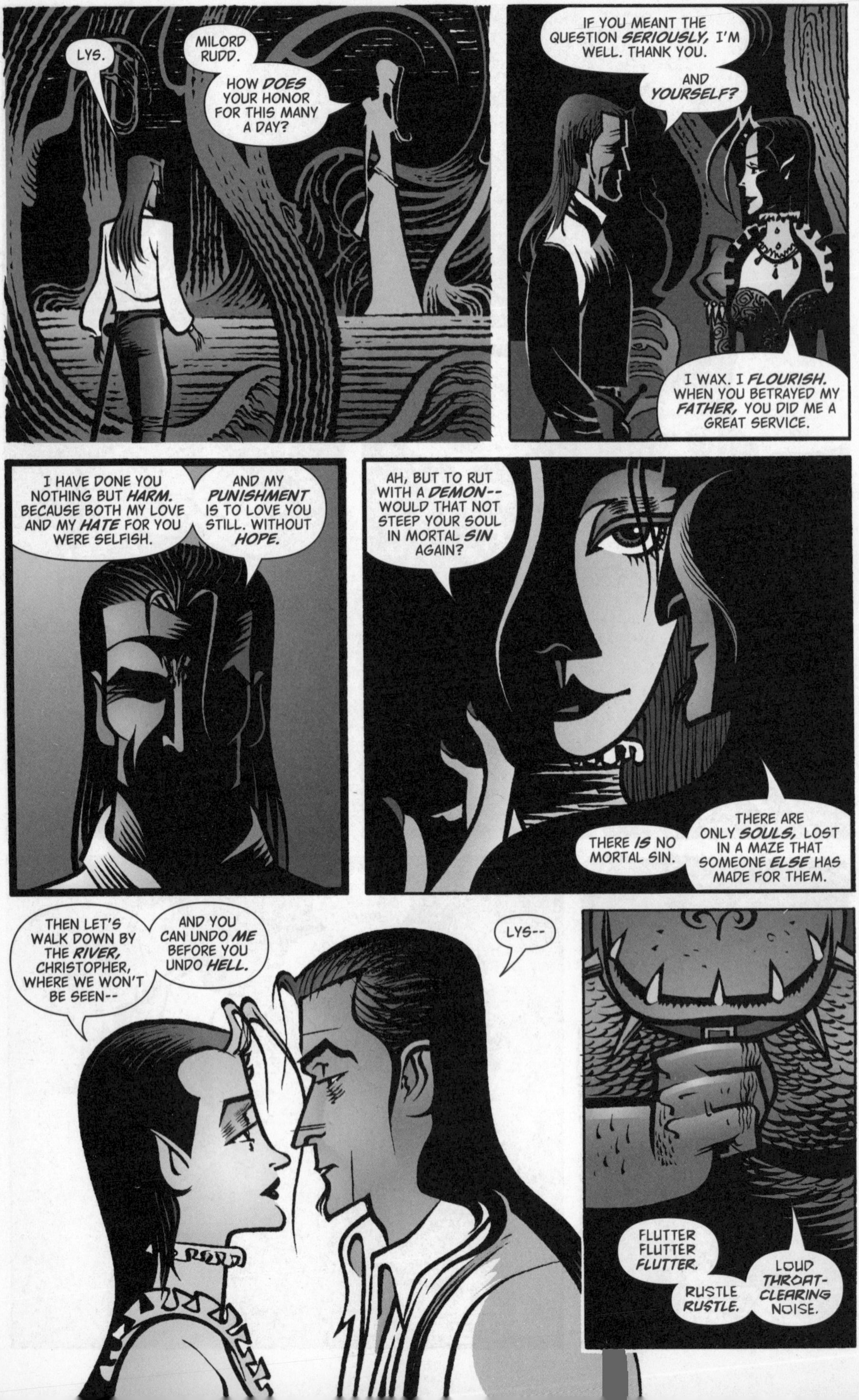
LYS.
MILORD RUDD.
HOW DOES YOUR HONOR FOR THIS MANY A DAY?
IF YOU MEANT THE QUESTION SERIOUSLY, I'M WELL. THANK YOU.
AND YOURSELF?
I WAX. I FLOURISH. WHEN YOU BETRAYED MY FATHER, YOU DID ME A GREAT SERVICE.
I HAVE DONE YOU NOTHING BUT HARM. BECAUSE BOTH MY LOVE AND MY HATE FOR YOU WERE SELFISH.
AND MY PUNISHMENT IS TO LOVE YOU STILL. WITHOUT HOPE.
AH, BUT TO RUT WITH A DEMON--WOULD THAT NOT STEEP YOUR SOUL IN MORTAL SIN AGAIN?
THERE IS NO MORTAL SIN.
THERE ARE ONLY SOULS, LOST IN A MAZE THAT SOMEONE ELSE HAS MADE FOR THEM.
THEN LET'S WALK DOWN BY THE RIVER, CHRISTOPHER, WHERE WE WON'T BE SEEN--
AND YOU CAN UNDO ME BEFORE YOU UNDO HELL.
LYS--
FLUTTER FLUTTER FLUTTER.
RUSTLE RUSTLE.
LOUD THROAT-CLEARING NOISE.

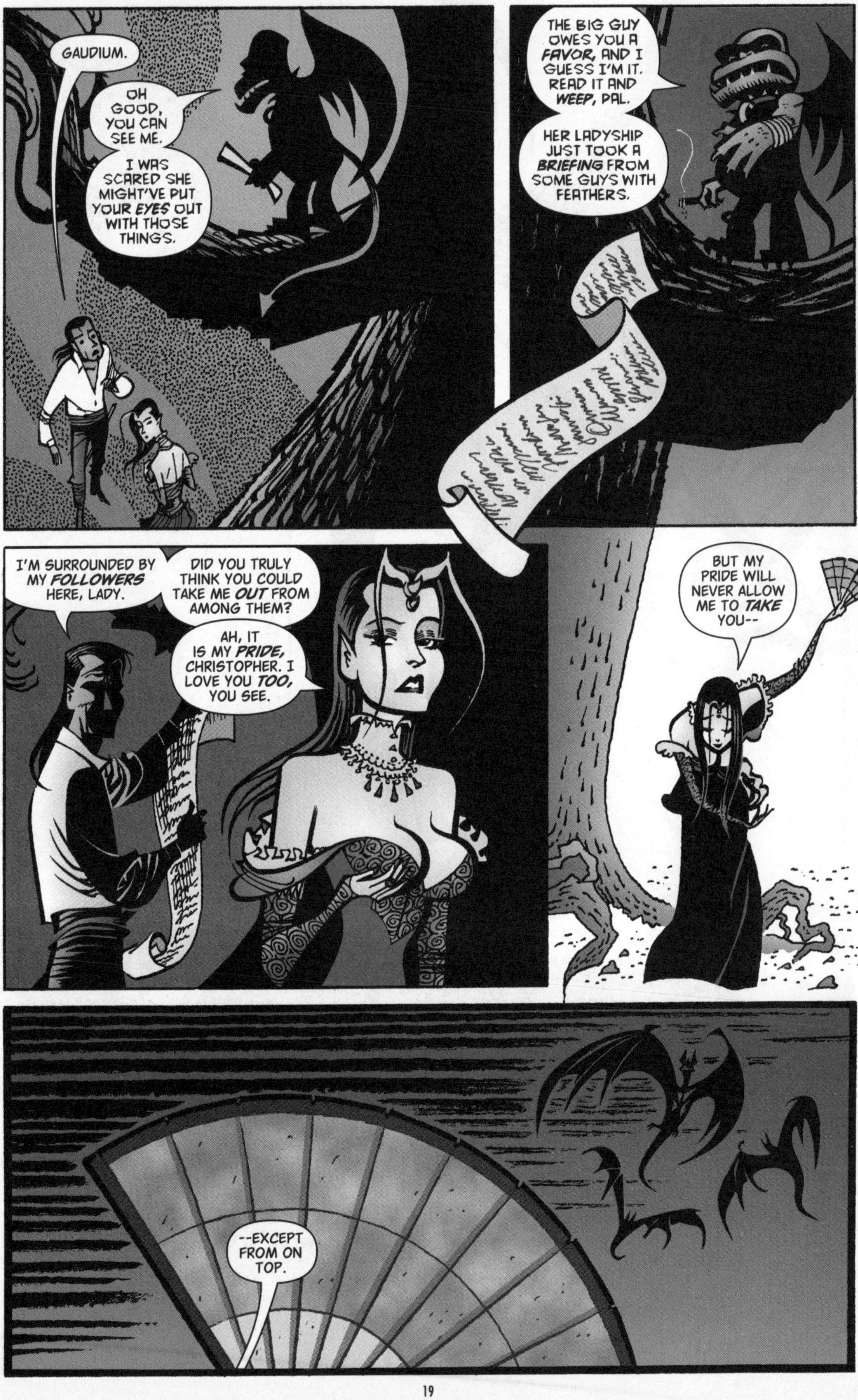
GAUDIUM.
OH GOOD, YOU CAN SEE ME.
I WAS SCARED SHE MIGHT'VE PUT YOUR EYES OUT WITH THOSE THINGS.
THE BIG GUY OWES YOU A FAVOR, AND I GUESS I'M IT. READ IT AND WEEP, PAL.
HER LADYSHIP JUST TOOK A BRIEFING FROM SOME GUYS WITH FEATHERS.
I'M SURROUNDED BY MY FOLLOWERS HERE, LADY.
DID YOU TRULY THINK YOU COULD TAKE ME OUT FROM AMONG THEM?
AH, IT IS MY PRIDE, CHRISTOPHER. I LOVE YOU TOO, YOU SEE.
BUT MY PRIDE WILL NEVER ALLOW ME TO TAKE YOU--
--EXCEPT FROM ON TOP.

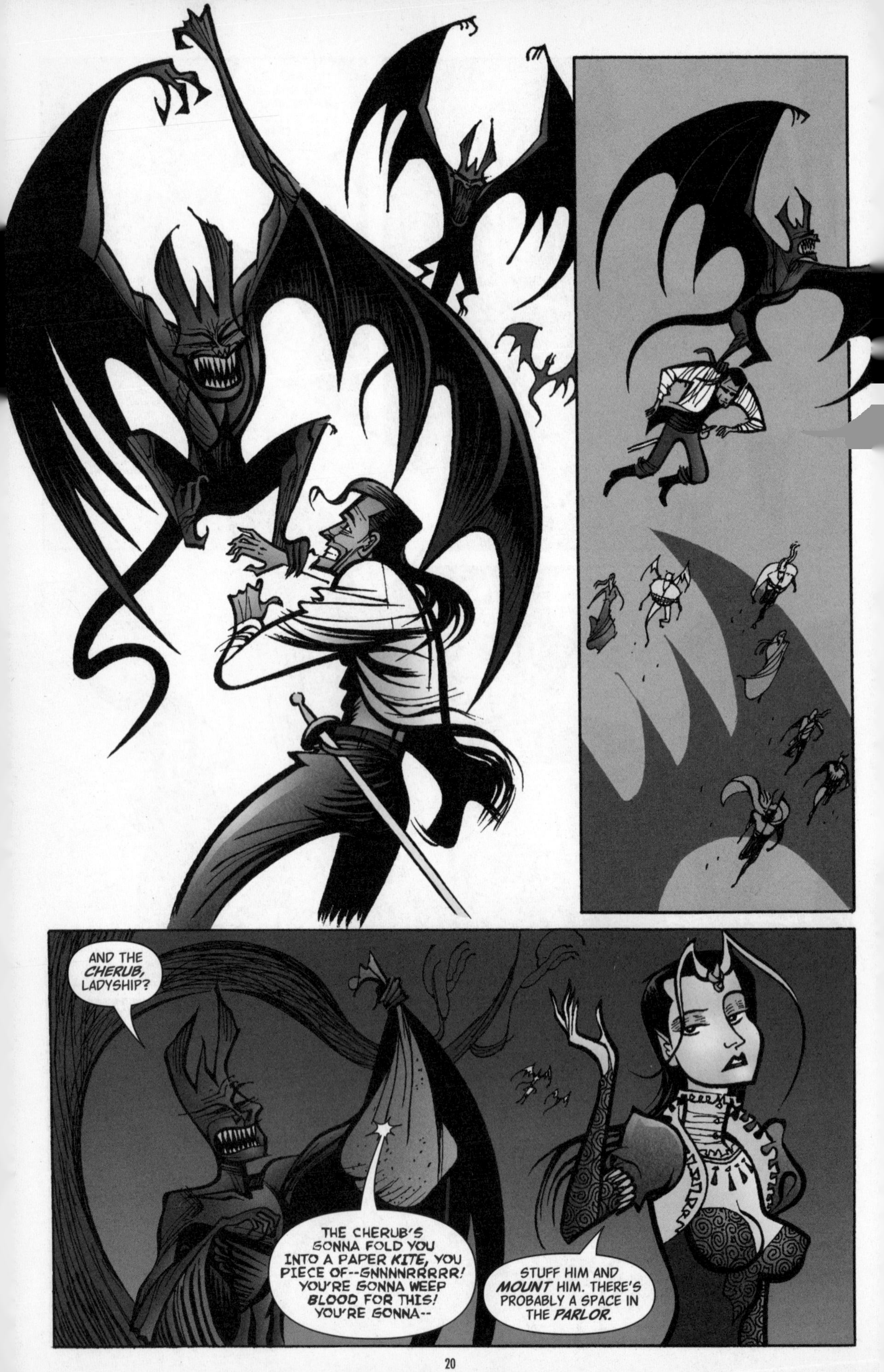
AND THE *CHERUB*, LADYSHIP?
THE CHERUB'S GONNA FOLD YOU INTO A PAPER *KITE*, YOU PIECE OF--GNNNNRRRRR! YOU'RE GONNA WEEP *BLOOD* FOR THIS! YOU'RE GONNA--
STUFF HIM AND *MOUNT* HIM. THERE'S PROBABLY A SPACE IN THE *PARLOR*.

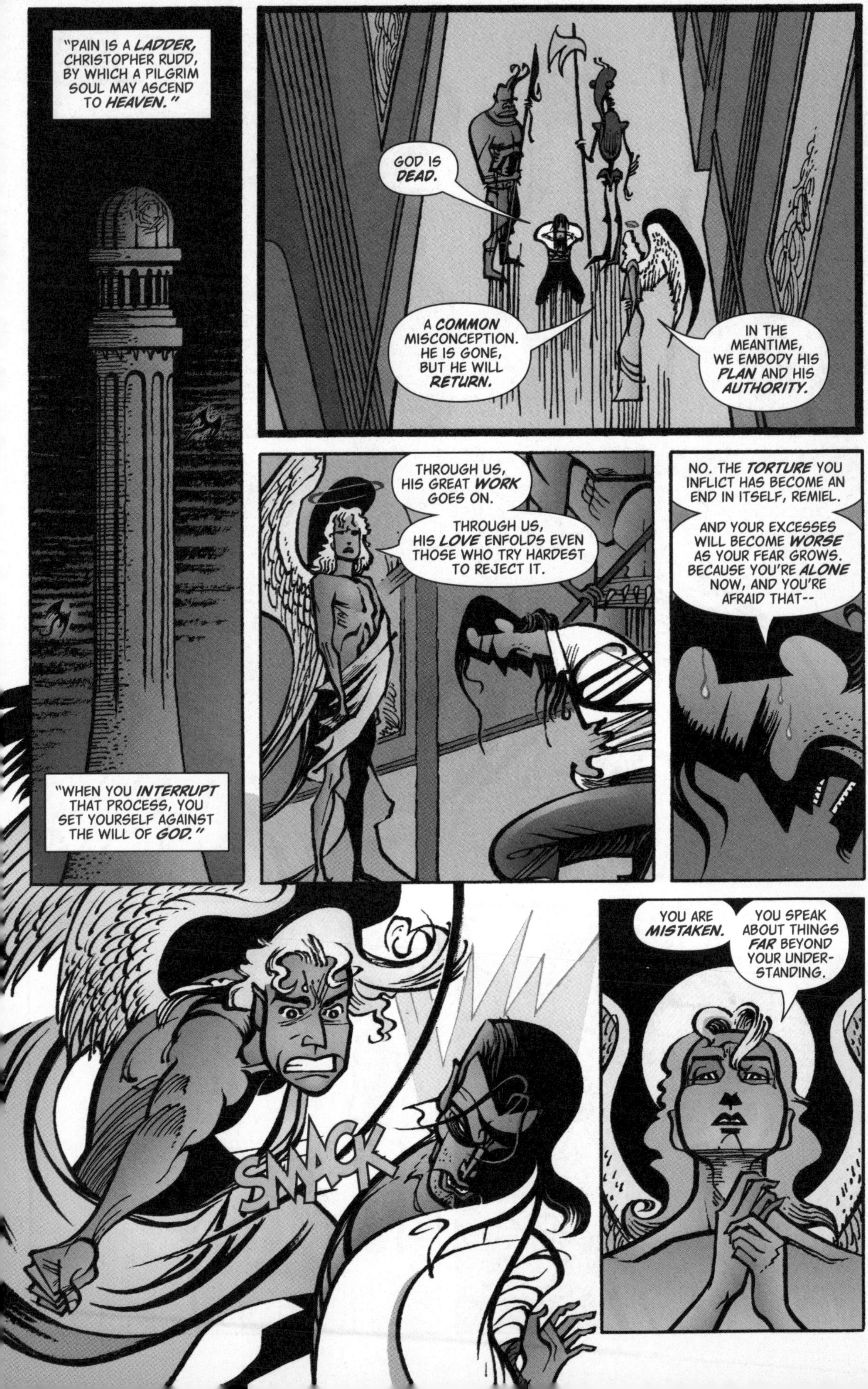
"PAIN IS A LADDER, CHRISTOPHER RUDD, BY WHICH A PILGRIM SOUL MAY ASCEND TO HEAVEN."
"WHEN YOU INTERRUPT THAT PROCESS, YOU SET YOURSELF AGAINST THE WILL OF GOD."
GOD IS DEAD.
A COMMON MISCONCEPTION. HE IS GONE, BUT HE WILL RETURN.
IN THE MEANTIME, WE EMBODY HIS PLAN AND HIS AUTHORITY.
THROUGH US, HIS GREAT WORK GOES ON.
THROUGH US, HIS LOVE ENFOLDS EVEN THOSE WHO TRY HARDEST TO REJECT IT.
NO. THE TORTURE YOU INFLICT HAS BECOME AN END IN ITSELF, REMIEL.
AND YOUR EXCESSES WILL BECOME WORSE AS YOUR FEAR GROWS. BECAUSE YOU'RE ALONE NOW, AND YOU'RE AFRAID THAT--
SMACK
YOU ARE MISTAKEN.
YOU SPEAK ABOUT THINGS FAR BEYOND YOUR UNDER-STANDING.

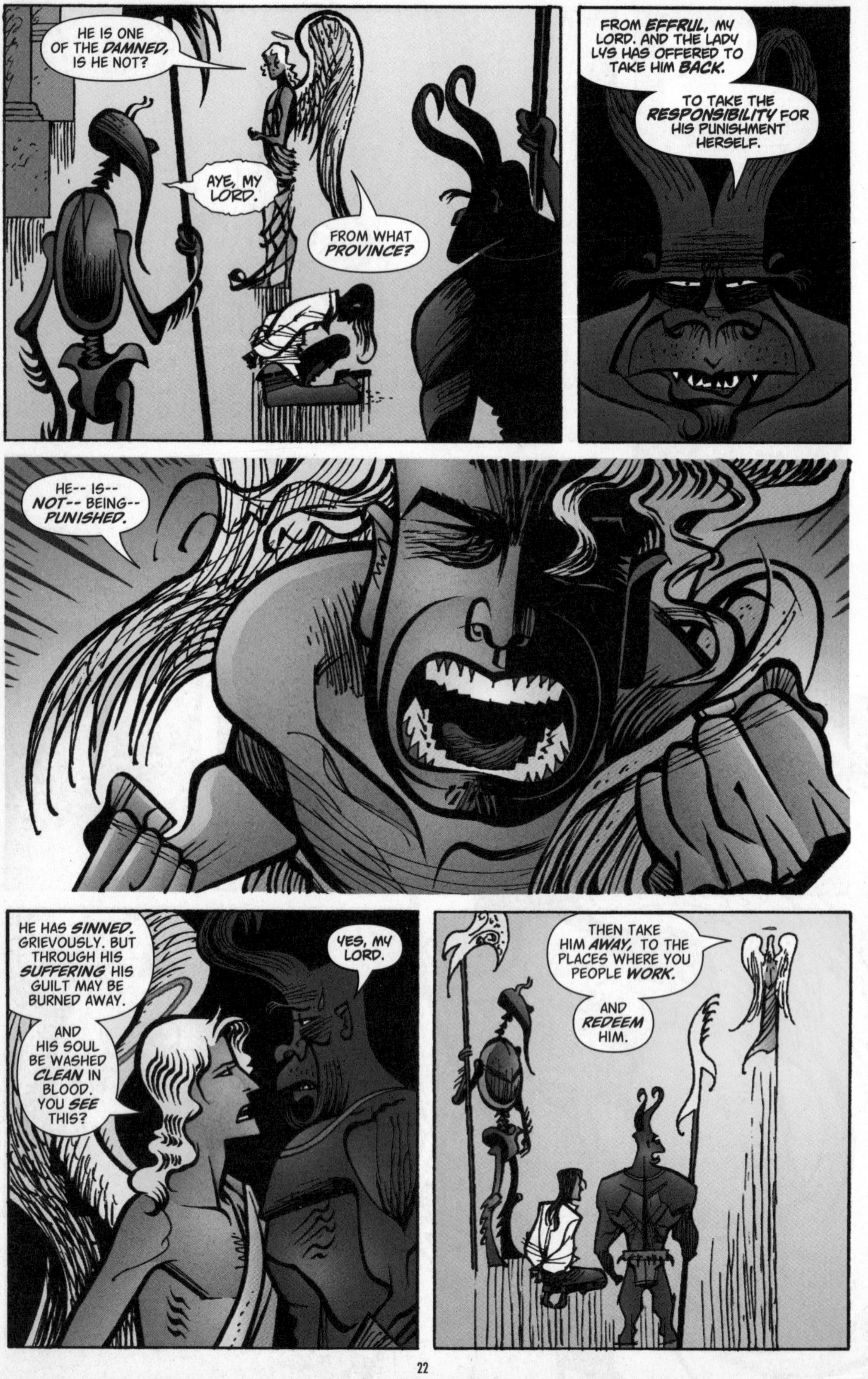
HE IS ONE OF THE DAMNED, IS HE NOT?
AYE, MY LORD.
FROM WHAT PROVINCE?
FROM EFFRUL, MY LORD. AND THE LADY LYS HAS OFFERED TO TAKE HIM BACK.
TO TAKE THE RESPONSIBILITY FOR HIS PUNISHMENT HERSELF.
HE-- IS-- NOT-- BEING-- PUNISHED.
HE HAS SINNED. GRIEVOUSLY. BUT THROUGH HIS SUFFERING HIS GUILT MAY BE BURNED AWAY.
AND HIS SOUL BE WASHED CLEAN IN BLOOD. YOU SEE THIS?
YES, MY LORD.
THEN TAKE HIM AWAY, TO THE PLACES WHERE YOU PEOPLE WORK.
AND REDEEM HIM.

IF THIS WERE A MOVIE, I THINK BY NOW WE'D HAVE REACHED THE END OF THE SECOND ACT.

HOW DO I WHAT?

I SAID, HOW DO YOU STUFF A CHERUB?

TAP TAP

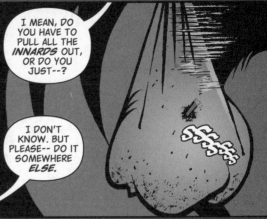

I MEAN, DO YOU HAVE TO PULL ALL THE INNARDS OUT, OR DO YOU JUST--?

I DON'T KNOW. BUT PLEASE-- DO IT SOMEWHERE ELSE.

THE PART WHERE EVERYTHING SEEMS MAXIMALLY FUCKED UP.

ONLY IT ISN'T, BECAUSE OUR CHARISMATIC HERO HAS GOT A PLAN.

WELL, COULD YOU LEND ME SOME TOOLS?

A SPATULA, OR--

...

SSSSSSSS

AAAURGH!

BUT BECAUSE I'M MORE CHARISMATIC THAN MOST, I FIGURE IT'S OKAY IF I JUST MAKE IT UP AS I GO ALONG.

TO SWITCH METAPHORS, IT WAS THE BOTTOM OF THE NINTH AND THE BASES WERE TOWERING INFERNOS. WHO'S GONNA STEP UP TO THE PLATE?

WHO ELSE?

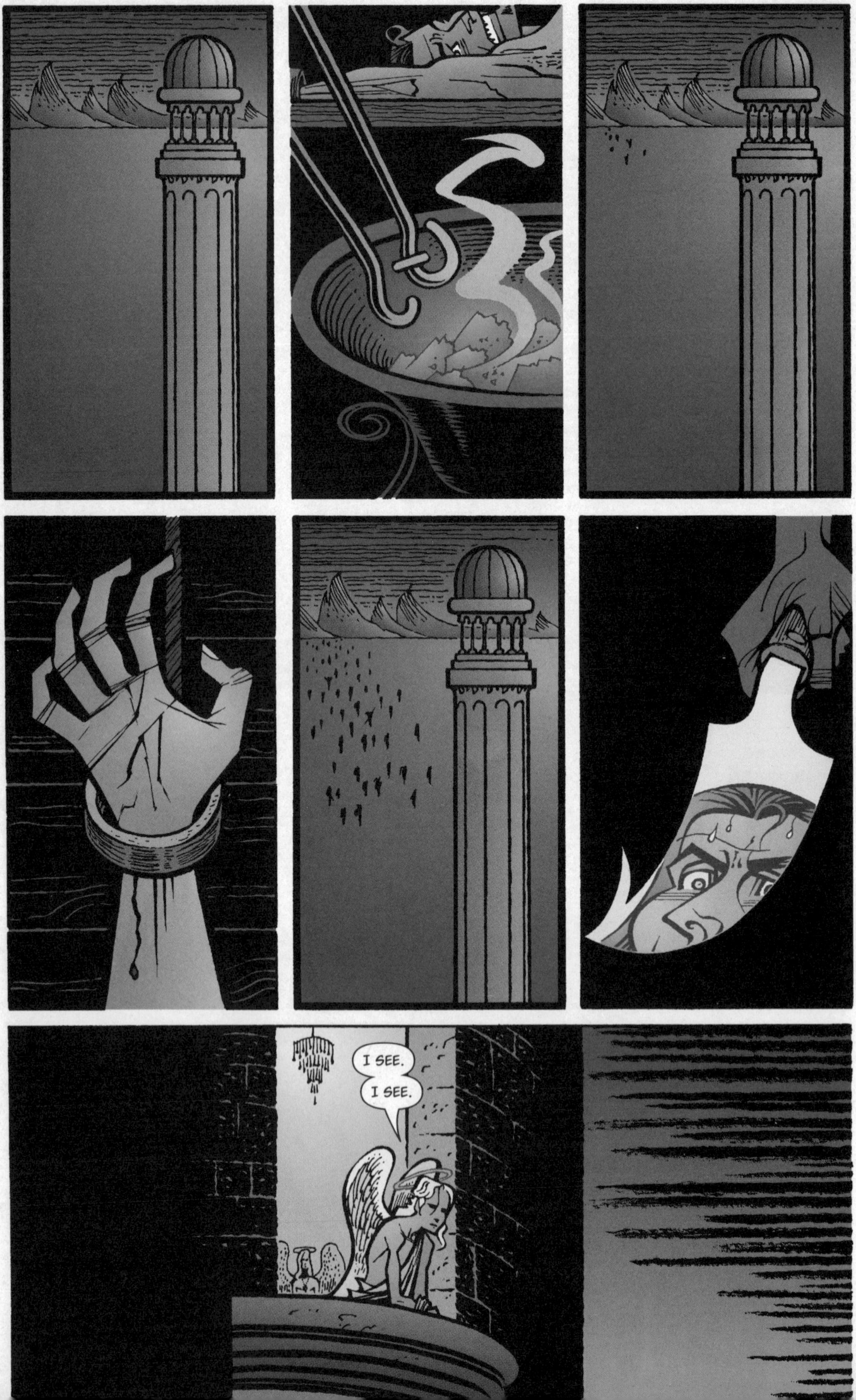
I SEE.
I SEE.

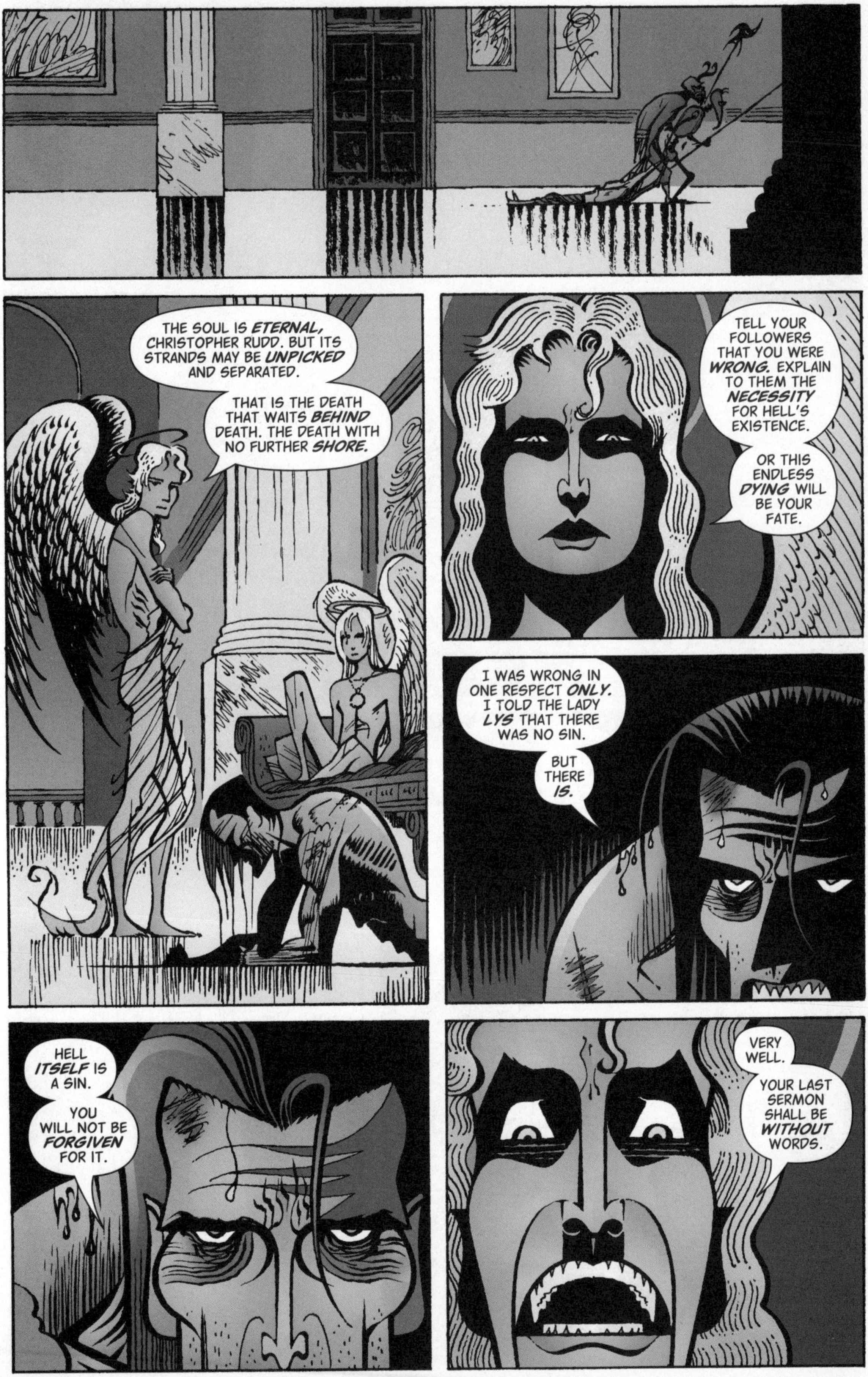
THE SOUL IS ETERNAL, CHRISTOPHER RUDD. BUT ITS STRANDS MAY BE UNPICKED AND SEPARATED.
THAT IS THE DEATH THAT WAITS BEHIND DEATH. THE DEATH WITH NO FURTHER SHORE.
TELL YOUR FOLLOWERS THAT YOU WERE WRONG. EXPLAIN TO THEM THE NECESSITY FOR HELL'S EXISTENCE.
OR THIS ENDLESS DYING WILL BE YOUR FATE.
I WAS WRONG IN ONE RESPECT ONLY. I TOLD THE LADY LYS THAT THERE WAS NO SIN.
BUT THERE IS.
HELL ITSELF IS A SIN.
YOU WILL NOT BE FORGIVEN FOR IT.
VERY WELL.
YOUR LAST SERMON SHALL BE WITHOUT WORDS.

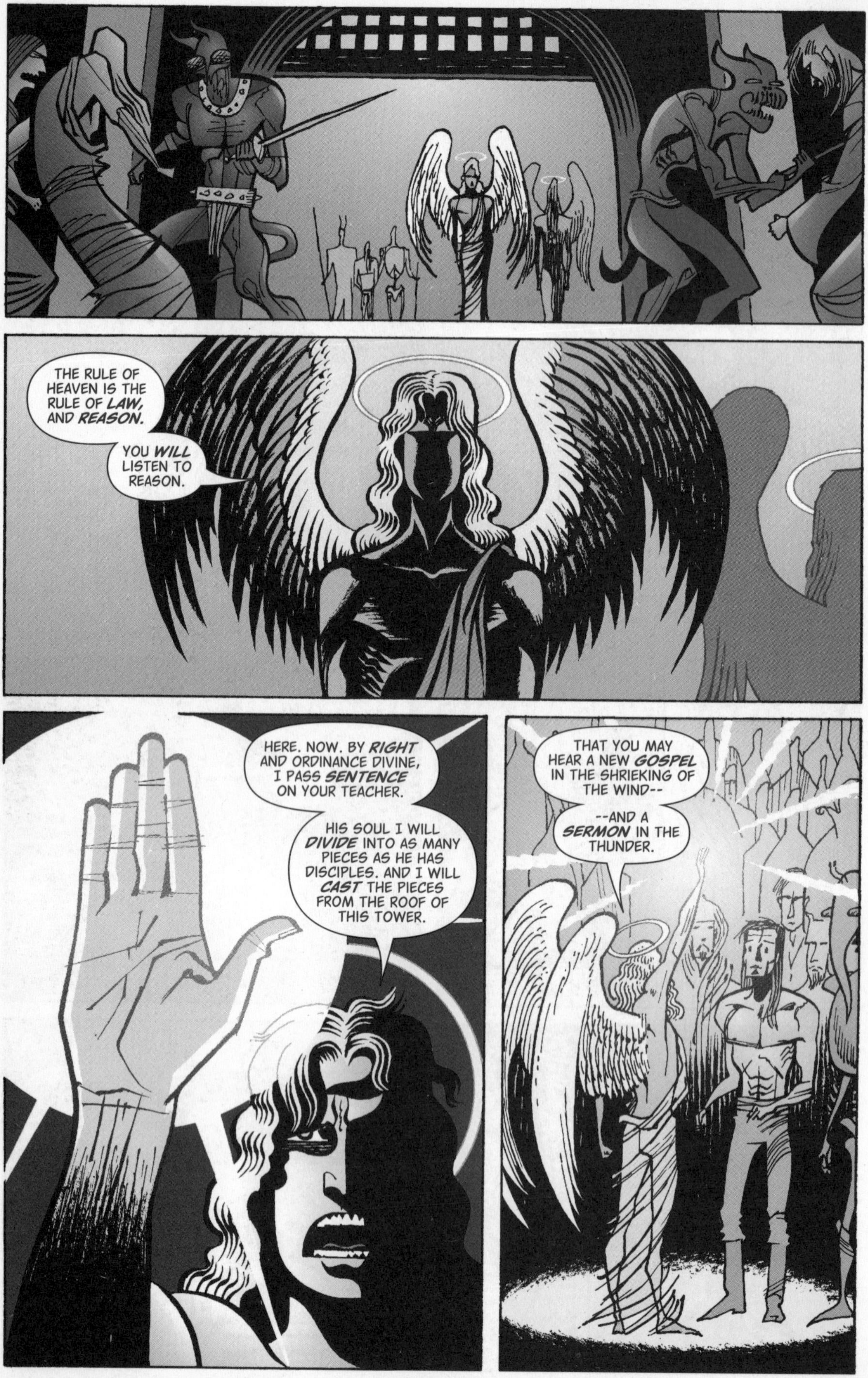

THE RULE OF HEAVEN IS THE RULE OF LAW, AND REASON.
YOU WILL LISTEN TO REASON.
HERE. NOW. BY RIGHT AND ORDINANCE DIVINE, I PASS SENTENCE ON YOUR TEACHER.
HIS SOUL I WILL DIVIDE INTO AS MANY PIECES AS HE HAS DISCIPLES. AND I WILL CAST THE PIECES FROM THE ROOF OF THIS TOWER.
THAT YOU MAY HEAR A NEW GOSPEL IN THE SHRIEKING OF THE WIND--
--AND A SERMON IN THE THUNDER.

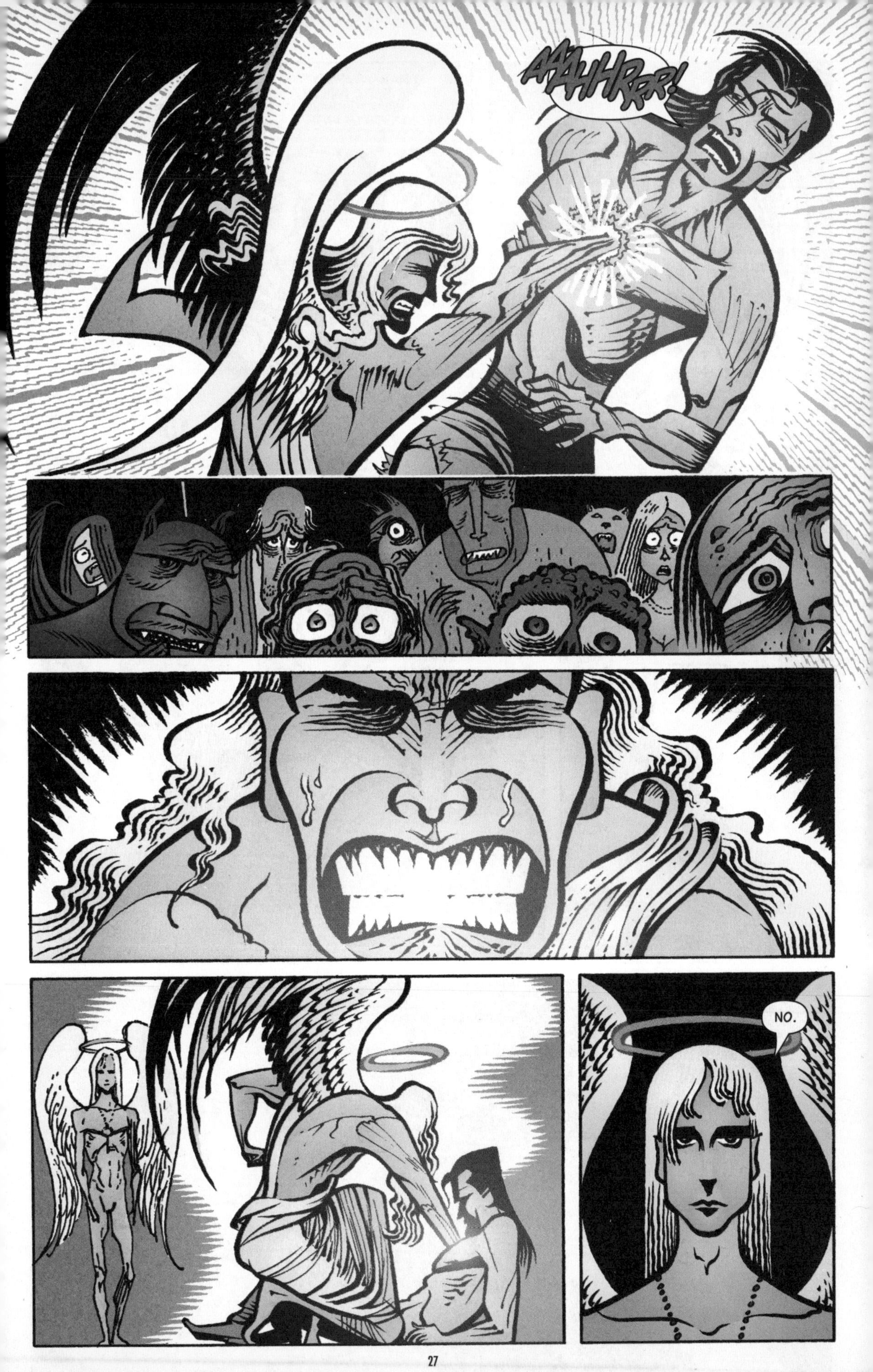
AAAHHRRRR!
NO.

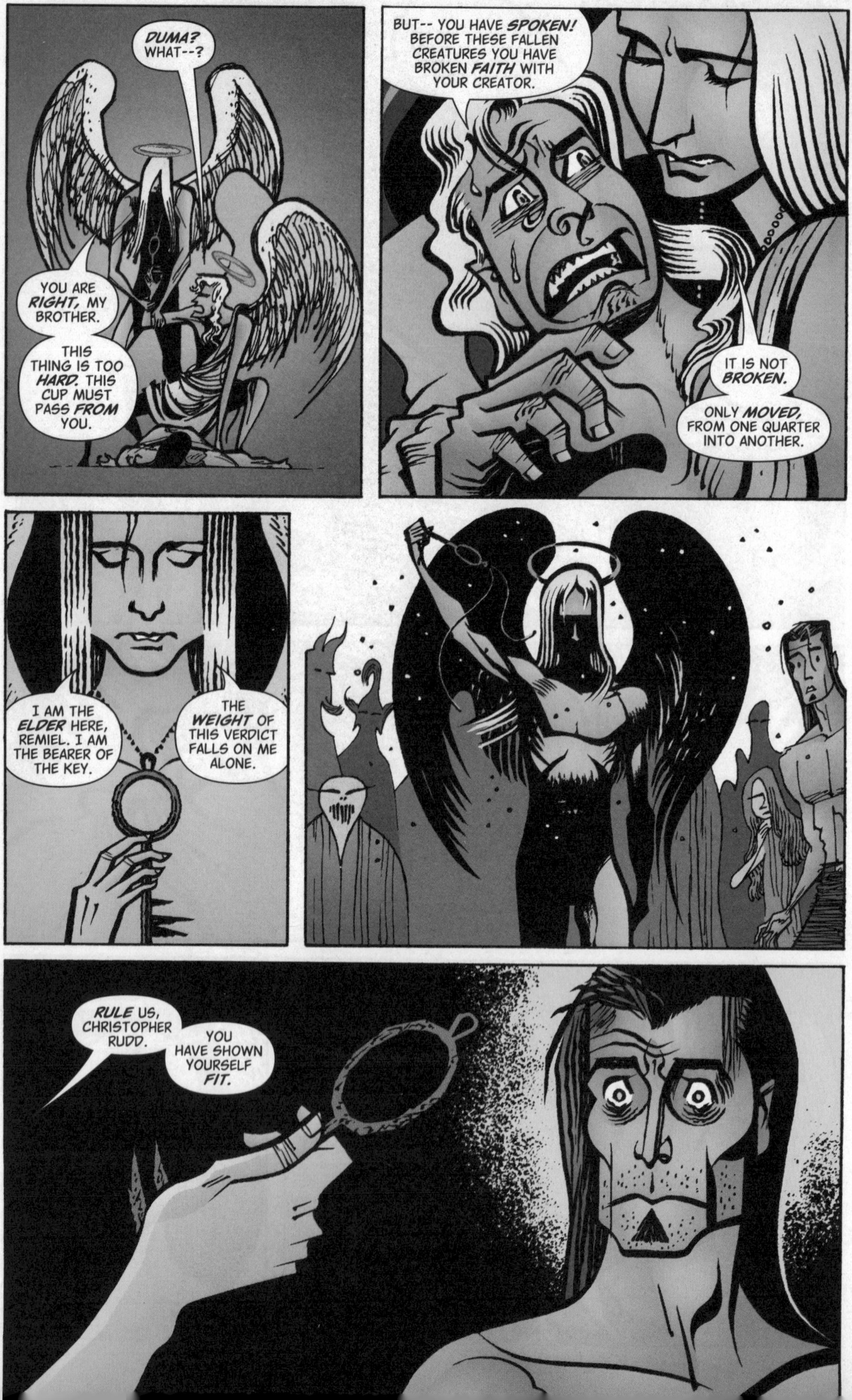
DUMA? WHAT--?
YOU ARE RIGHT, MY BROTHER.
THIS THING IS TOO HARD. THIS CUP MUST PASS FROM YOU.
BUT-- YOU HAVE SPOKEN! BEFORE THESE FALLEN CREATURES YOU HAVE BROKEN FAITH WITH YOUR CREATOR.
IT IS NOT BROKEN.
ONLY MOVED, FROM ONE QUARTER INTO ANOTHER.
I AM THE ELDER HERE, REMIEL. I AM THE BEARER OF THE KEY.
THE WEIGHT OF THIS VERDICT FALLS ON ME ALONE.
RULE US, CHRISTOPHER RUDD.
YOU HAVE SHOWN YOURSELF FIT.

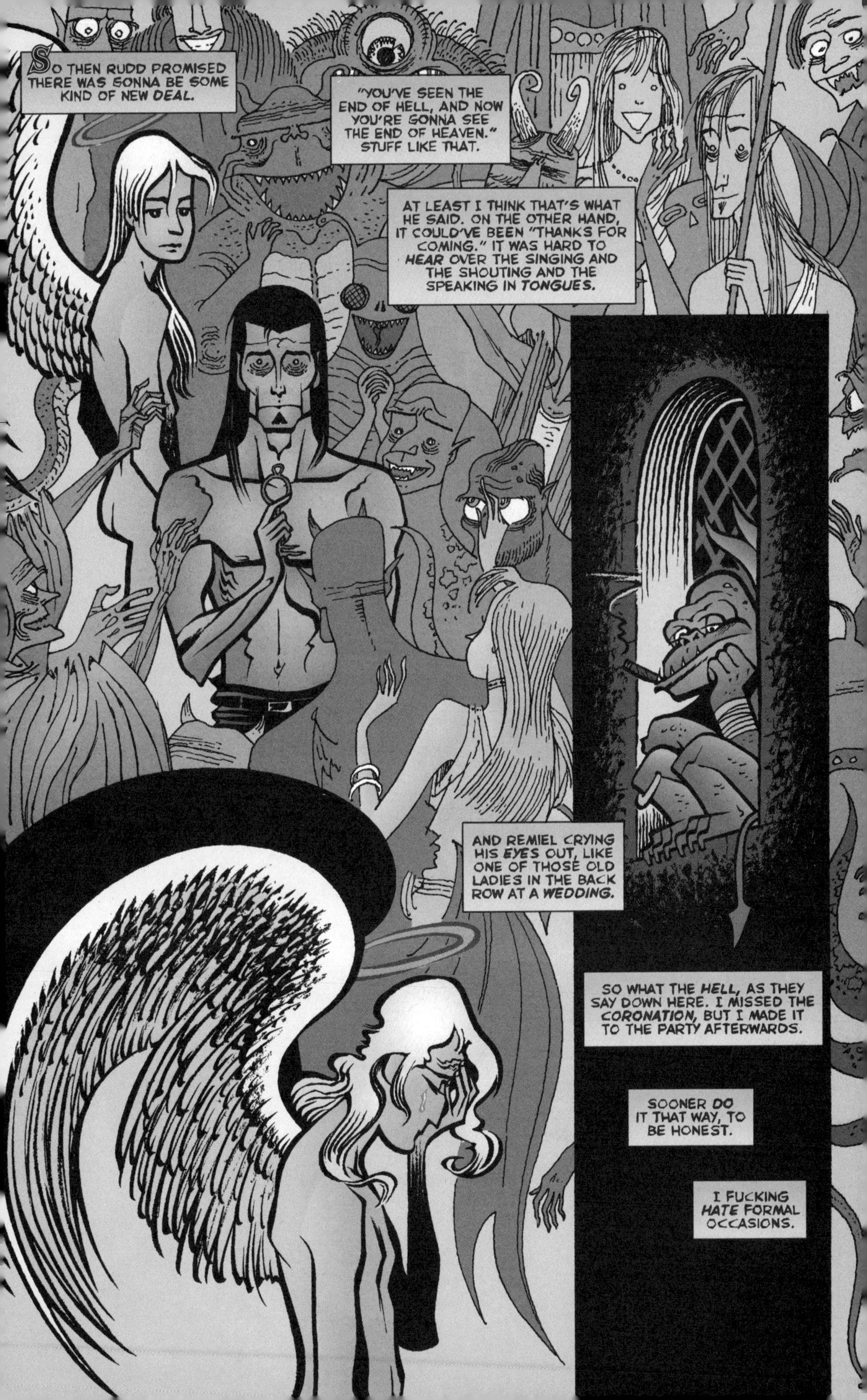
SO THEN RUDD PROMISED THERE WAS GONNA BE SOME KIND OF NEW DEAL.
"YOU'VE SEEN THE END OF HELL, AND NOW YOU'RE GONNA SEE THE END OF HEAVEN." STUFF LIKE THAT.
AT LEAST I THINK THAT'S WHAT HE SAID. ON THE OTHER HAND, IT COULD'VE BEEN "THANKS FOR COMING." IT WAS HARD TO HEAR OVER THE SINGING AND THE SHOUTING AND THE SPEAKING IN TONGUES.
AND REMIEL CRYING HIS EYES OUT, LIKE ONE OF THOSE OLD LADIES IN THE BACK ROW AT A WEDDING.
SO WHAT THE HELL, AS THEY SAY DOWN HERE. I MISSED THE CORONATION, BUT I MADE IT TO THE PARTY AFTERWARDS.
SOONER DO IT THAT WAY, TO BE HONEST.
I FUCKING HATE FORMAL OCCASIONS.

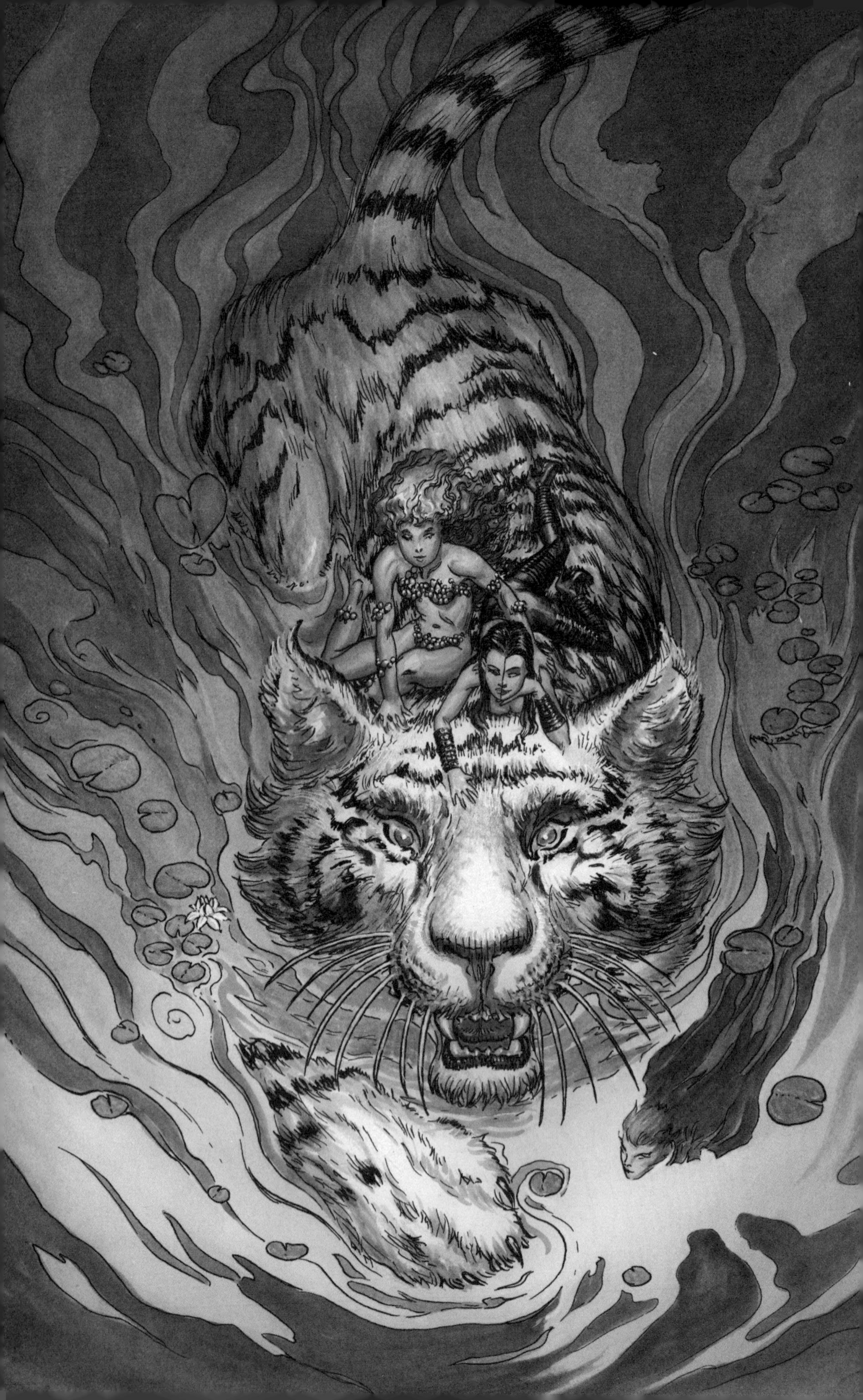

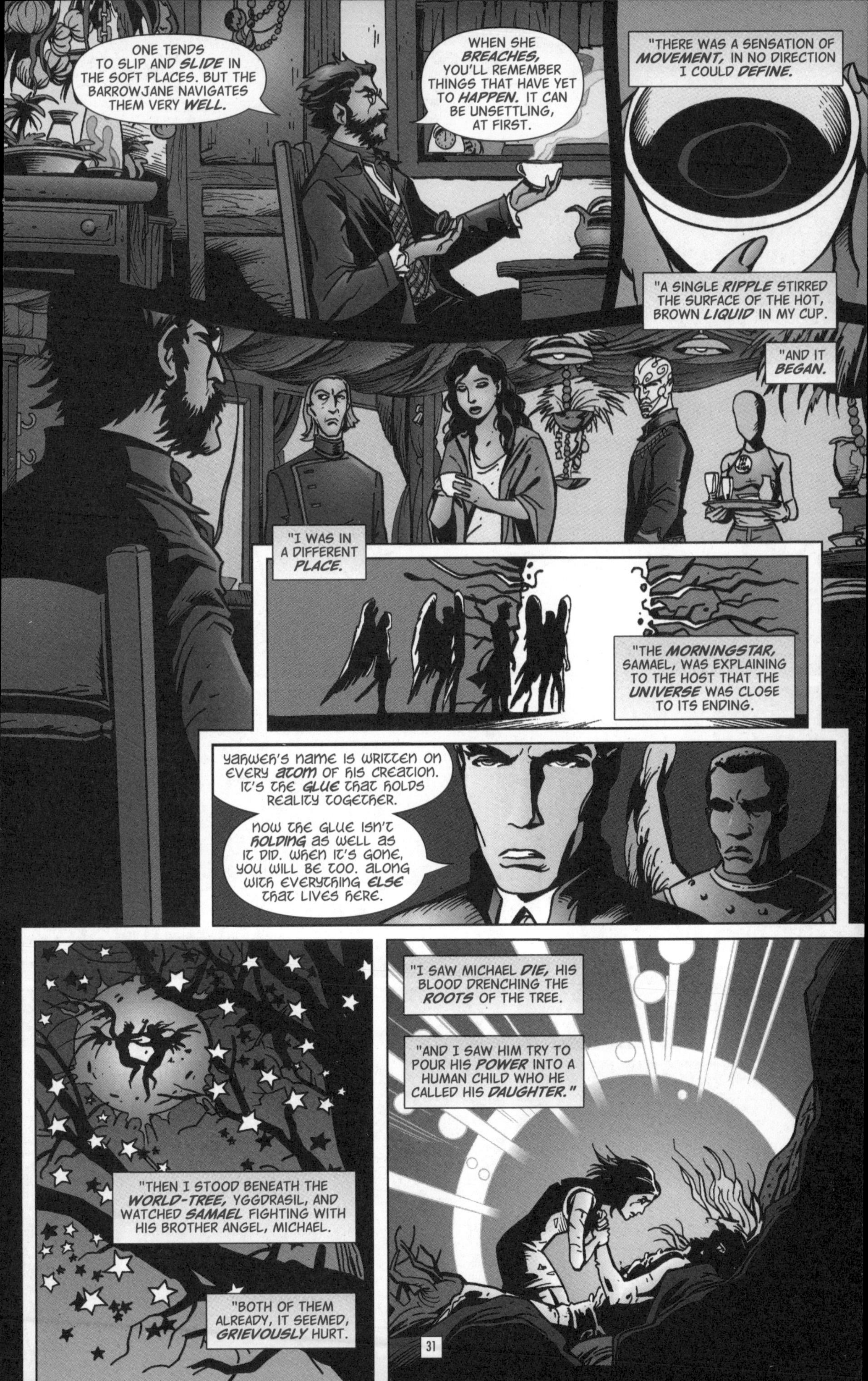
ONE TENDS TO SLIP AND *SLIDE* IN THE SOFT PLACES. BUT THE BARROWJANE NAVIGATES THEM VERY *WELL.*
WHEN SHE *BREACHES,* YOU'LL REMEMBER THINGS THAT HAVE YET TO *HAPPEN.* IT CAN BE UNSETTLING, AT FIRST.
"THERE WAS A SENSATION OF *MOVEMENT,* IN NO DIRECTION I COULD *DEFINE.*
"A SINGLE *RIPPLE* STIRRED THE SURFACE OF THE HOT, BROWN *LIQUID* IN MY CUP.
"AND IT *BEGAN.*
"I WAS IN A DIFFERENT *PLACE.*
"THE *MORNINGSTAR,* SAMAEL, WAS EXPLAINING TO THE HOST THAT THE *UNIVERSE* WAS CLOSE TO ITS ENDING.
YAHWEH'S NAME IS WRITTEN ON EVERY *ATOM* OF HIS CREATION. IT'S THE *GLUE* THAT HOLDS REALITY TOGETHER.
NOW THE GLUE ISN'T *HOLDING* AS WELL AS IT DID. WHEN IT'S GONE, YOU WILL BE TOO. ALONG WITH EVERYTHING *ELSE* THAT LIVES HERE.
"THEN I STOOD BENEATH THE *WORLD-TREE,* YGGDRASIL, AND WATCHED *SAMAEL* FIGHTING WITH HIS BROTHER ANGEL, MICHAEL.
"BOTH OF THEM ALREADY, IT SEEMED, *GRIEVOUSLY* HURT.
"I SAW MICHAEL *DIE,* HIS BLOOD DRENCHING THE *ROOTS* OF THE TREE.
"AND I SAW HIM TRY TO POUR HIS *POWER* INTO A HUMAN CHILD WHO HE CALLED HIS *DAUGHTER."*

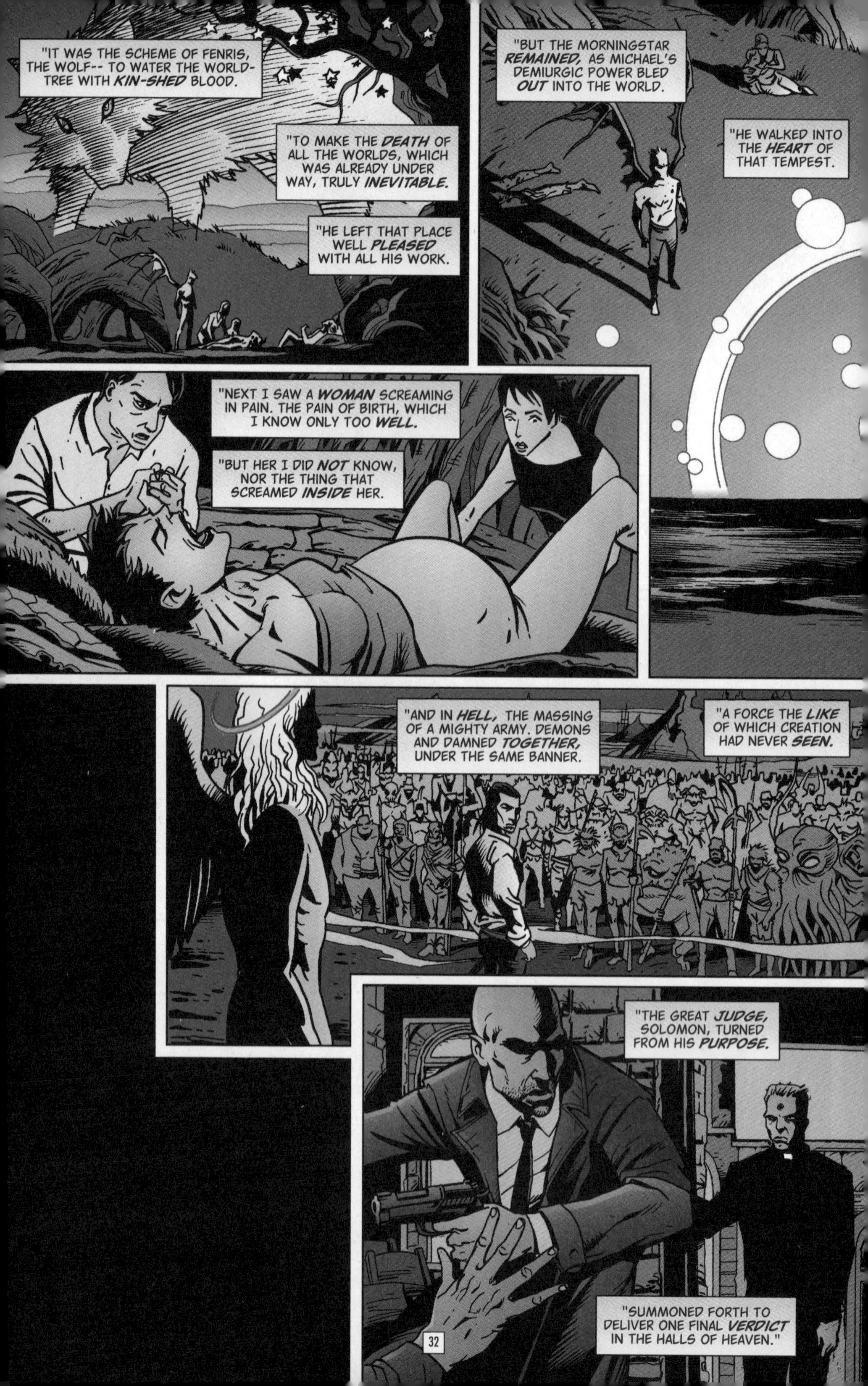
"IT WAS THE SCHEME OF FENRIS, THE WOLF-- TO WATER THE WORLD-TREE WITH KIN-SHED BLOOD.
"TO MAKE THE DEATH OF ALL THE WORLDS, WHICH WAS ALREADY UNDER WAY, TRULY INEVITABLE.
"HE LEFT THAT PLACE WELL PLEASED WITH ALL HIS WORK.
"BUT THE MORNINGSTAR REMAINED, AS MICHAEL'S DEMIURGIC POWER BLED OUT INTO THE WORLD.
"HE WALKED INTO THE HEART OF THAT TEMPEST.
"NEXT I SAW A WOMAN SCREAMING IN PAIN. THE PAIN OF BIRTH, WHICH I KNOW ONLY TOO WELL.
"BUT HER I DID NOT KNOW, NOR THE THING THAT SCREAMED INSIDE HER.
"AND IN HELL, THE MASSING OF A MIGHTY ARMY. DEMONS AND DAMNED TOGETHER, UNDER THE SAME BANNER.
"A FORCE THE LIKE OF WHICH CREATION HAD NEVER SEEN.
"THE GREAT JUDGE, SOLOMON, TURNED FROM HIS PURPOSE.
"SUMMONED FORTH TO DELIVER ONE FINAL VERDICT IN THE HALLS OF HEAVEN."

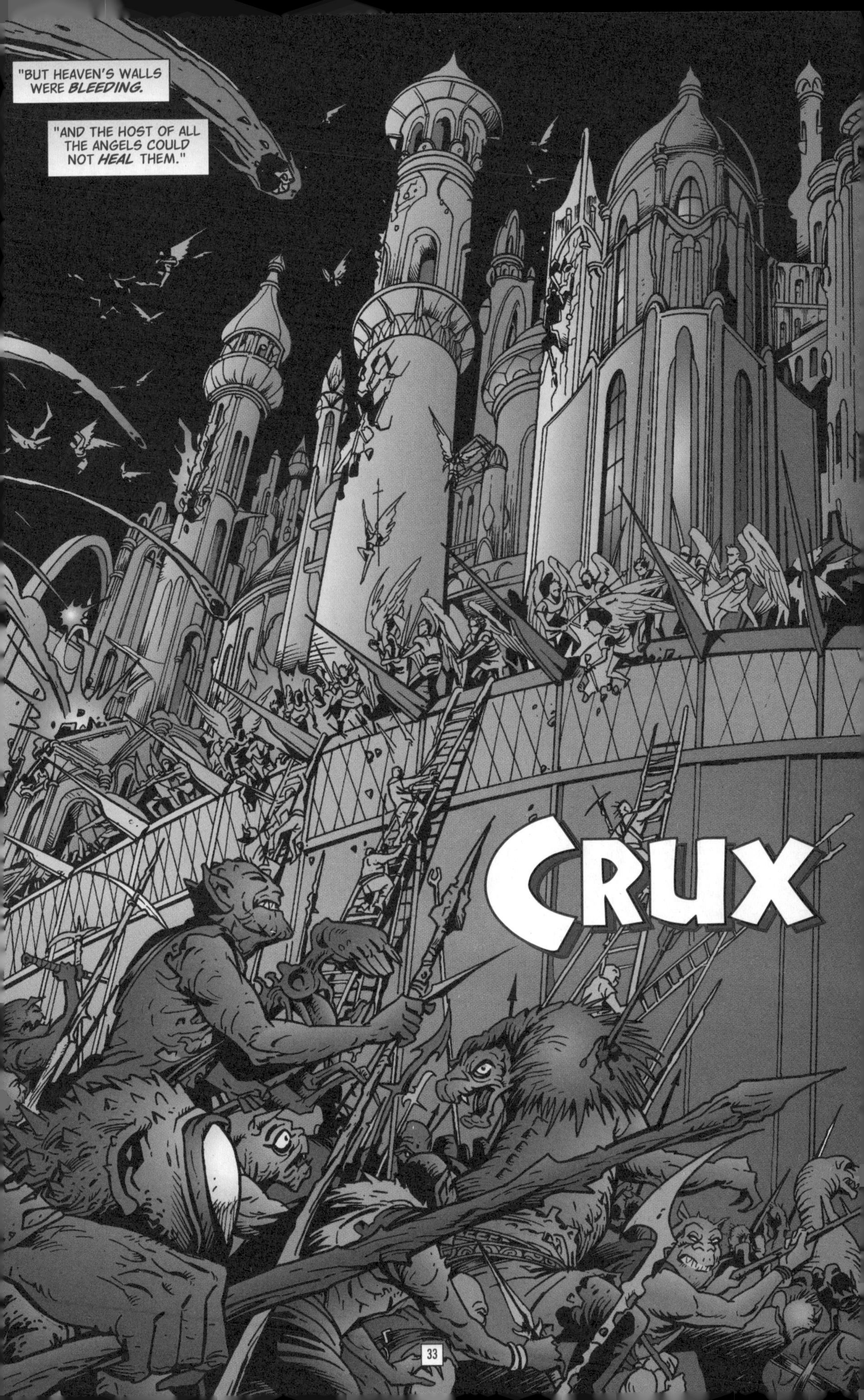
"BUT HEAVEN'S WALLS WERE *BLEEDING.*
"AND THE HOST OF ALL THE ANGELS COULD NOT *HEAL* THEM."
CRUX

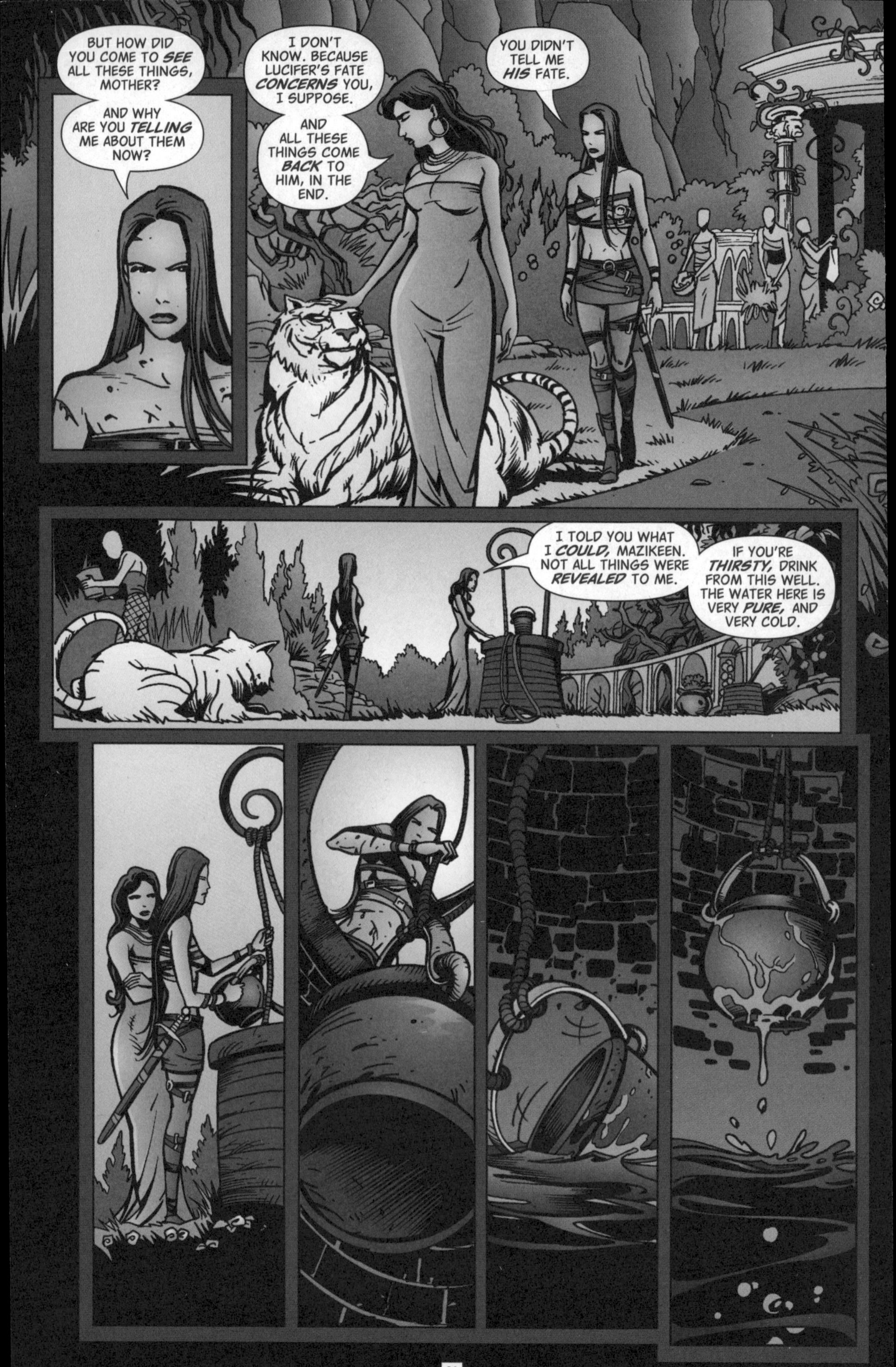
BUT HOW DID YOU COME TO SEE ALL THESE THINGS, MOTHER?
AND WHY ARE YOU TELLING ME ABOUT THEM NOW?
I DON'T KNOW. BECAUSE LUCIFER'S FATE CONCERNS YOU, I SUPPOSE.
AND ALL THESE THINGS COME BACK TO HIM, IN THE END.
YOU DIDN'T TELL ME HIS FATE.
I TOLD YOU WHAT I COULD, MAZIKEEN. NOT ALL THINGS WERE REVEALED TO ME.
IF YOU'RE THIRSTY, DRINK FROM THIS WELL. THE WATER HERE IS VERY PURE, AND VERY COLD.

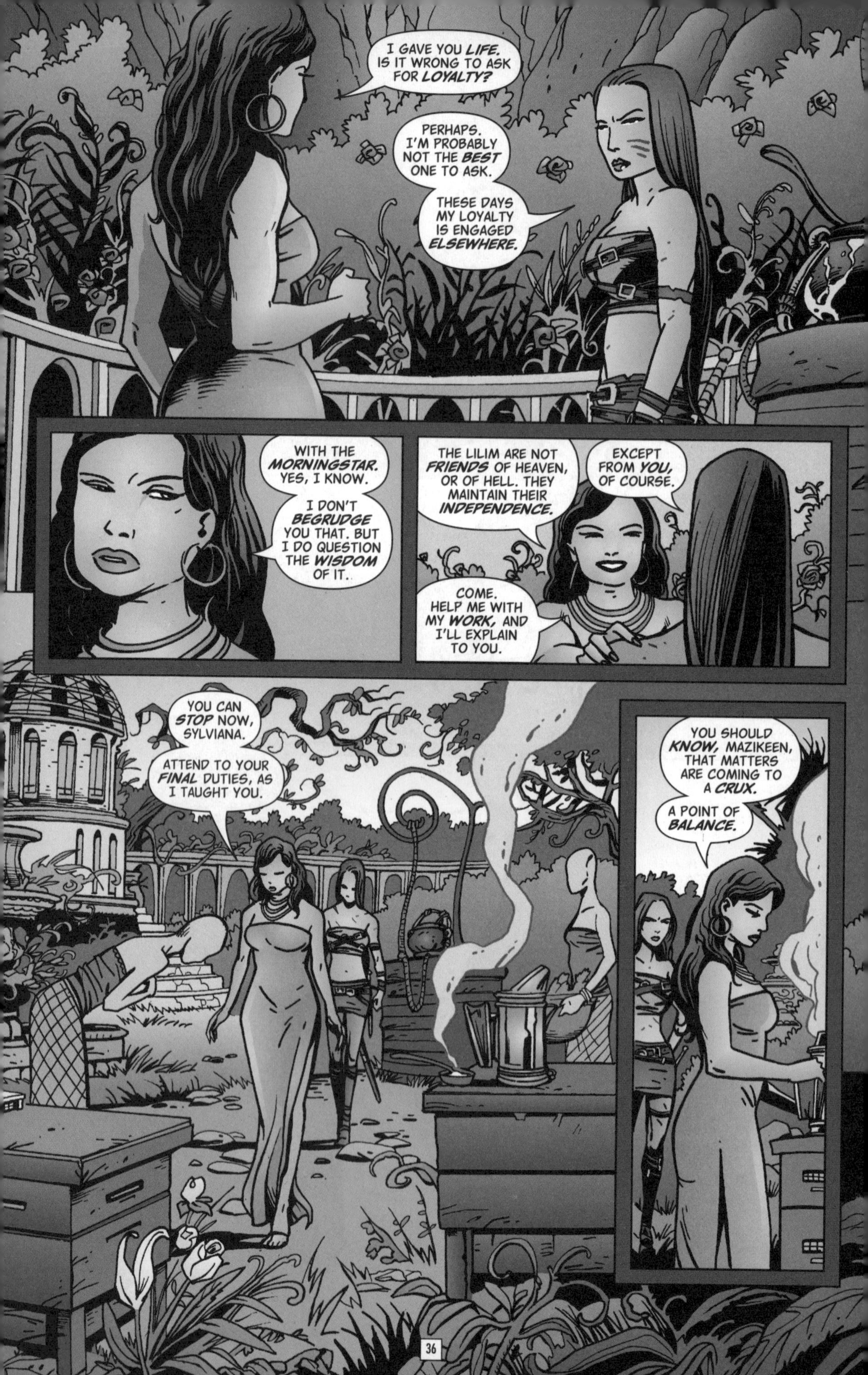
I GAVE YOU LIFE. IS IT WRONG TO ASK FOR LOYALTY?
PERHAPS. I'M PROBABLY NOT THE BEST ONE TO ASK.
THESE DAYS MY LOYALTY IS ENGAGED ELSEWHERE.
WITH THE MORNINGSTAR. YES, I KNOW.
I DON'T BEGRUDGE YOU THAT. BUT I DO QUESTION THE WISDOM OF IT.
THE LILIM ARE NOT FRIENDS OF HEAVEN, OR OF HELL. THEY MAINTAIN THEIR INDEPENDENCE.
EXCEPT FROM YOU, OF COURSE.
COME. HELP ME WITH MY WORK, AND I'LL EXPLAIN TO YOU.
YOU CAN STOP NOW, SYLVIANA.
ATTEND TO YOUR FINAL DUTIES, AS I TAUGHT YOU.
YOU SHOULD KNOW, MAZIKEEN, THAT MATTERS ARE COMING TO A CRUX.
A POINT OF BALANCE.

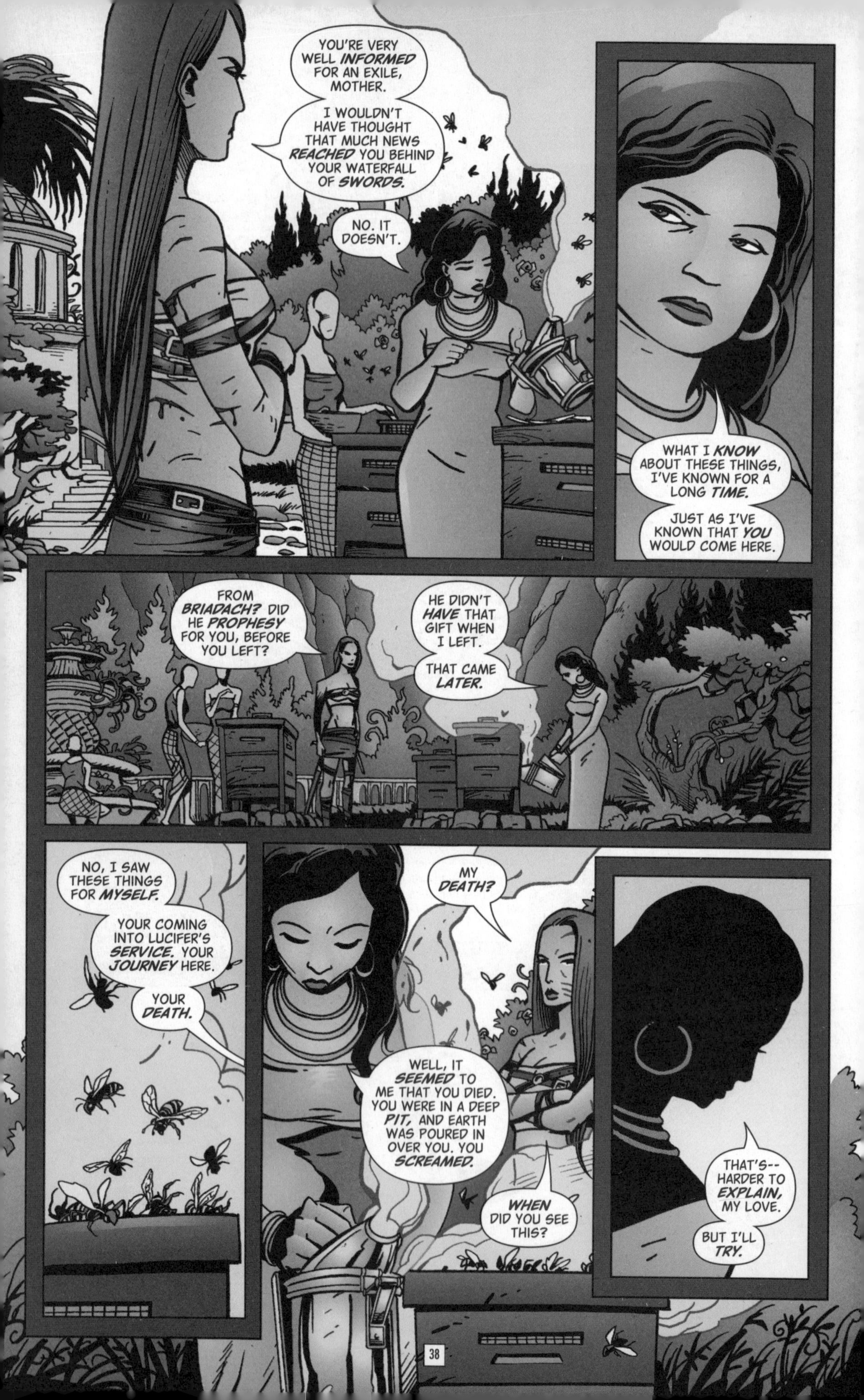
YOU'RE VERY WELL INFORMED FOR AN EXILE, MOTHER.
I WOULDN'T HAVE THOUGHT THAT MUCH NEWS REACHED YOU BEHIND YOUR WATERFALL OF SWORDS.
NO. IT DOESN'T.
WHAT I KNOW ABOUT THESE THINGS, I'VE KNOWN FOR A LONG TIME.
JUST AS I'VE KNOWN THAT YOU WOULD COME HERE.
FROM BRIADACH? DID HE PROPHESY FOR YOU, BEFORE YOU LEFT?
HE DIDN'T HAVE THAT GIFT WHEN I LEFT.
THAT CAME LATER.
NO, I SAW THESE THINGS FOR MYSELF.
YOUR COMING INTO LUCIFER'S SERVICE. YOUR JOURNEY HERE.
YOUR DEATH.
MY DEATH?
WELL, IT SEEMED TO ME THAT YOU DIED. YOU WERE IN A DEEP PIT, AND EARTH WAS POURED IN OVER YOU. YOU SCREAMED.
WHEN DID YOU SEE THIS?
THAT'S-- HARDER TO EXPLAIN, MY LOVE.
BUT I'LL TRY.

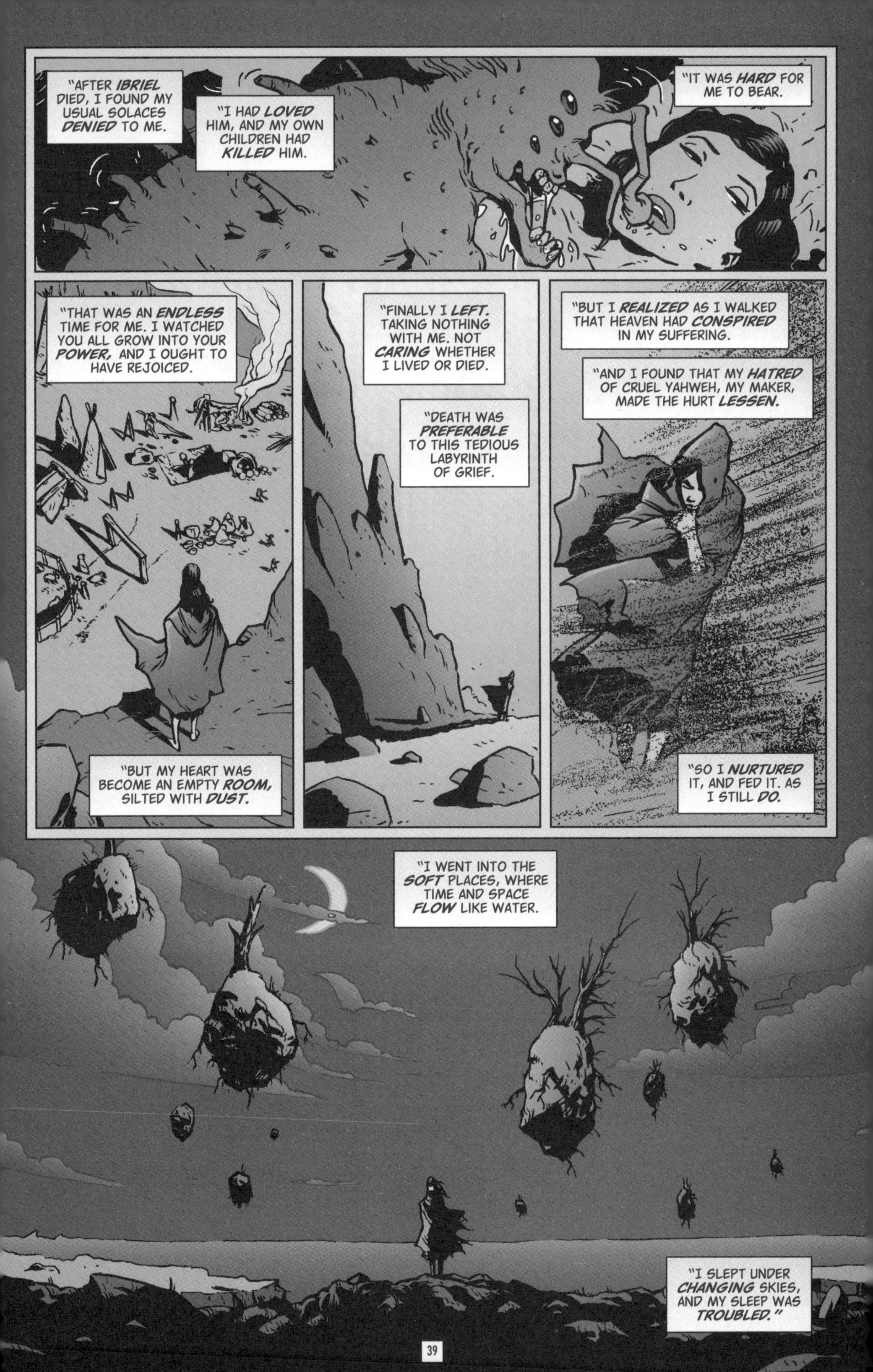
"AFTER IBRIEL DIED, I FOUND MY USUAL SOLACES DENIED TO ME.
"I HAD LOVED HIM, AND MY OWN CHILDREN HAD KILLED HIM.
"IT WAS HARD FOR ME TO BEAR.
"THAT WAS AN ENDLESS TIME FOR ME. I WATCHED YOU ALL GROW INTO YOUR POWER, AND I OUGHT TO HAVE REJOICED.
"BUT MY HEART WAS BECOME AN EMPTY ROOM, SILTED WITH DUST.
"FINALLY I LEFT. TAKING NOTHING WITH ME. NOT CARING WHETHER I LIVED OR DIED.
"DEATH WAS PREFERABLE TO THIS TEDIOUS LABYRINTH OF GRIEF.
"BUT I REALIZED AS I WALKED THAT HEAVEN HAD CONSPIRED IN MY SUFFERING.
"AND I FOUND THAT MY HATRED OF CRUEL YAHWEH, MY MAKER, MADE THE HURT LESSEN.
"SO I NURTURED IT, AND FED IT. AS I STILL DO.
"I WENT INTO THE SOFT PLACES, WHERE TIME AND SPACE FLOW LIKE WATER.
"I SLEPT UNDER CHANGING SKIES, AND MY SLEEP WAS TROUBLED."

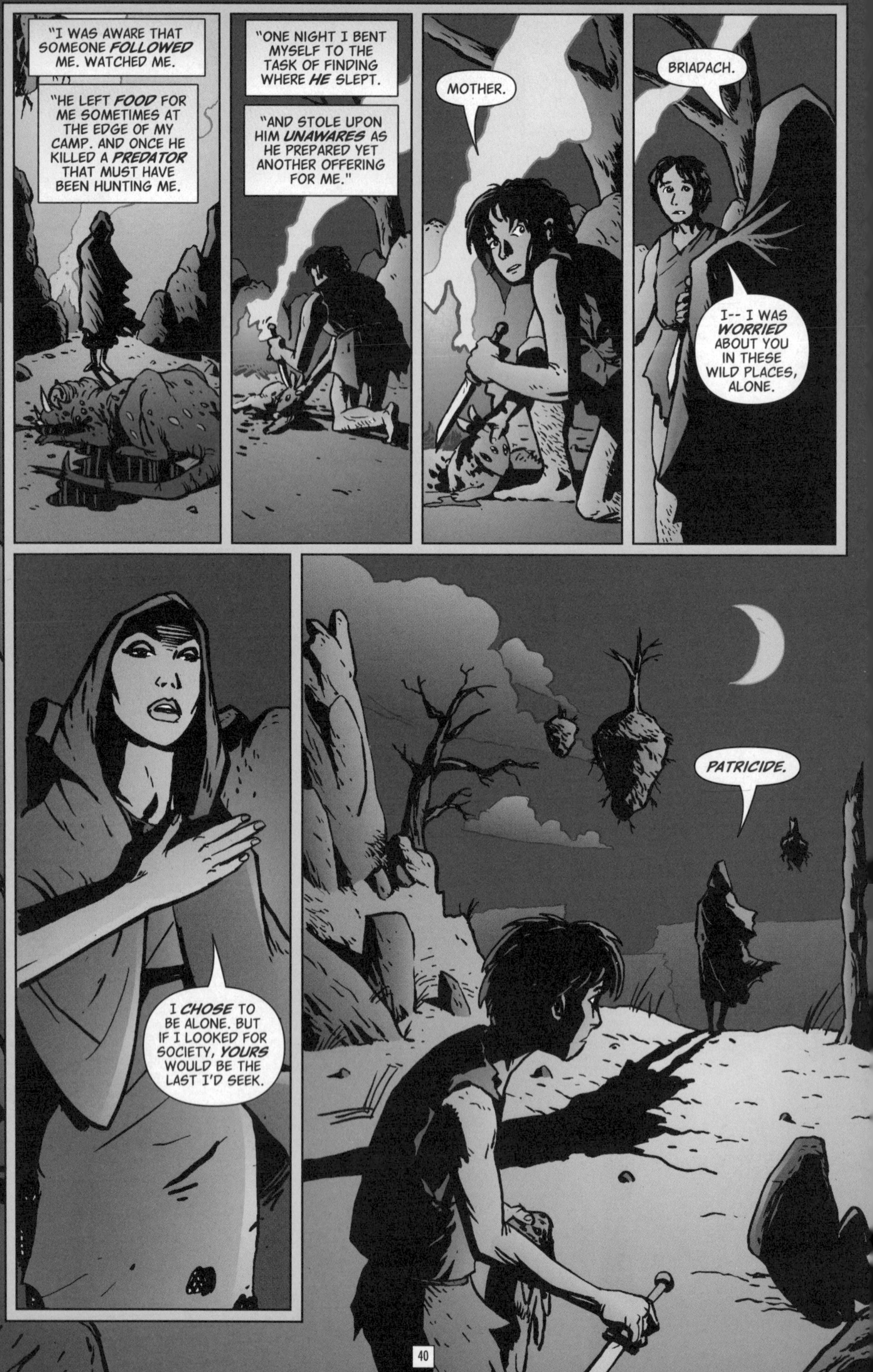
"I WAS AWARE THAT SOMEONE *FOLLOWED* ME. WATCHED ME.
"HE LEFT *FOOD* FOR ME SOMETIMES AT THE EDGE OF MY CAMP. AND ONCE HE KILLED A *PREDATOR* THAT MUST HAVE BEEN HUNTING ME.
"ONE NIGHT I BENT MYSELF TO THE TASK OF FINDING WHERE *HE* SLEPT.
"AND STOLE UPON HIM *UNAWARES* AS HE PREPARED YET ANOTHER OFFERING FOR ME."
MOTHER.
BRIADACH.
I-- I WAS *WORRIED* ABOUT YOU IN THESE WILD PLACES, ALONE.
I *CHOSE* TO BE ALONE. BUT IF I LOOKED FOR SOCIETY, *YOURS* WOULD BE THE LAST I'D SEEK.
PATRICIDE.

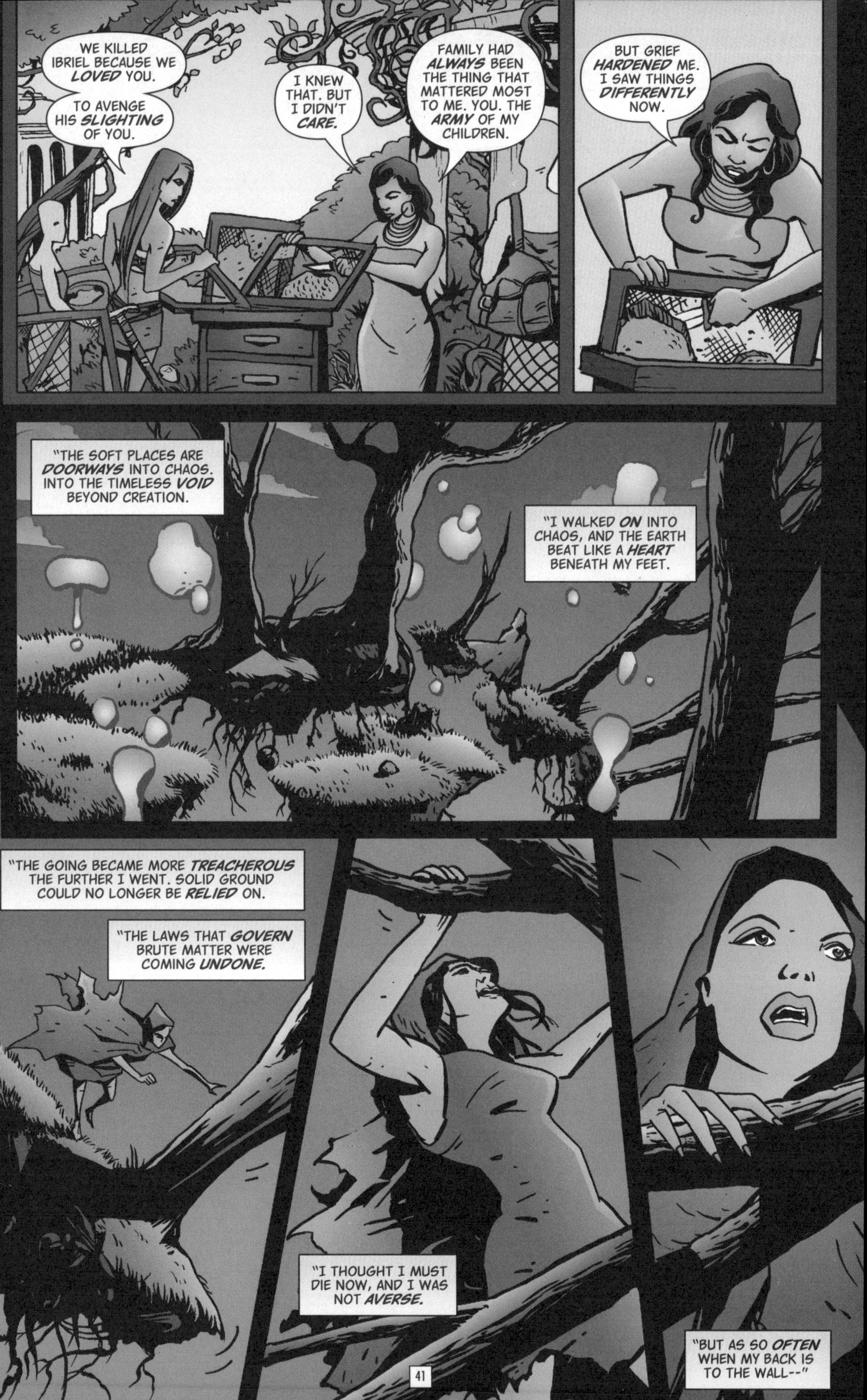
WE KILLED IBRIEL BECAUSE WE LOVED YOU.
TO AVENGE HIS SLIGHTING OF YOU.
I KNEW THAT. BUT I DIDN'T CARE.
FAMILY HAD ALWAYS BEEN THE THING THAT MATTERED MOST TO ME. YOU. THE ARMY OF MY CHILDREN.
BUT GRIEF HARDENED ME. I SAW THINGS DIFFERENTLY NOW.
"THE SOFT PLACES ARE DOORWAYS INTO CHAOS. INTO THE TIMELESS VOID BEYOND CREATION.
"I WALKED ON INTO CHAOS, AND THE EARTH BEAT LIKE A HEART BENEATH MY FEET.
"THE GOING BECAME MORE TREACHEROUS THE FURTHER I WENT. SOLID GROUND COULD NO LONGER BE RELIED ON.
"THE LAWS THAT GOVERN BRUTE MATTER WERE COMING UNDONE.
"I THOUGHT I MUST DIE NOW, AND I WAS NOT AVERSE.
"BUT AS SO OFTEN WHEN MY BACK IS TO THE WALL--"

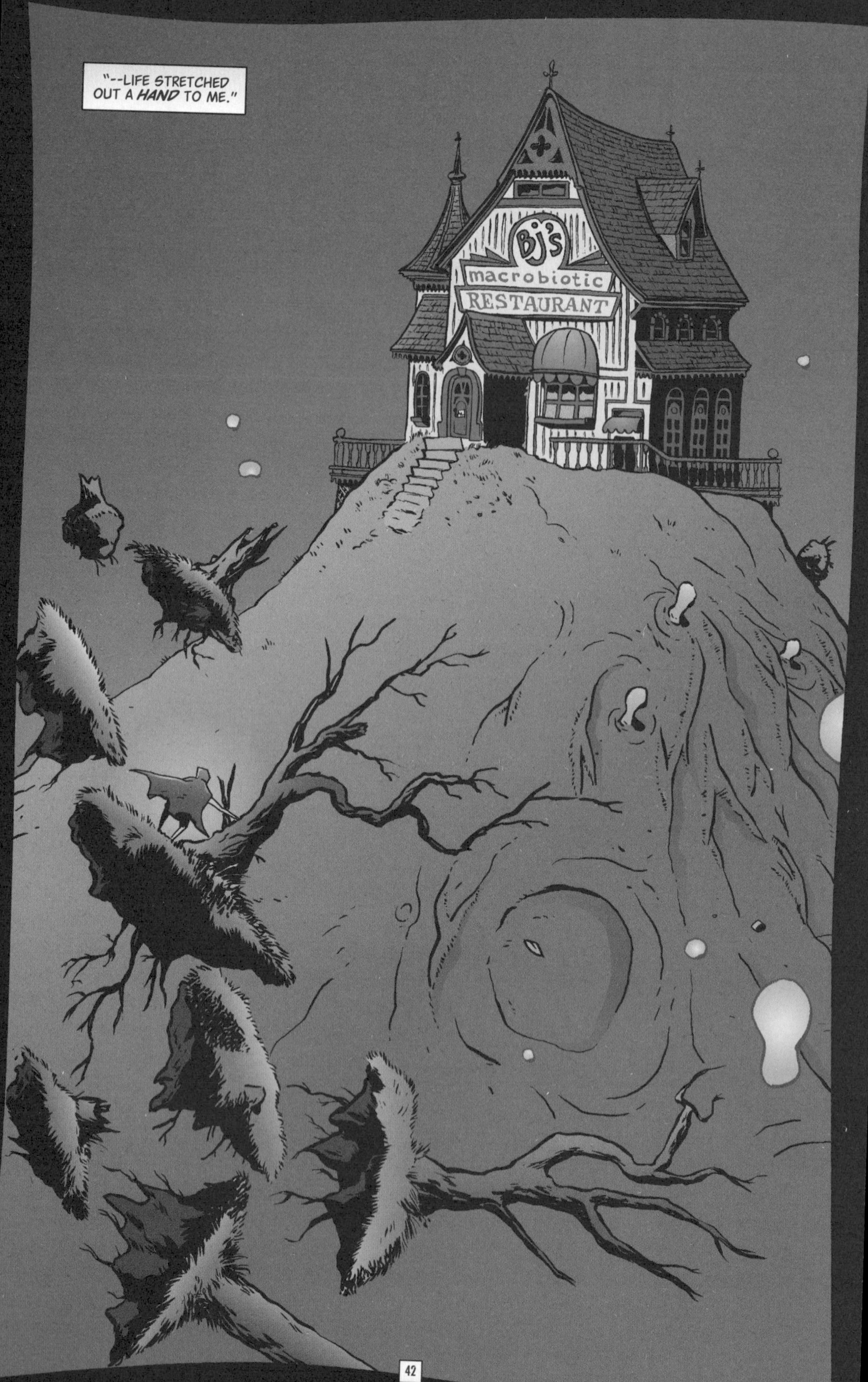
"--LIFE STRETCHED OUT A *HAND* TO ME."
BJ's
macrobiotic
RESTAURANT

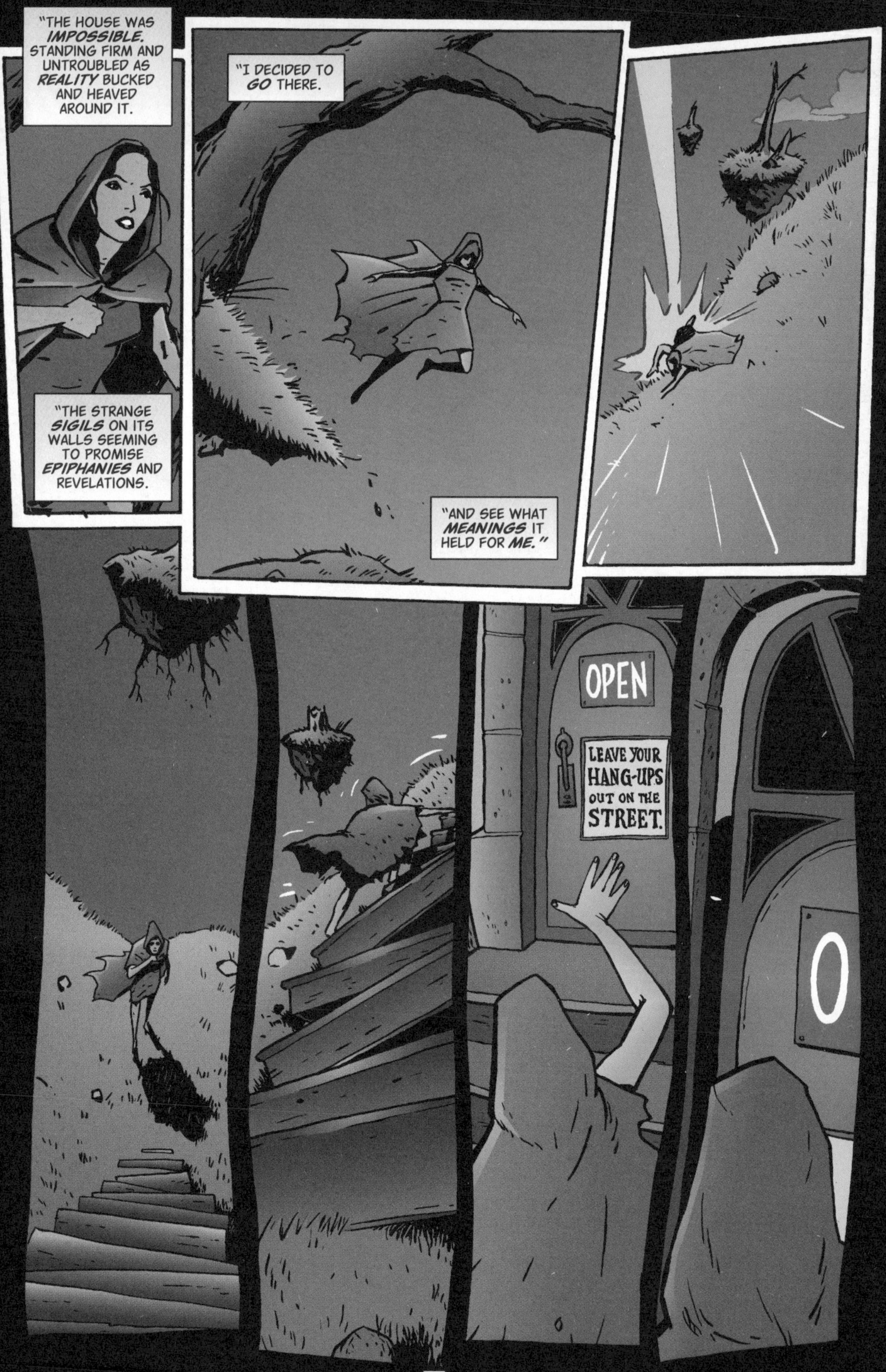
"THE HOUSE WAS IMPOSSIBLE. STANDING FIRM AND UNTROUBLED AS REALITY BUCKED AND HEAVED AROUND IT.
"THE STRANGE SIGILS ON ITS WALLS SEEMING TO PROMISE EPIPHANIES AND REVELATIONS.
"I DECIDED TO GO THERE.
"AND SEE WHAT MEANINGS IT HELD FOR ME."
OPEN
LEAVE YOUR HANG-UPS OUT ON THE STREET.

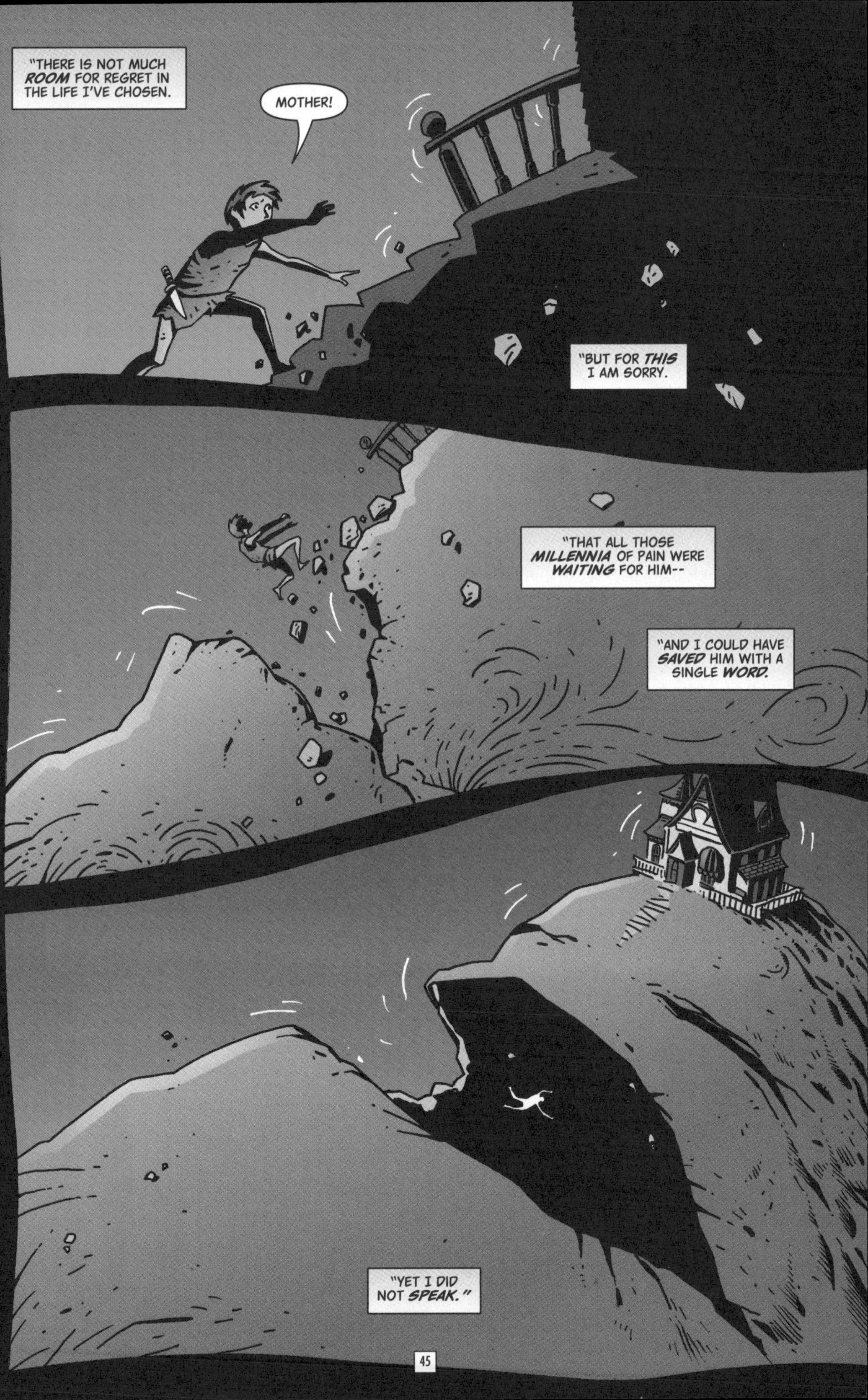
"THERE IS NOT MUCH ROOM FOR REGRET IN THE LIFE I'VE CHOSEN.
MOTHER!
"BUT FOR THIS I AM SORRY.
"THAT ALL THOSE MILLENNIA OF PAIN WERE WAITING FOR HIM--
"AND I COULD HAVE SAVED HIM WITH A SINGLE WORD.
"YET I DID NOT SPEAK."

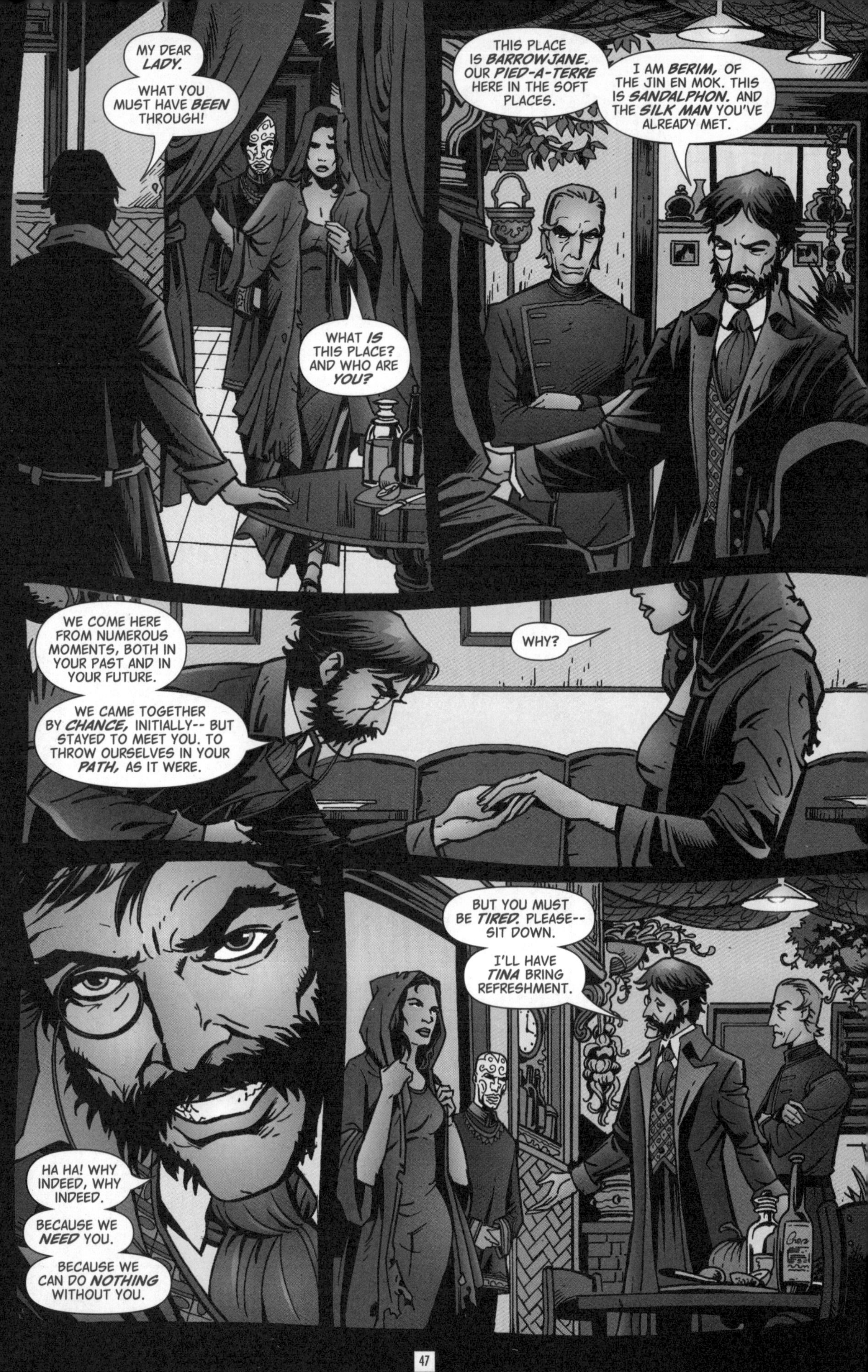
MY DEAR *LADY.*
WHAT YOU MUST HAVE *BEEN* THROUGH!
WHAT *IS* THIS PLACE? AND WHO ARE *YOU?*
THIS PLACE IS *BARROWJANE.* OUR *PIED-A-TERRE* HERE IN THE SOFT PLACES.
I AM *BERIM,* OF THE JIN EN MOK. THIS IS *SANDALPHON.* AND THE *SILK MAN* YOU'VE ALREADY MET.
WE COME HERE FROM NUMEROUS MOMENTS, BOTH IN YOUR PAST AND IN YOUR FUTURE.
WE CAME TOGETHER BY *CHANCE,* INITIALLY-- BUT STAYED TO MEET YOU. TO THROW OURSELVES IN YOUR *PATH,* AS IT WERE.
WHY?
HA HA! WHY INDEED, WHY INDEED.
BECAUSE WE *NEED* YOU.
BECAUSE WE CAN DO *NOTHING* WITHOUT YOU.
BUT YOU MUST BE *TIRED.* PLEASE-- SIT DOWN.
I'LL HAVE *TINA* BRING REFRESHMENT.

THIS HOUSE-- WHAT IS IT *MADE* FROM? IT SEEMS TO *BREATHE*.

IT *DOES* BREATHE. THE BARROWJANE IS A LIVING *ENTITY*.

SHE HOUSES US AND FEEDS US, AND *SLIVERS* OF HER SUBSTANCE SERVE US.

BUT SHE'S OLD, AND HER ABILITY TO CAMOUFLAGE HERSELF HAS FALLEN *OFF* SOMEWHAT.

TEA AND *CAKE*, TINA.

SURE.

UMM... THE ANGEL LOOKS LIKE HE'S GONNA *DIE*. DID YOU WANT TO *SPEAK* TO HIM AGAIN?

HI, I AM TINA

HMM. ACTUALLY, I SUPPOSE *LILITH'S* ARRIVAL MAKES HIM A LITTLE-- *IRRELEVANT*.

THEN LET'S BE *RID* OF HIM.

VERY WELL, THEN. I'LL *DO* IT.

I *SAID* I WOULD, AND I'M A MAN OF MY *WORD*.

I BELIEVE THAT YOU *TOO*, DEAR LADY, HAVE A CERTAIN *ANIMUS* AGAINST THE HOST OF HEAVEN.

I HATE THEM. I HATE THEM *ALL*, SAVE ONLY *SAMAEL*.

FOR SOME REASON THE PROXIMITY OF *ANGELS* MAKES ME THINK OF *DEATH*.

JUST SO. IN THAT CASE, I THINK YOU MAY *ENJOY* THIS.

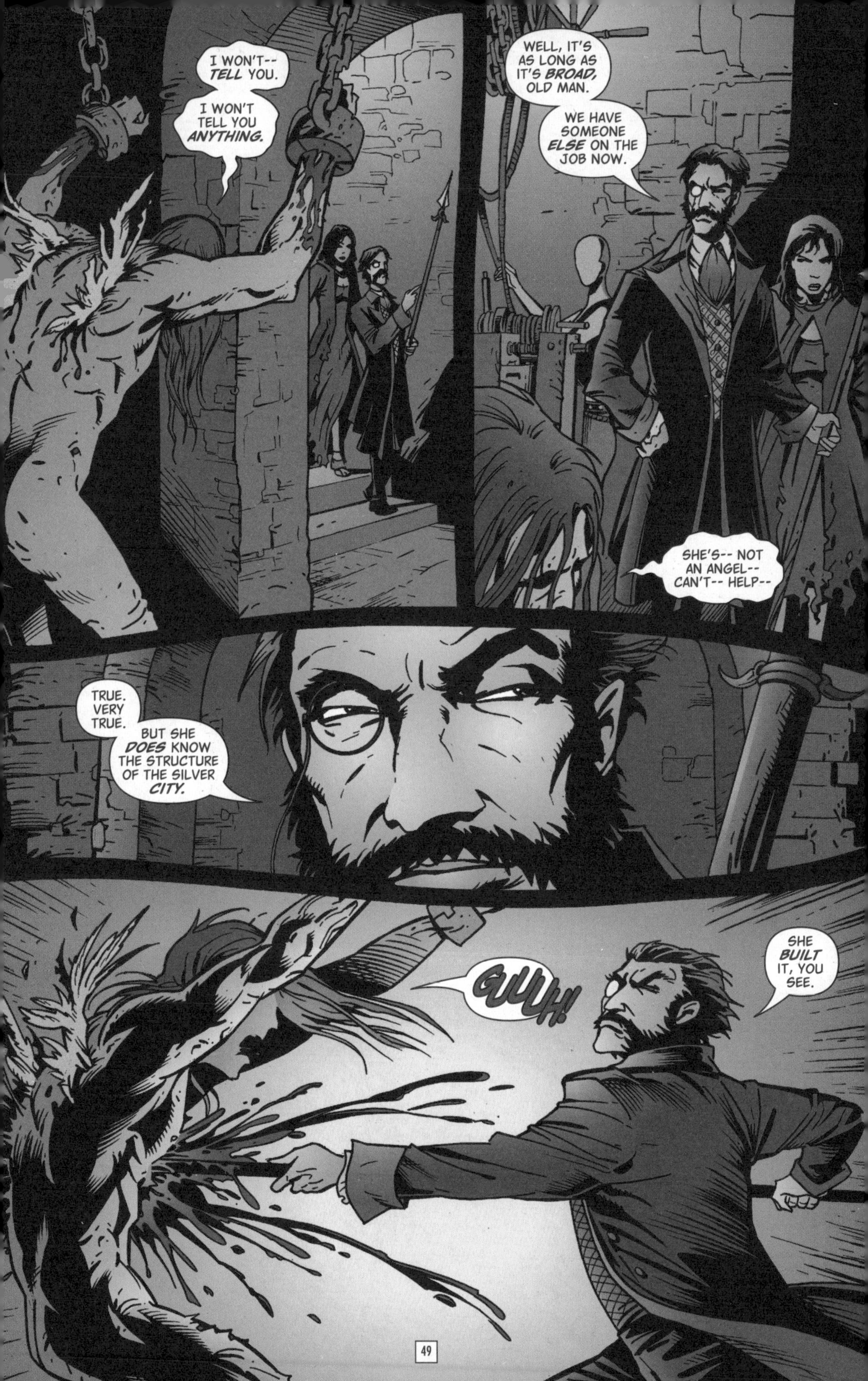
I WON'T-- TELL YOU.
I WON'T TELL YOU ANYTHING.
WELL, IT'S AS LONG AS IT'S BROAD, OLD MAN.
WE HAVE SOMEONE ELSE ON THE JOB NOW.
SHE'S-- NOT AN ANGEL-- CAN'T-- HELP--
TRUE. VERY TRUE.
BUT SHE DOES KNOW THE STRUCTURE OF THE SILVER CITY.
GUUH!
SHE BUILT IT, YOU SEE.

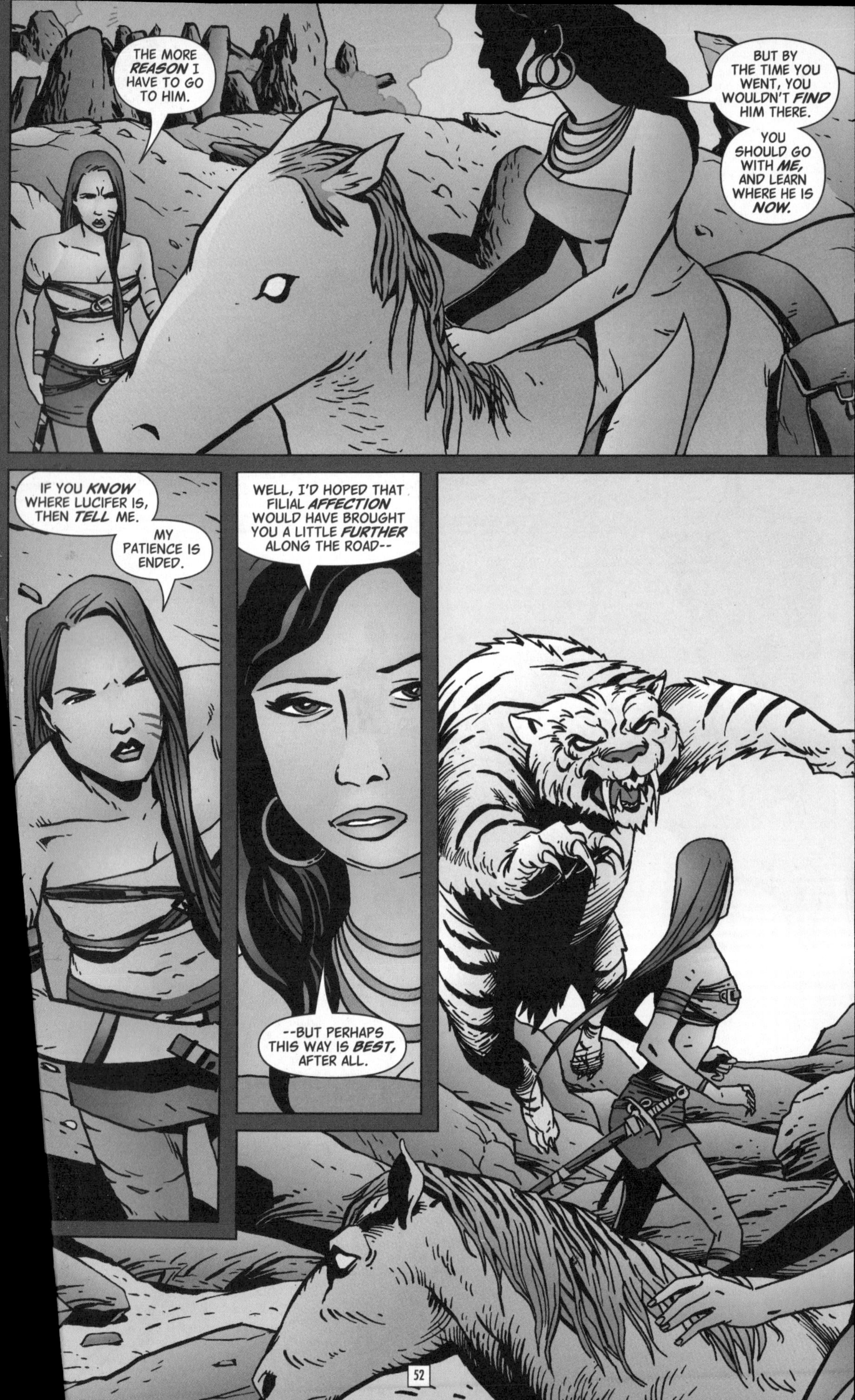
THE MORE REASON I HAVE TO GO TO HIM.
BUT BY THE TIME YOU WENT, YOU WOULDN'T FIND HIM THERE.
YOU SHOULD GO WITH ME, AND LEARN WHERE HE IS NOW.
IF YOU KNOW WHERE LUCIFER IS, THEN TELL ME.
MY PATIENCE IS ENDED.
WELL, I'D HOPED THAT FILIAL AFFECTION WOULD HAVE BROUGHT YOU A LITTLE FURTHER ALONG THE ROAD--
--BUT PERHAPS THIS WAY IS BEST, AFTER ALL.

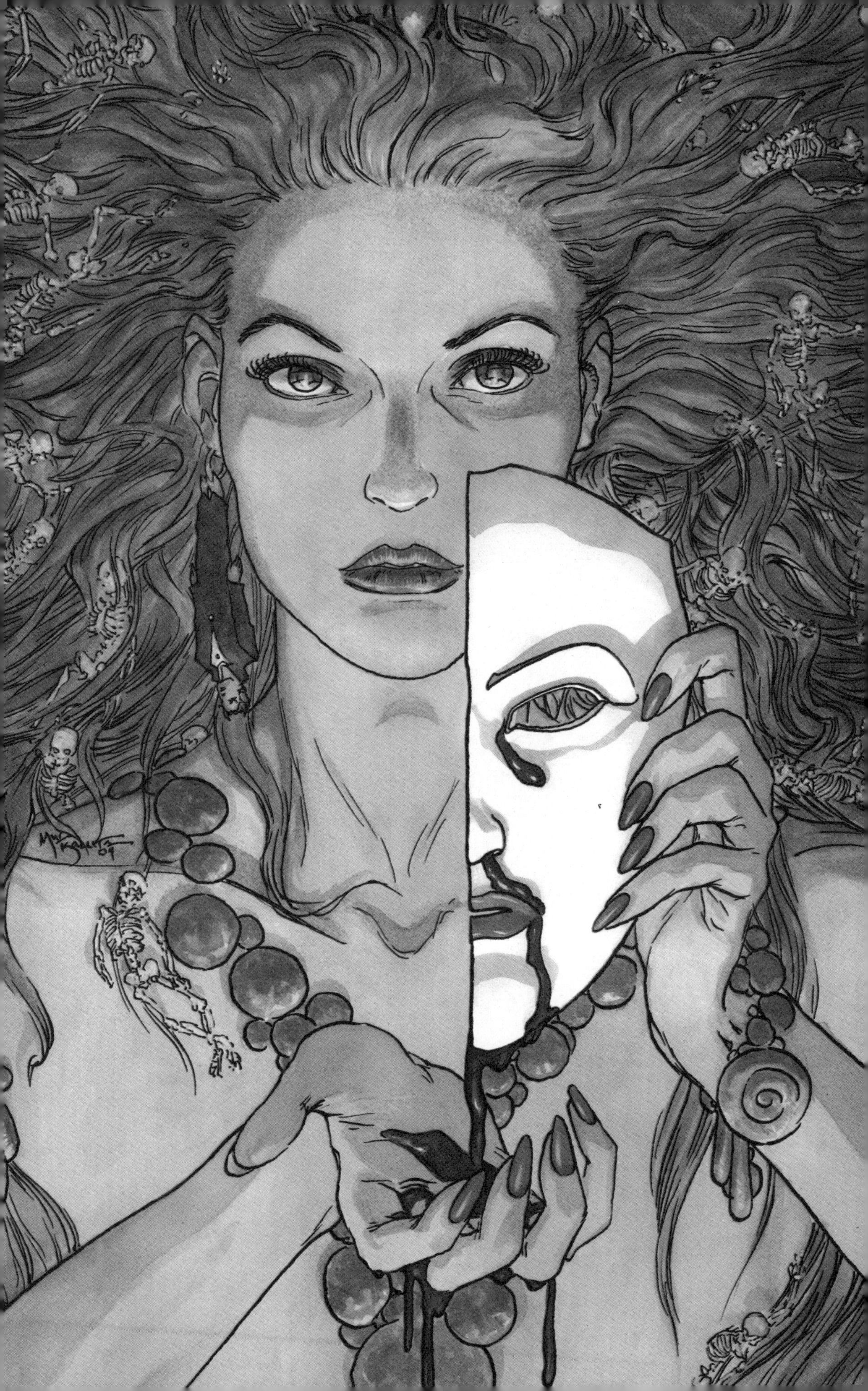

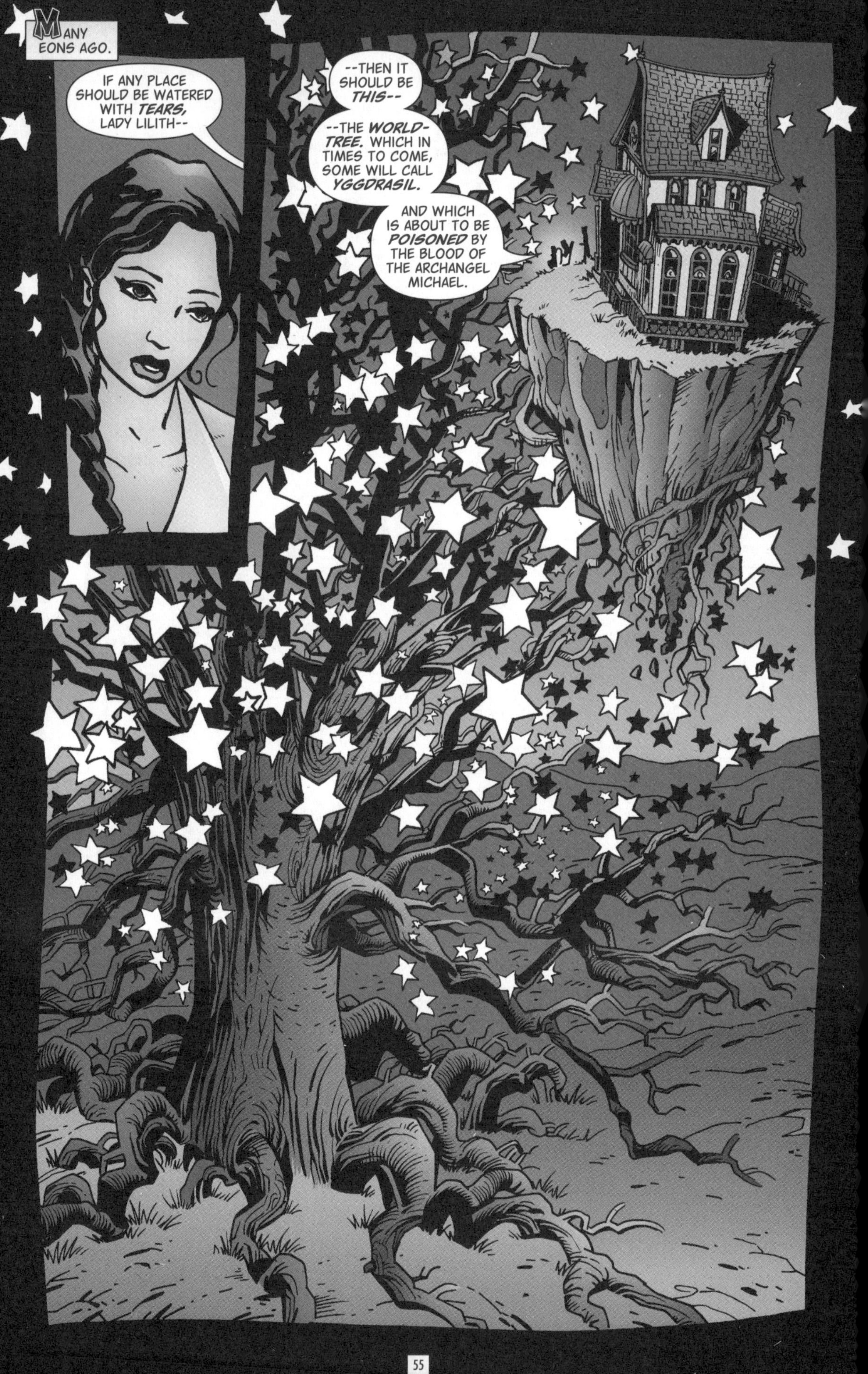
MANY EONS AGO.
IF ANY PLACE SHOULD BE WATERED WITH TEARS, LADY LILITH--
--THEN IT SHOULD BE THIS--
--THE WORLD-TREE. WHICH IN TIMES TO COME, SOME WILL CALL YGGDRASIL.
AND WHICH IS ABOUT TO BE POISONED BY THE BLOOD OF THE ARCHANGEL MICHAEL.

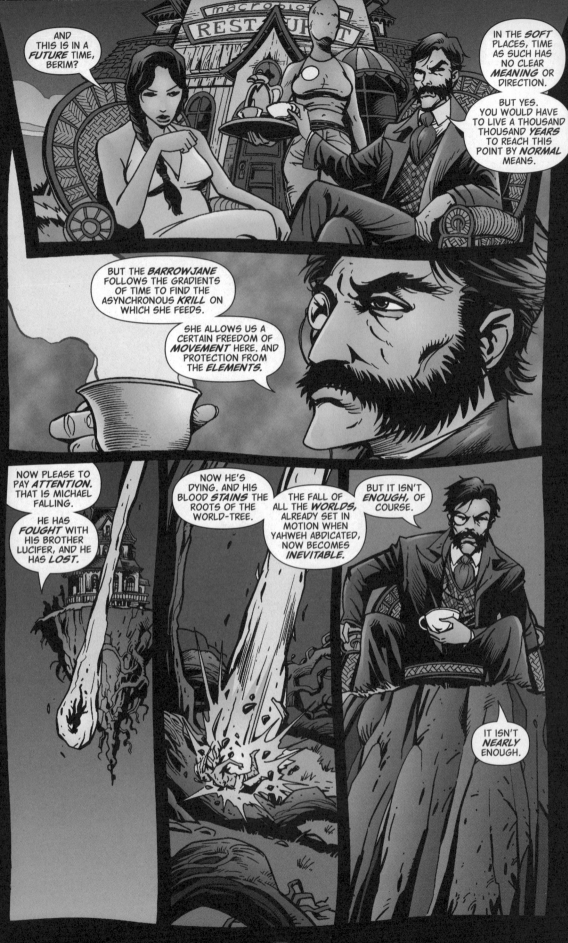

AND THIS IS IN A *FUTURE* TIME, BERIM?

IN THE *SOFT* PLACES, TIME AS SUCH HAS NO CLEAR *MEANING* OR DIRECTION.

BUT YES. YOU WOULD HAVE TO LIVE A THOUSAND THOUSAND *YEARS* TO REACH THIS POINT BY *NORMAL* MEANS.

BUT THE *BARROWJANE* FOLLOWS THE GRADIENTS OF TIME TO FIND THE ASYNCHRONOUS *KRILL* ON WHICH SHE FEEDS.

SHE ALLOWS US A CERTAIN FREEDOM OF *MOVEMENT* HERE. AND PROTECTION FROM THE *ELEMENTS*.

NOW PLEASE TO PAY *ATTENTION*. THAT IS MICHAEL FALLING.

HE HAS *FOUGHT* WITH HIS BROTHER LUCIFER, AND HE HAS *LOST*.

NOW HE'S DYING. AND HIS BLOOD *STAINS* THE ROOTS OF THE WORLD-TREE.

THE FALL OF ALL THE *WORLDS*, ALREADY SET IN MOTION WHEN YAHWEH ABDICATED, NOW BECOMES *INEVITABLE*.

BUT IT ISN'T *ENOUGH*, OF COURSE.

IT ISN'T *NEARLY* ENOUGH.

THERE IS A *POWER* WITHIN ME. THE *DUNAMIS DEMIURGOS.* GOD'S POWER.

WHEN I DIE, IT WILL POUR *OUT* OF ME AND OVERWHELM EVERYTHING THAT *EXISTS.*

I'M DYING *NOW,* ELAINE.

YOU HAVE TO *TAKE* THE POWER FROM ME.

TAKE IT-- TAKE IT *FROM* YOU?

SHE'S NOT *STRONG* ENOUGH. IT WILL *DESTROY* HER.

I CAN THINK OF NO OTHER *WAY.*

FATHER. OH GOD, I'M SORRY I NEVER *CAME* TO YOU. NEVER TRIED TO TALK--

IT WOULD HAVE DONE NO *GOOD.* I WAS *PROUD,* AND STUBBORN.

I COULD HAVE SOUGHT *YOU* OUT. I COULD HAVE--

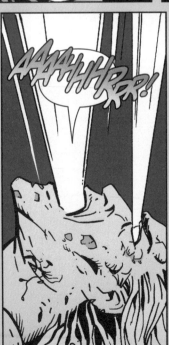

AAAHHHRR!

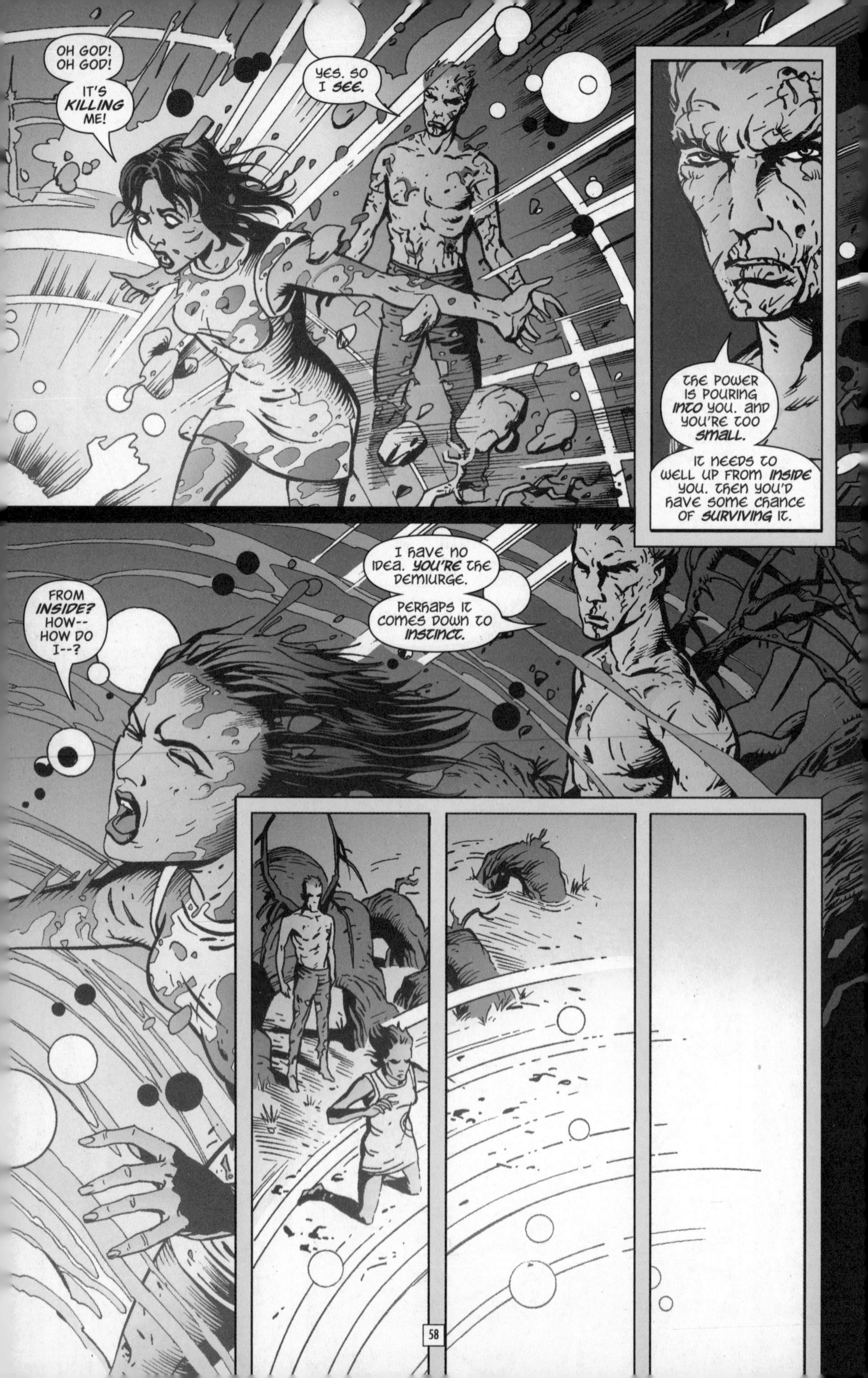
OH GOD! OH GOD!
IT'S KILLING ME!
YES. SO I SEE.
THE POWER IS POURING INTO YOU. AND YOU'RE TOO SMALL.
IT NEEDS TO WELL UP FROM INSIDE YOU. THEN YOU'D HAVE SOME CHANCE OF SURVIVING IT.
FROM INSIDE? HOW-- HOW DO I--?
I HAVE NO IDEA. YOU'RE THE DEMIURGE.
PERHAPS IT COMES DOWN TO INSTINCT.

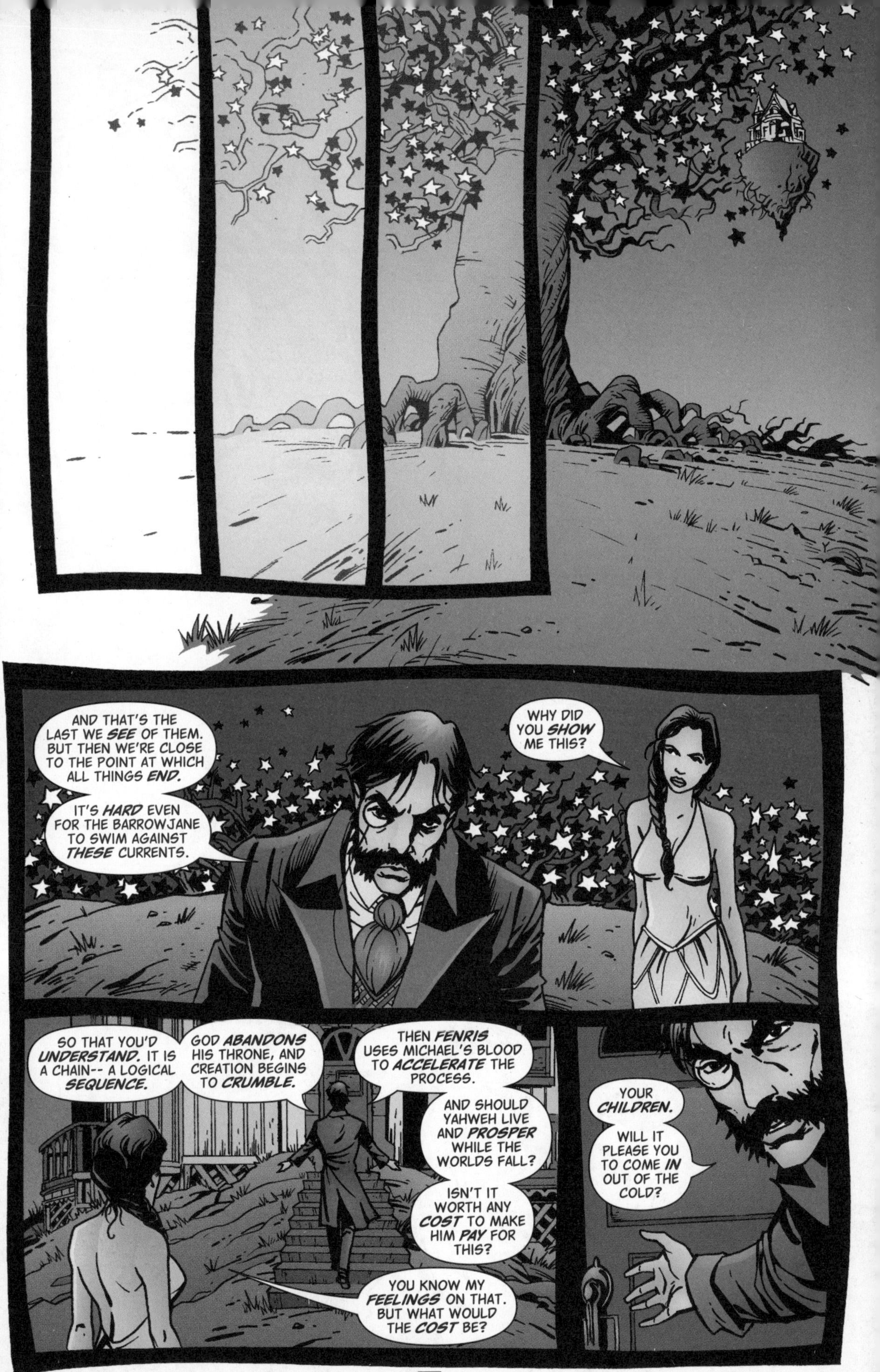
AND THAT'S THE LAST WE SEE OF THEM. BUT THEN WE'RE CLOSE TO THE POINT AT WHICH ALL THINGS END.
IT'S HARD EVEN FOR THE BARROWJANE TO SWIM AGAINST THESE CURRENTS.
WHY DID YOU SHOW ME THIS?
SO THAT YOU'D UNDERSTAND. IT IS A CHAIN-- A LOGICAL SEQUENCE.
GOD ABANDONS HIS THRONE, AND CREATION BEGINS TO CRUMBLE.
THEN FENRIS USES MICHAEL'S BLOOD TO ACCELERATE THE PROCESS.
AND SHOULD YAHWEH LIVE AND PROSPER WHILE THE WORLDS FALL?
ISN'T IT WORTH ANY COST TO MAKE HIM PAY FOR THIS?
YOU KNOW MY FEELINGS ON THAT. BUT WHAT WOULD THE COST BE?
YOUR CHILDREN.
WILL IT PLEASE YOU TO COME IN OUT OF THE COLD?

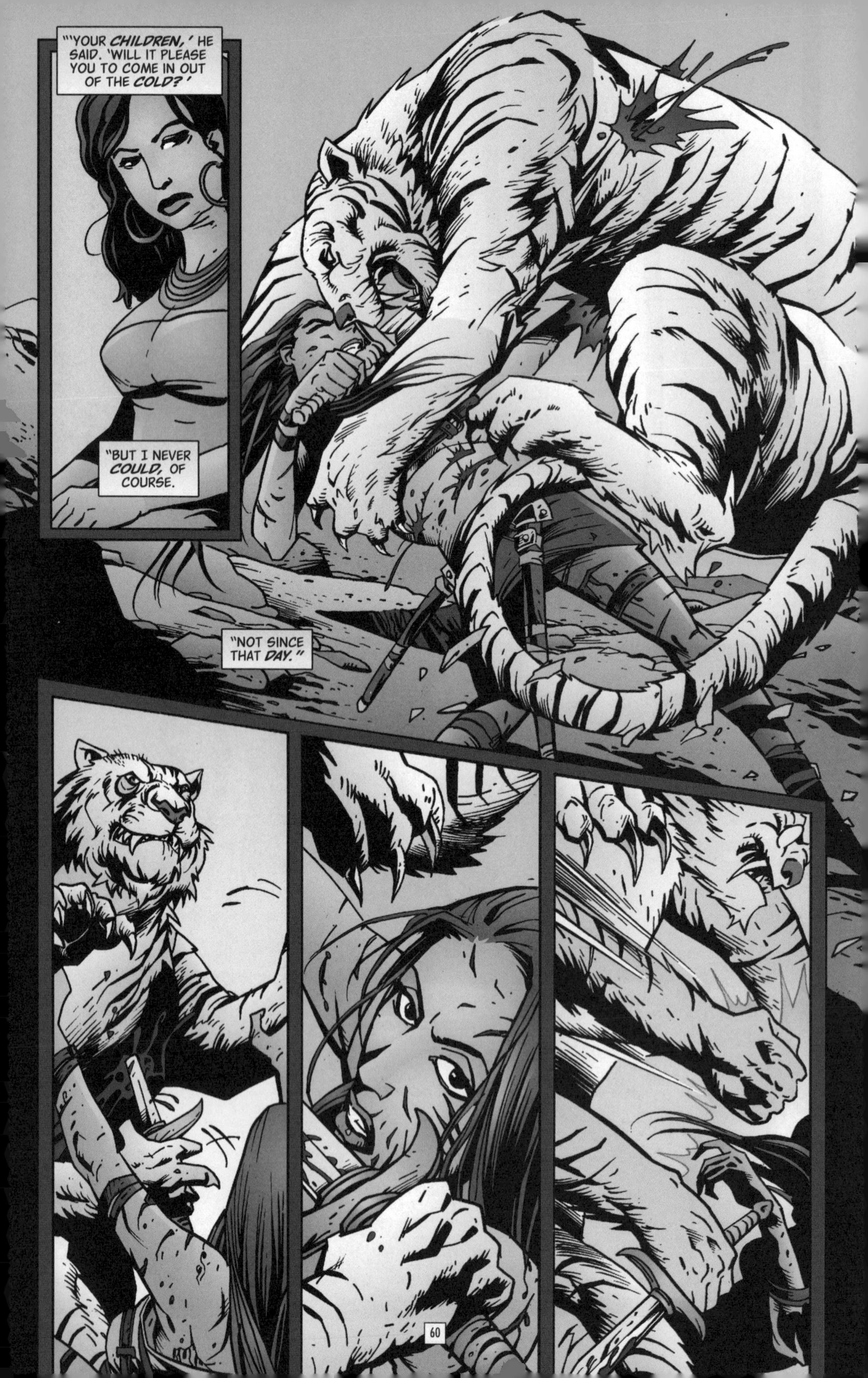
"'YOUR CHILDREN,' HE SAID. 'WILL IT PLEASE YOU TO COME IN OUT OF THE COLD?'
"BUT I NEVER COULD, OF COURSE.
"NOT SINCE THAT DAY."

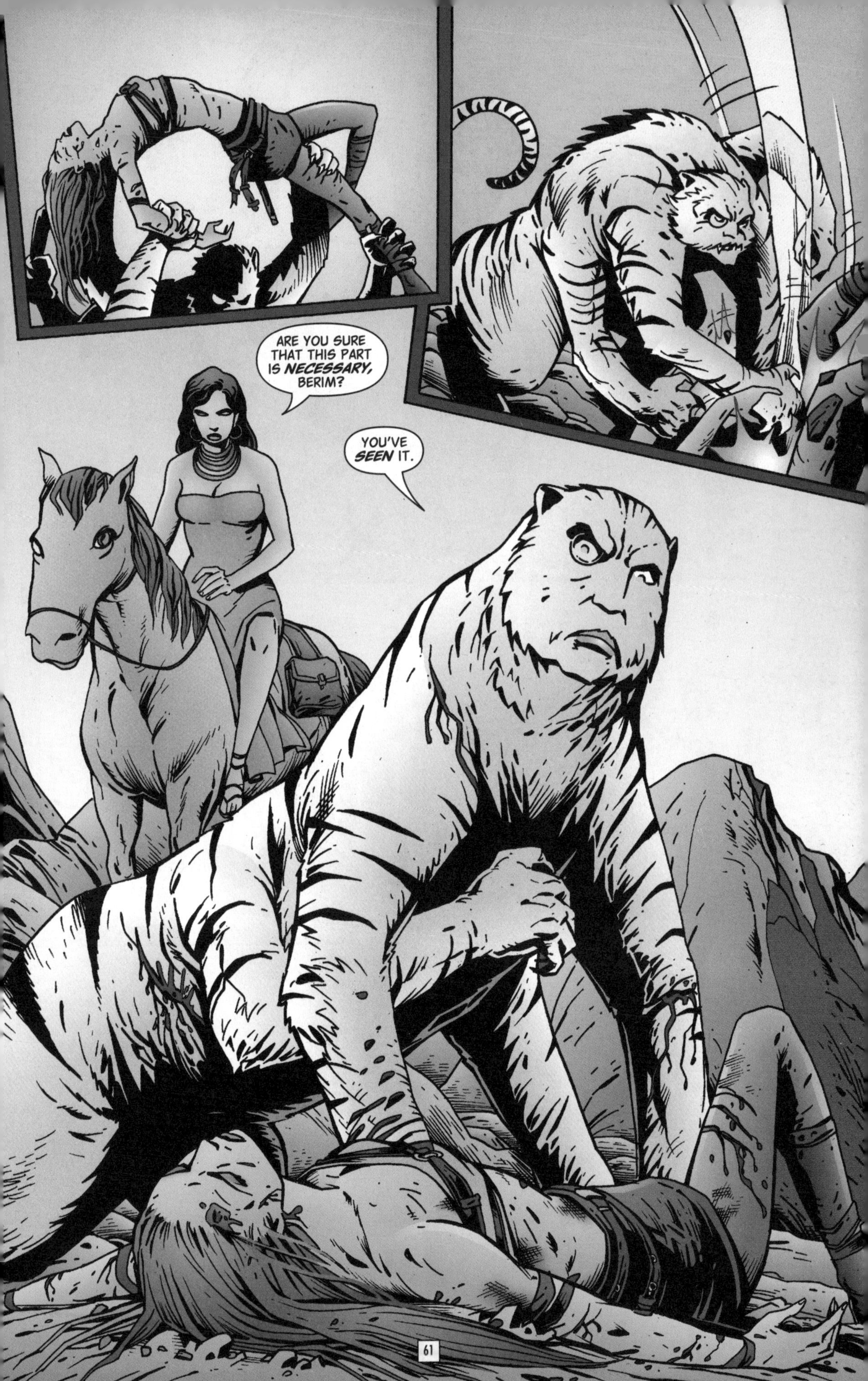
ARE YOU SURE THAT THIS PART IS *NECESSARY,* BERIM?
YOU'VE *SEEN* IT.

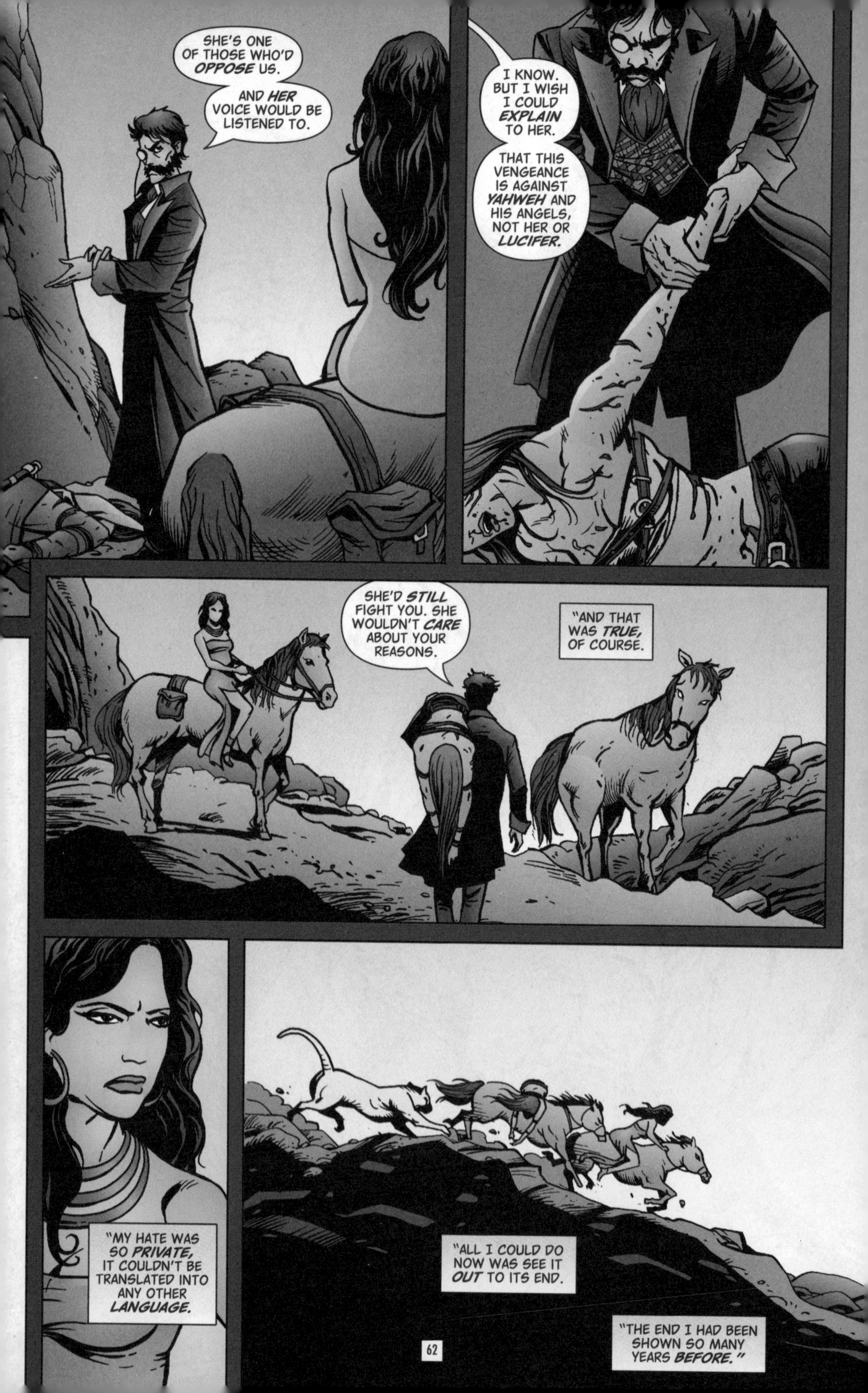

SHE'S ONE OF THOSE WHO'D OPPOSE US.
AND HER VOICE WOULD BE LISTENED TO.
I KNOW. BUT I WISH I COULD EXPLAIN TO HER.
THAT THIS VENGEANCE IS AGAINST YAHWEH AND HIS ANGELS, NOT HER OR LUCIFER.
SHE'D STILL FIGHT YOU. SHE WOULDN'T CARE ABOUT YOUR REASONS.
"AND THAT WAS TRUE, OF COURSE.
"MY HATE WAS SO PRIVATE, IT COULDN'T BE TRANSLATED INTO ANY OTHER LANGUAGE.
"ALL I COULD DO NOW WAS SEE IT OUT TO ITS END.
"THE END I HAD BEEN SHOWN SO MANY YEARS BEFORE."

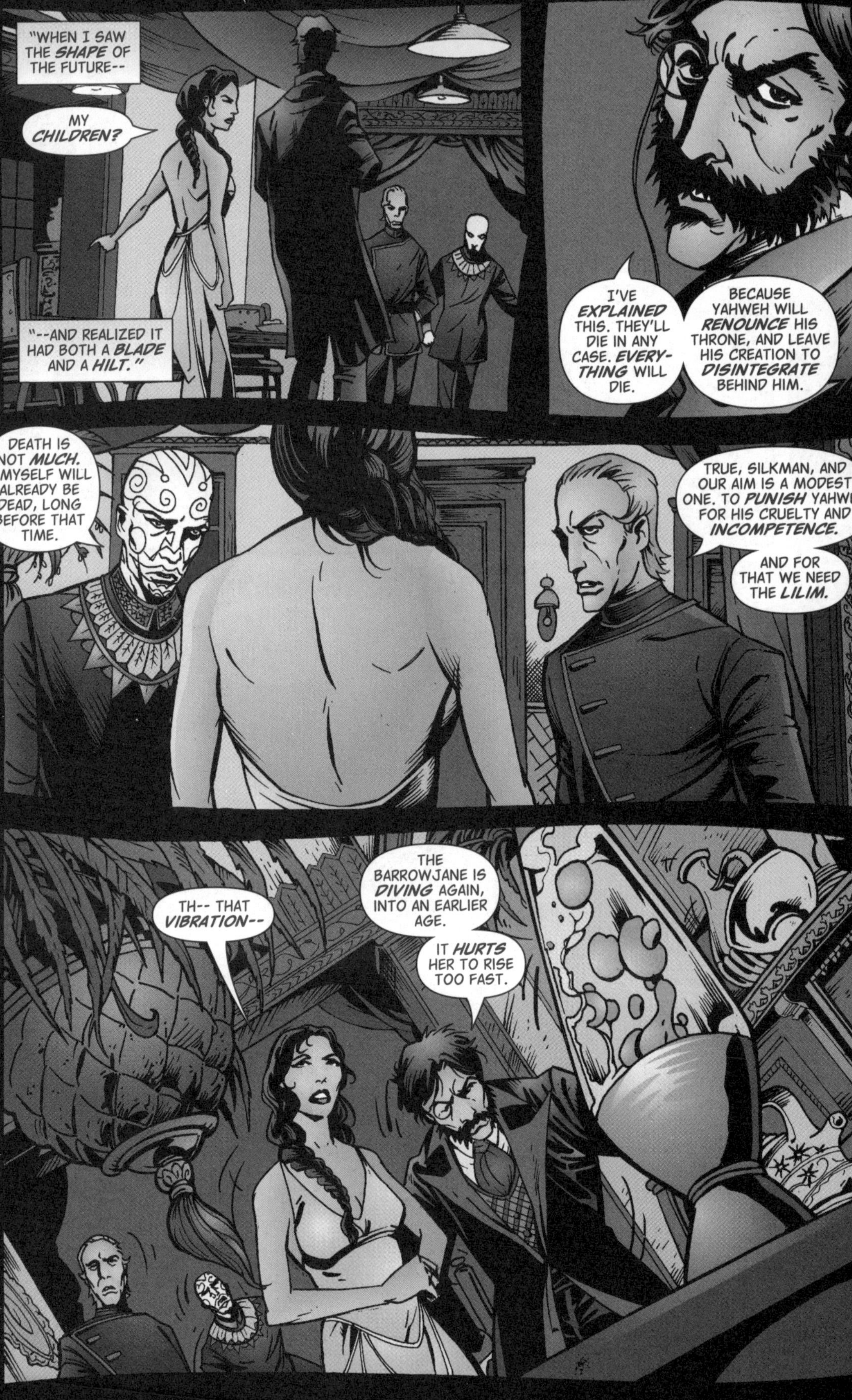
"WHEN I SAW THE SHAPE OF THE FUTURE--
MY CHILDREN?
"--AND REALIZED IT HAD BOTH A BLADE AND A HILT."
I'VE EXPLAINED THIS. THEY'LL DIE IN ANY CASE. EVERYTHING WILL DIE.
BECAUSE YAHWEH WILL RENOUNCE HIS THRONE, AND LEAVE HIS CREATION TO DISINTEGRATE BEHIND HIM.
DEATH IS NOT MUCH. I MYSELF WILL ALREADY BE DEAD, LONG BEFORE THAT TIME.
TRUE, SILKMAN, AND OUR AIM IS A MODEST ONE. TO PUNISH YAHWEH FOR HIS CRUELTY AND INCOMPETENCE.
AND FOR THAT WE NEED THE LILIM.
TH-- THAT VIBRATION--
THE BARROWJANE IS DIVING AGAIN, INTO AN EARLIER AGE.
IT HURTS HER TO RISE TOO FAST.

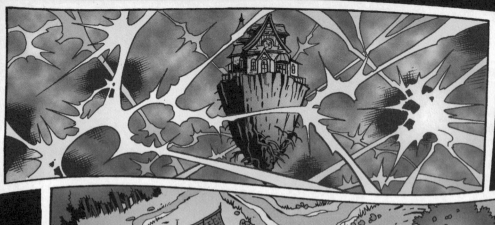

EDEN GARDEN. WE'VE COME FROM THE *END* OF TIME TO ITS *BEGINNING.*

THERE *IS* NO BEGINNING. THIS OCEAN HAS NO *FLOOR.*

BUT WHEN YOU *LEAVE,* IT WOULD BE BEST IF YOU WERE *CLOSE* TO THE POINT AT WHICH YOU ENTERED.

"THE POWER IS TOO *FIERCE* AND CORROSIVE.

"AND SHE IS TOO *FRAIL* A VESSEL.

"AS I SAID, WE HAVE NOT *FOUND* HER ON TIME'S FURTHER SHORE.

"SHE IS *SWALLOWED* BY THE POWER, AND SHE DOES NOT *EMERGE* AGAIN.

"WE BELIEVE SHE IS *DISMANTLED* BY IT.

"SHE *IS*, AFTER ALL, PARTLY OF *HUMAN* FLESH.

"AND IN THAT *FURNACE*, FLESH IS LIKE *CHAFF* IN A HURRICANE.

"WHAT COULD SHE *HAVE* TO SET AGAINST THAT WIND OF FIRE?

"HER *WILL?* HER HOPE? HER SMATTERING OF HALF-GLIMPSED *WISDOM?*

"NOTHING.

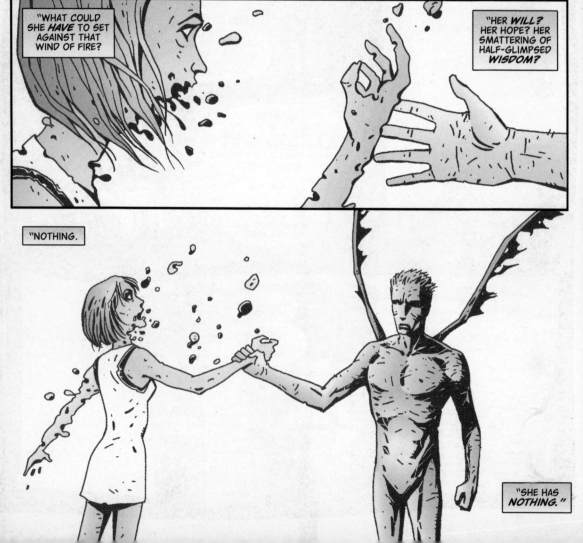

"SHE HAS *NOTHING.*"

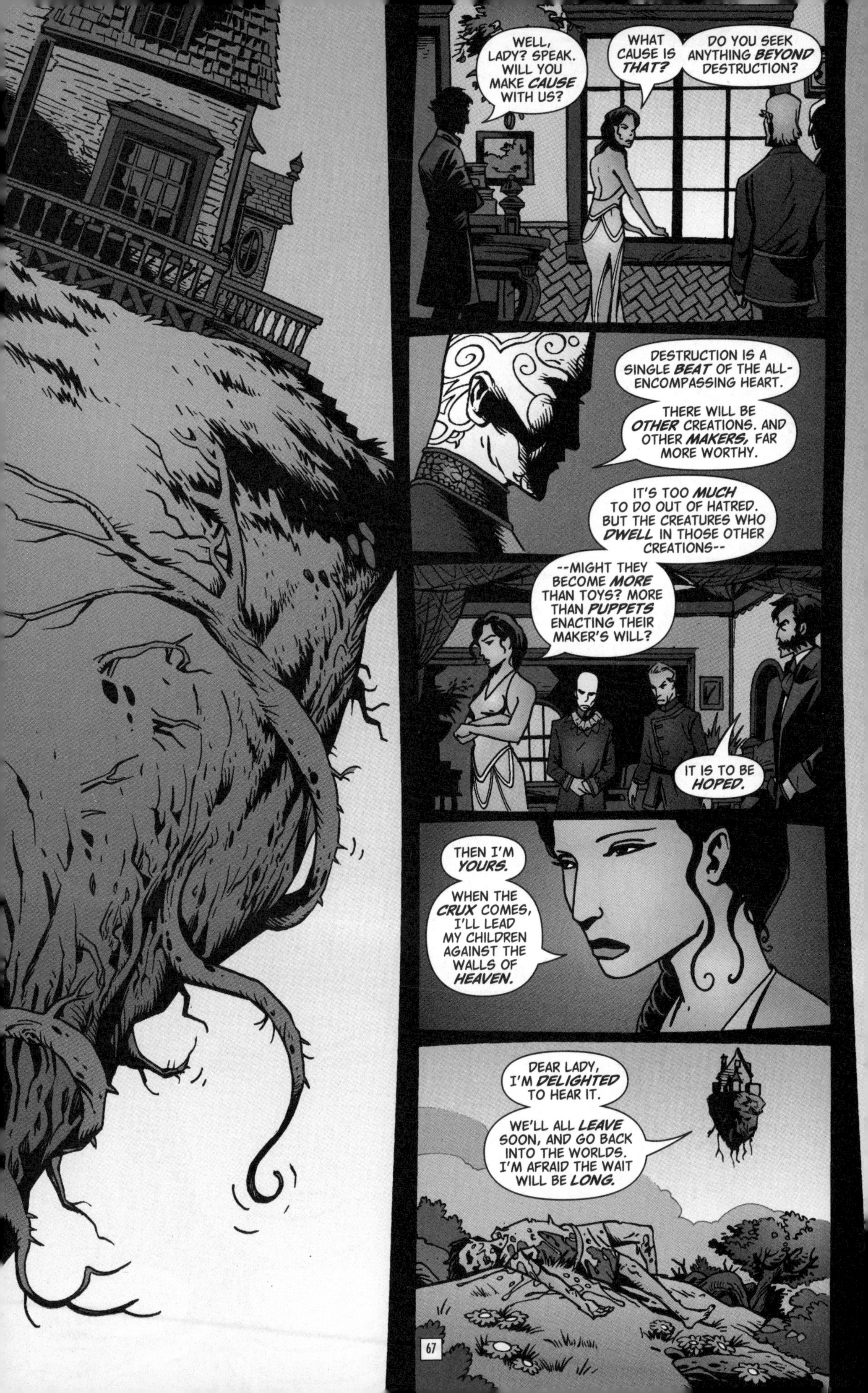
WELL, LADY? SPEAK. WILL YOU MAKE CAUSE WITH US?
WHAT CAUSE IS THAT?
DO YOU SEEK ANYTHING BEYOND DESTRUCTION?
DESTRUCTION IS A SINGLE BEAT OF THE ALL-ENCOMPASSING HEART.
THERE WILL BE OTHER CREATIONS. AND OTHER MAKERS, FAR MORE WORTHY.
IT'S TOO MUCH TO DO OUT OF HATRED. BUT THE CREATURES WHO DWELL IN THOSE OTHER CREATIONS--
--MIGHT THEY BECOME MORE THAN TOYS? MORE THAN PUPPETS ENACTING THEIR MAKER'S WILL?
IT IS TO BE HOPED.
THEN I'M YOURS.
WHEN THE CRUX COMES, I'LL LEAD MY CHILDREN AGAINST THE WALLS OF HEAVEN.
DEAR LADY, I'M DELIGHTED TO HEAR IT.
WE'LL ALL LEAVE SOON, AND GO BACK INTO THE WORLDS. I'M AFRAID THE WAIT WILL BE LONG.

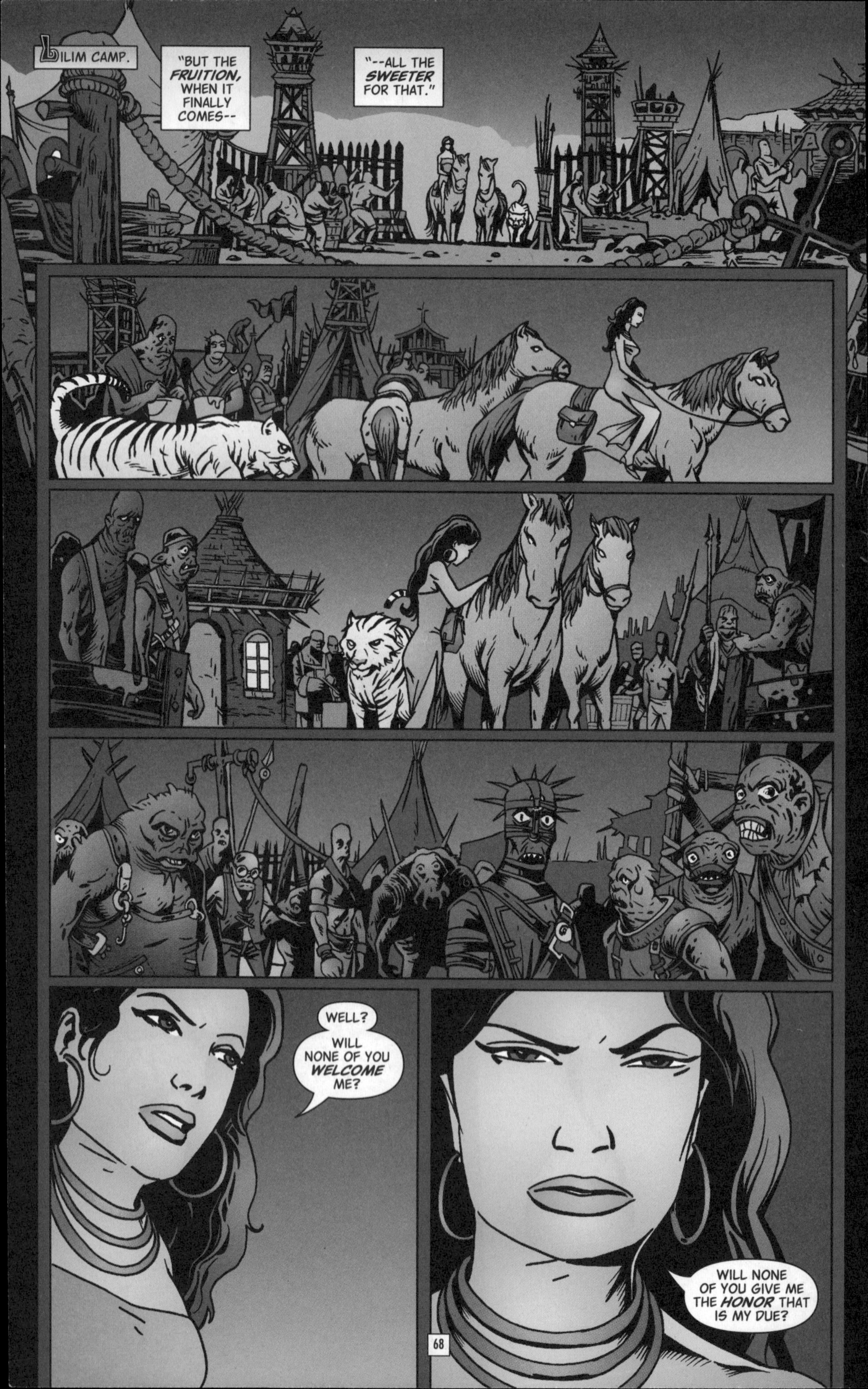
LILIM CAMP.
"BUT THE FRUITION, WHEN IT FINALLY COMES--
"--ALL THE SWEETER FOR THAT."
WELL? WILL NONE OF YOU WELCOME ME?
WILL NONE OF YOU GIVE ME THE HONOR THAT IS MY DUE?

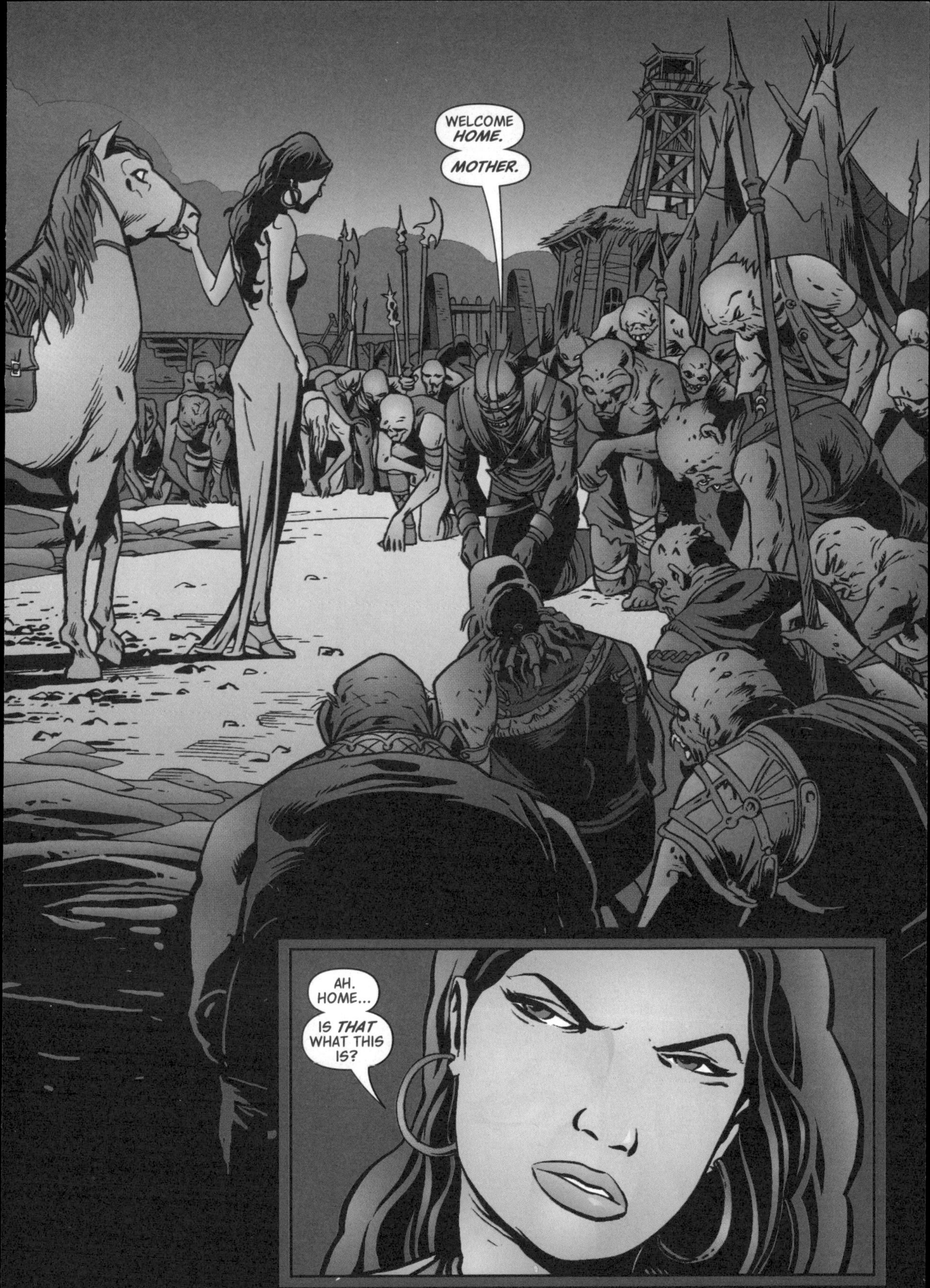
WELCOME *HOME.*
MOTHER.
AH. HOME...
IS *THAT* WHAT THIS IS?

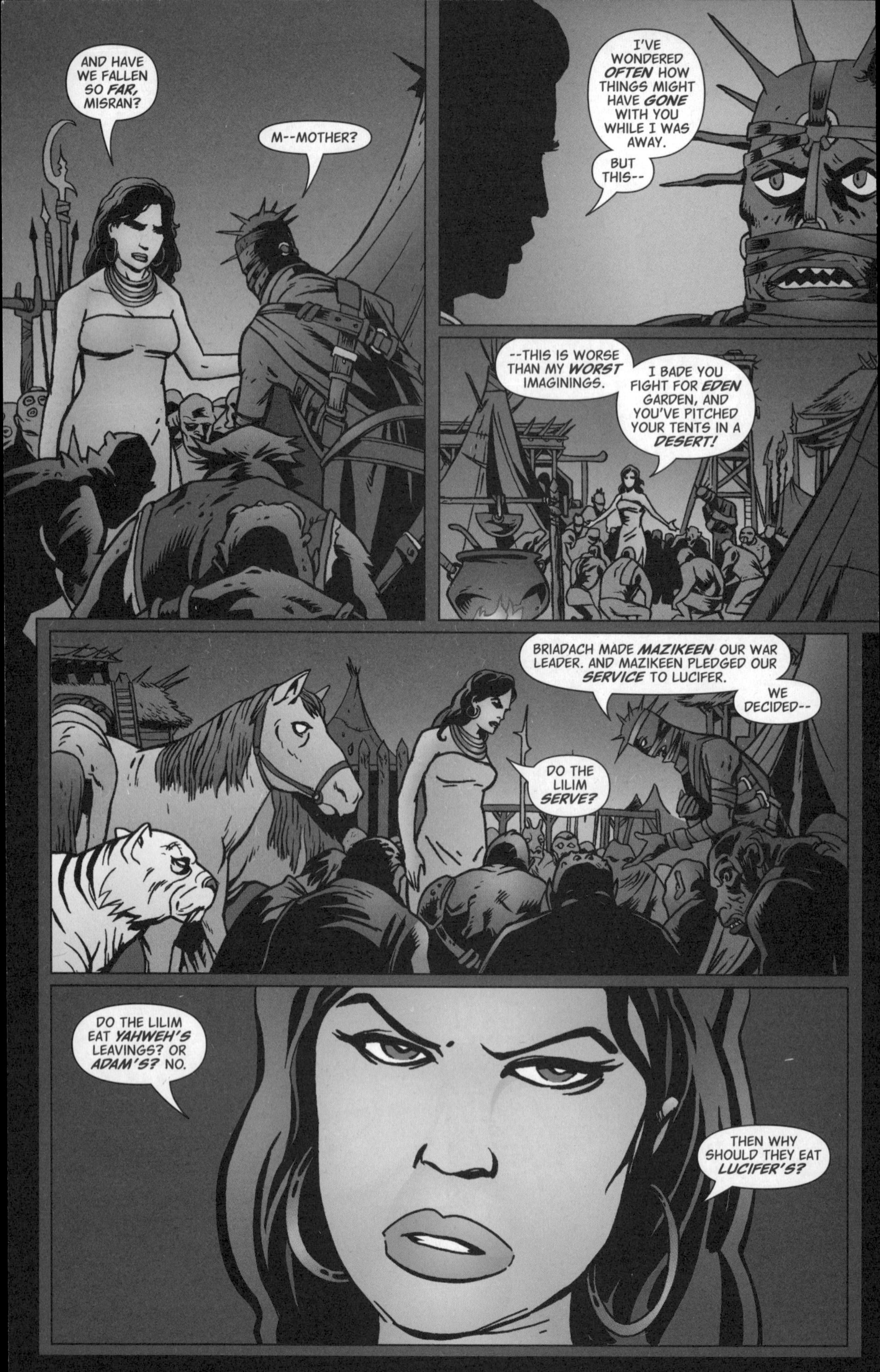
AND HAVE WE FALLEN SO FAR, MISRAN?
M--MOTHER?
I'VE WONDERED OFTEN HOW THINGS MIGHT HAVE GONE WITH YOU WHILE I WAS AWAY.
BUT THIS--
--THIS IS WORSE THAN MY WORST IMAGININGS.
I BADE YOU FIGHT FOR EDEN GARDEN, AND YOU'VE PITCHED YOUR TENTS IN A DESERT!
BRIADACH MADE MAZIKEEN OUR WAR LEADER. AND MAZIKEEN PLEDGED OUR SERVICE TO LUCIFER.
WE DECIDED--
DO THE LILIM SERVE?
DO THE LILIM EAT YAHWEH'S LEAVINGS? OR ADAM'S? NO.
THEN WHY SHOULD THEY EAT LUCIFER'S?

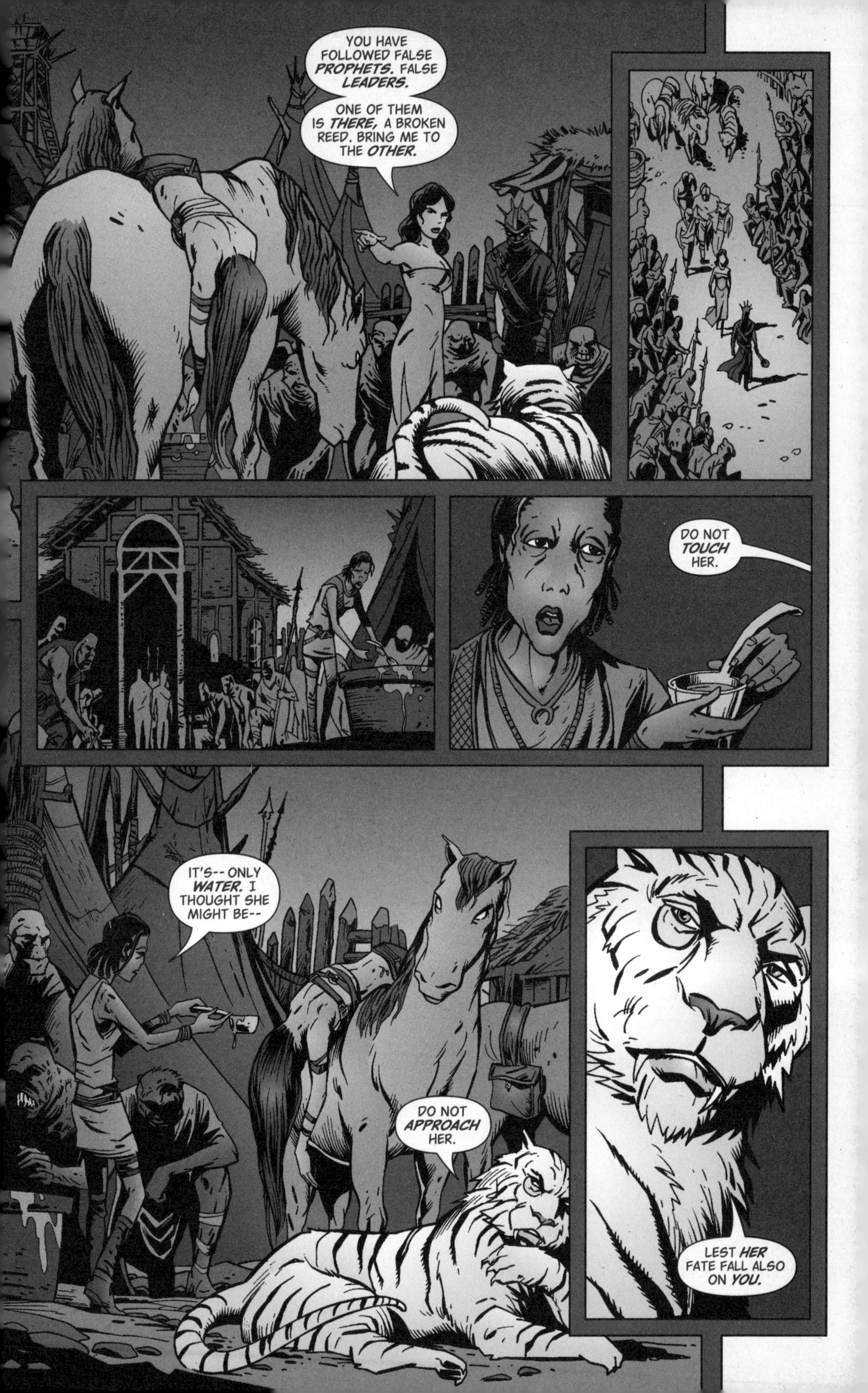
YOU HAVE FOLLOWED FALSE PROPHETS. FALSE LEADERS.
ONE OF THEM IS THERE, A BROKEN REED. BRING ME TO THE OTHER.
DO NOT TOUCH HER.
IT'S-- ONLY WATER. I THOUGHT SHE MIGHT BE--
DO NOT APPROACH HER.
LEST HER FATE FALL ALSO ON YOU.

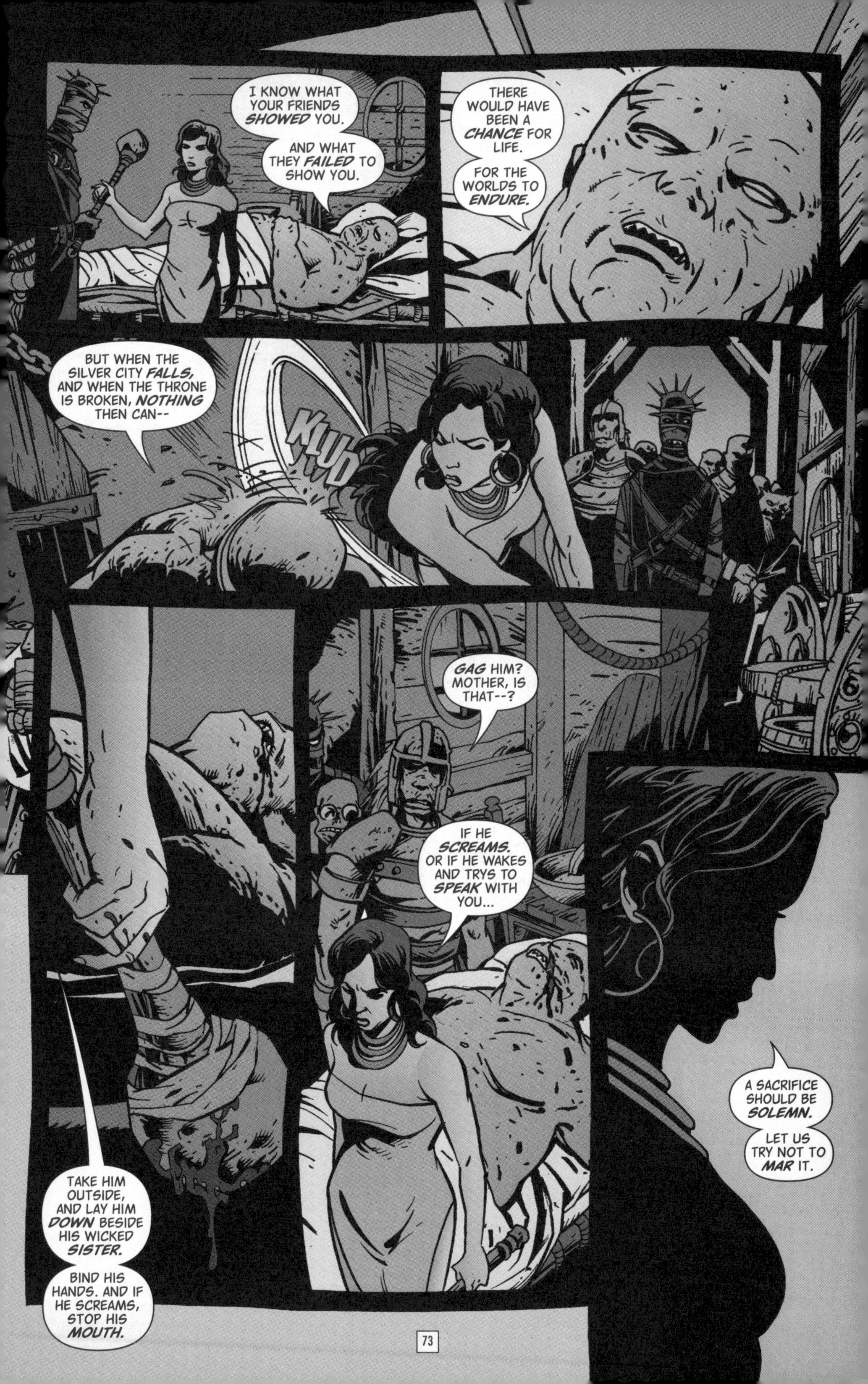
I KNOW WHAT YOUR FRIENDS SHOWED YOU.
AND WHAT THEY FAILED TO SHOW YOU.
THERE WOULD HAVE BEEN A CHANCE FOR LIFE.
FOR THE WORLDS TO ENDURE.
BUT WHEN THE SILVER CITY FALLS, AND WHEN THE THRONE IS BROKEN, NOTHING THEN CAN--
KLUD
GAG HIM? MOTHER, IS THAT--?
IF HE SCREAMS. OR IF HE WAKES AND TRYS TO SPEAK WITH YOU...
A SACRIFICE SHOULD BE SOLEMN.
LET US TRY NOT TO MAR IT.
TAKE HIM OUTSIDE, AND LAY HIM DOWN BESIDE HIS WICKED SISTER.
BIND HIS HANDS. AND IF HE SCREAMS, STOP HIS MOUTH.

OH, THANK *GOD!*

IT'S STILL *THERE!*

LUCIFER, IT'S *ALL* STILL THERE!

THANK *WHO?*

THERE'S *GROUND.* AND *SKY.* EVERYTHING.

TO TOUCH. TO *BREATHE.*

YOU CAN'T *AFFORD* THEM, ELAINE.

I CAN'T--?

NO. KEEP IT *SIMPLE.* KEEP IT *DOWN* TO ONE THING.

NO *REFRACTION* OF THE LIGHT. NO MOVING *PARTS.*

BELIEVE ME, THIS IS *HARDER* THAN IT LOOKS.

IMAGINE A *SPACE.*

THIS IS A SPACE. WHERE WE ARE. THIS IS--

THIS IS THE *ABSENCE* OF SPACE. PUSH *AGAINST* IT.

MAKE IT BACK *AWAY* FROM YOU. SO THAT YOU CAN *FILL* IT.

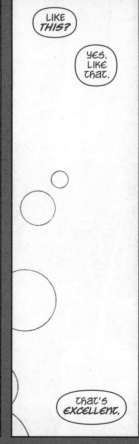

LIKE *THIS?*

YES. LIKE THAT.

THAT'S *EXCELLENT.*

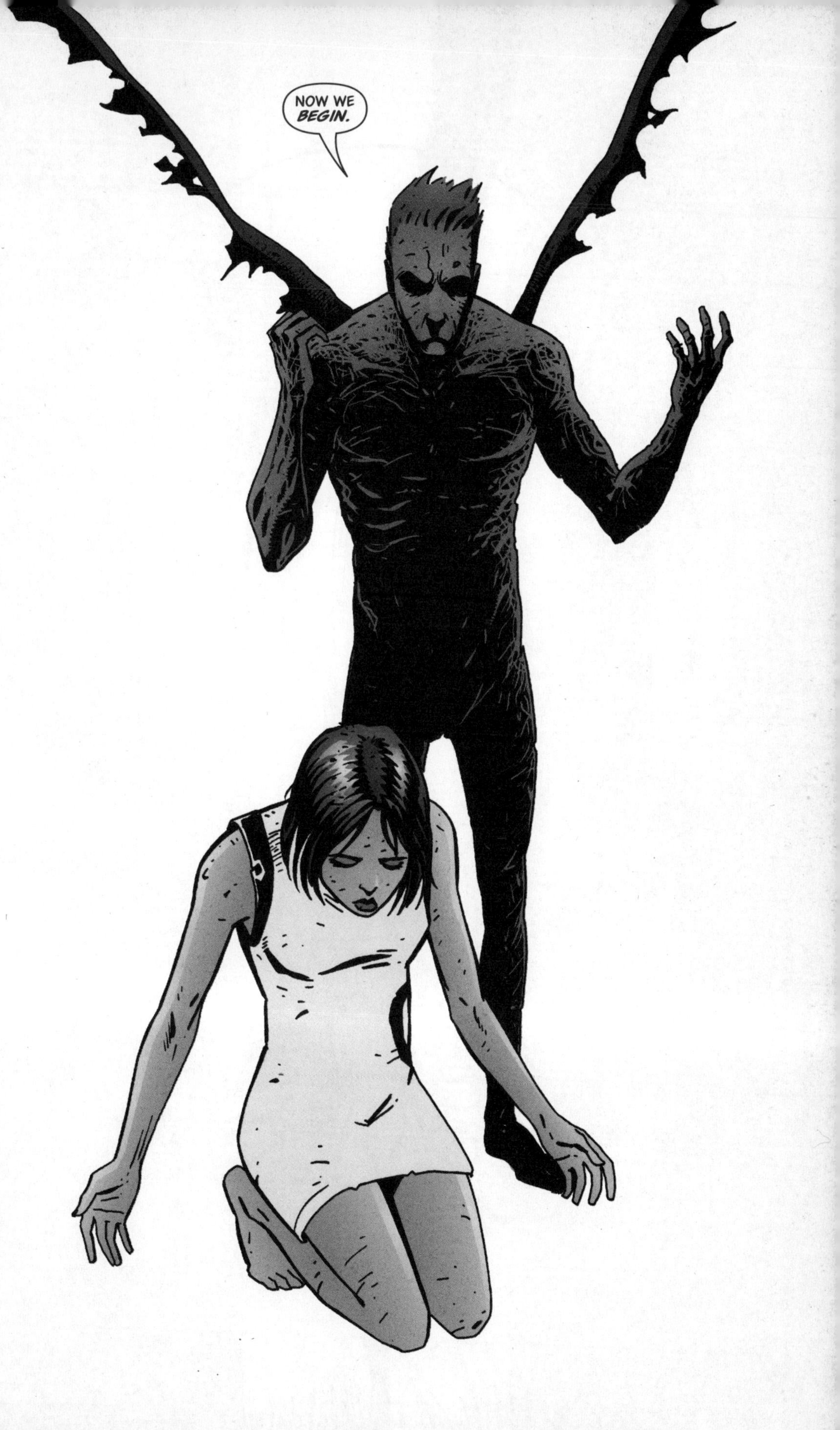
NOW WE *BEGIN.*

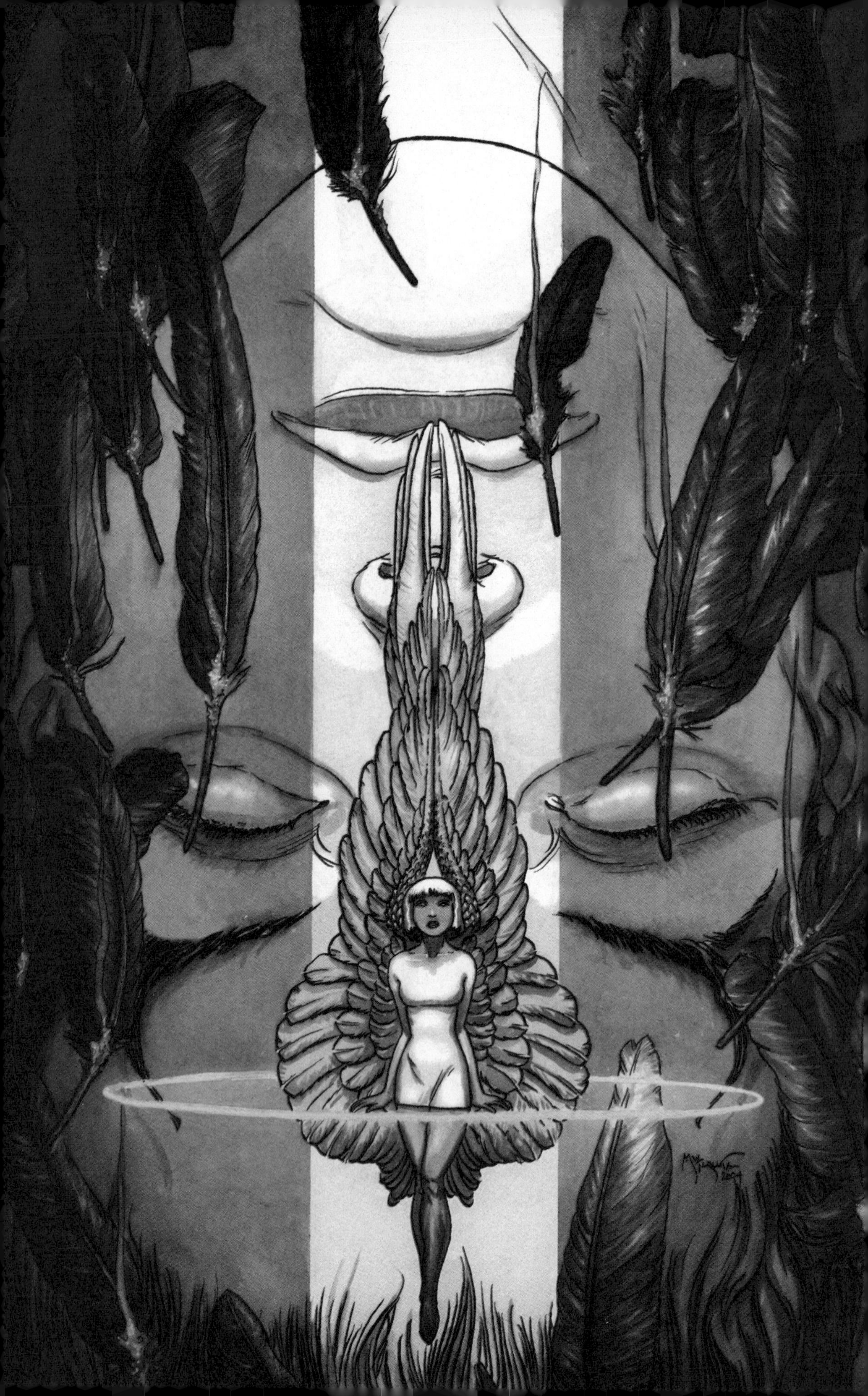

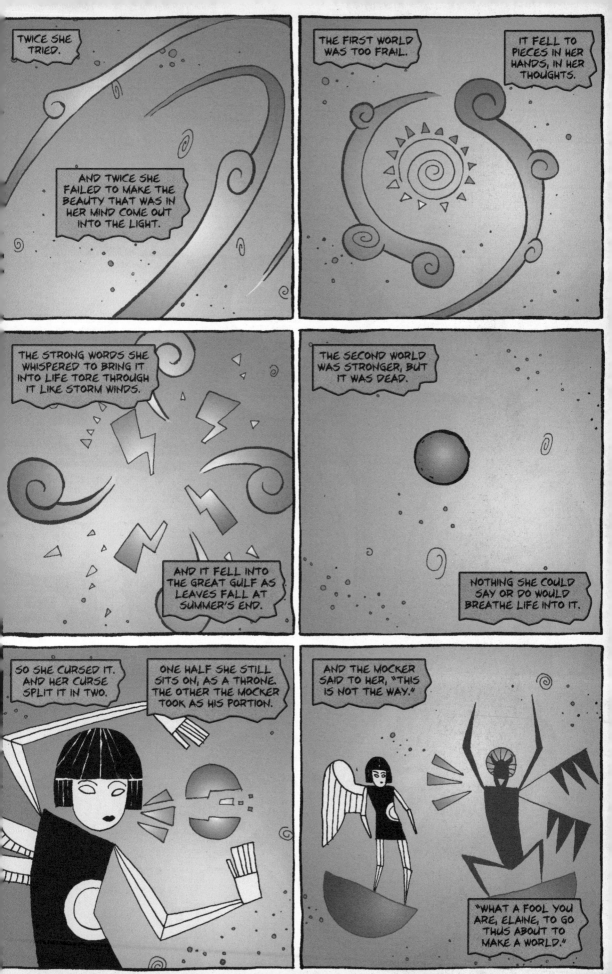

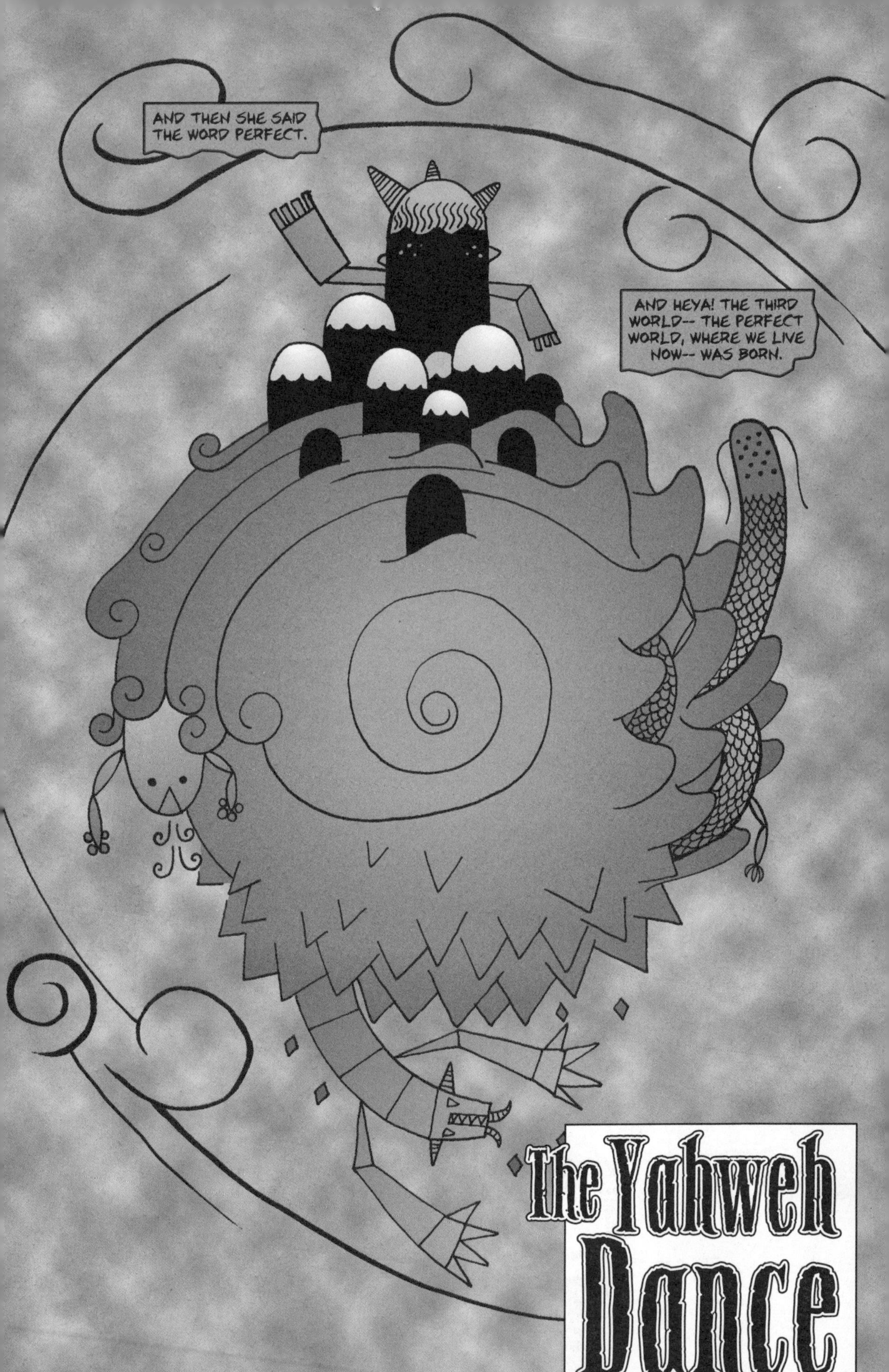
AND THEN SHE SAID THE WORD PERFECT.
AND HEYA! THE THIRD WORLD-- THE PERFECT WORLD, WHERE WE LIVE NOW-- WAS BORN.
The Yahweh Dance

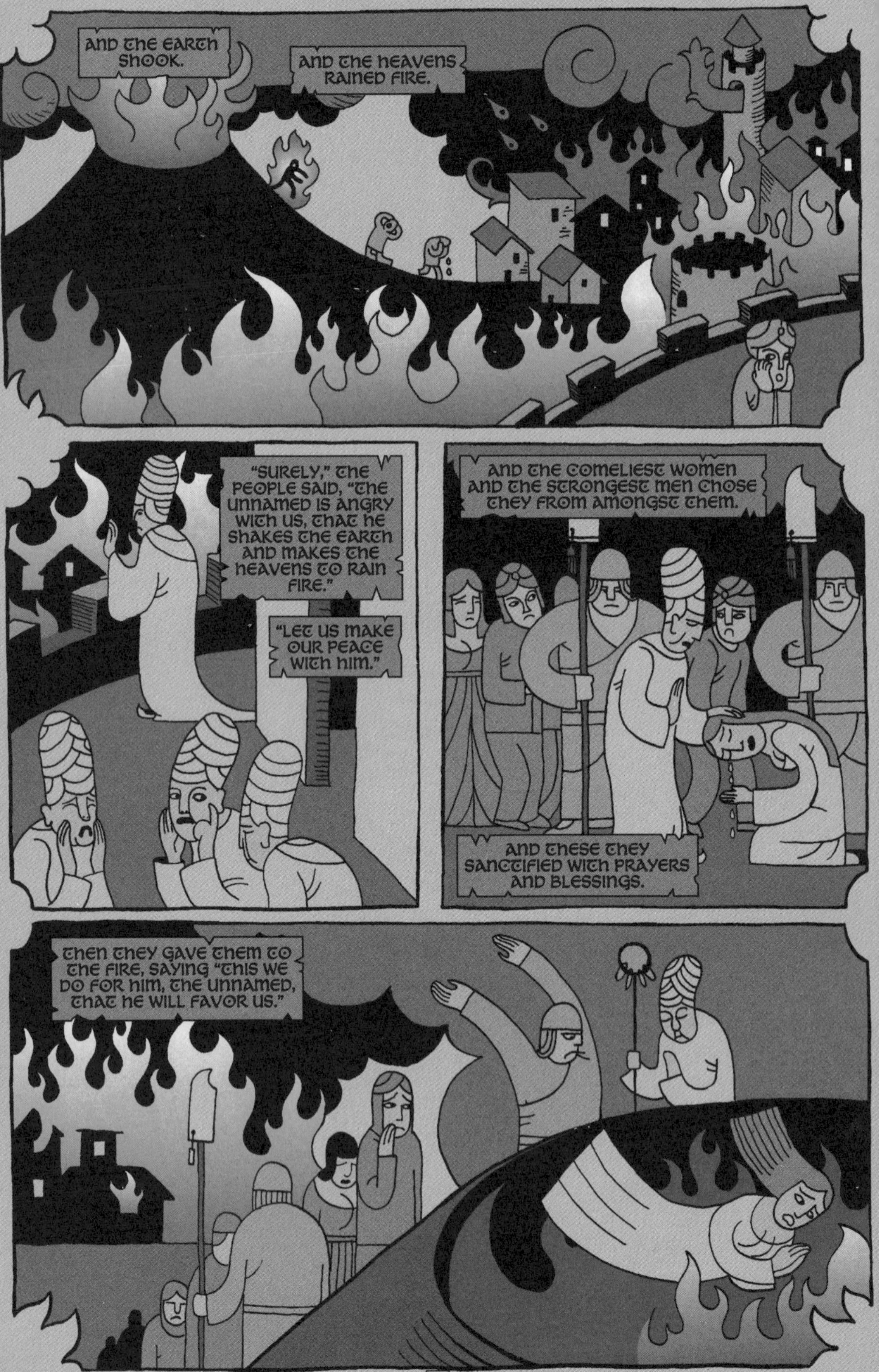
AND THE EARTH SHOOK.
AND THE HEAVENS RAINED FIRE.
"SURELY," THE PEOPLE SAID, "THE UNNAMED IS ANGRY WITH US, THAT HE SHAKES THE EARTH AND MAKES THE HEAVENS TO RAIN FIRE."
"LET US MAKE OUR PEACE WITH HIM."
AND THE COMELIEST WOMEN AND THE STRONGEST MEN CHOSE THEY FROM AMONGST THEM.
AND THESE THEY SANCTIFIED WITH PRAYERS AND BLESSINGS.
THEN THEY GAVE THEM TO THE FIRE, SAYING "THIS WE DO FOR HIM, THE UNNAMED, THAT HE WILL FAVOR US."

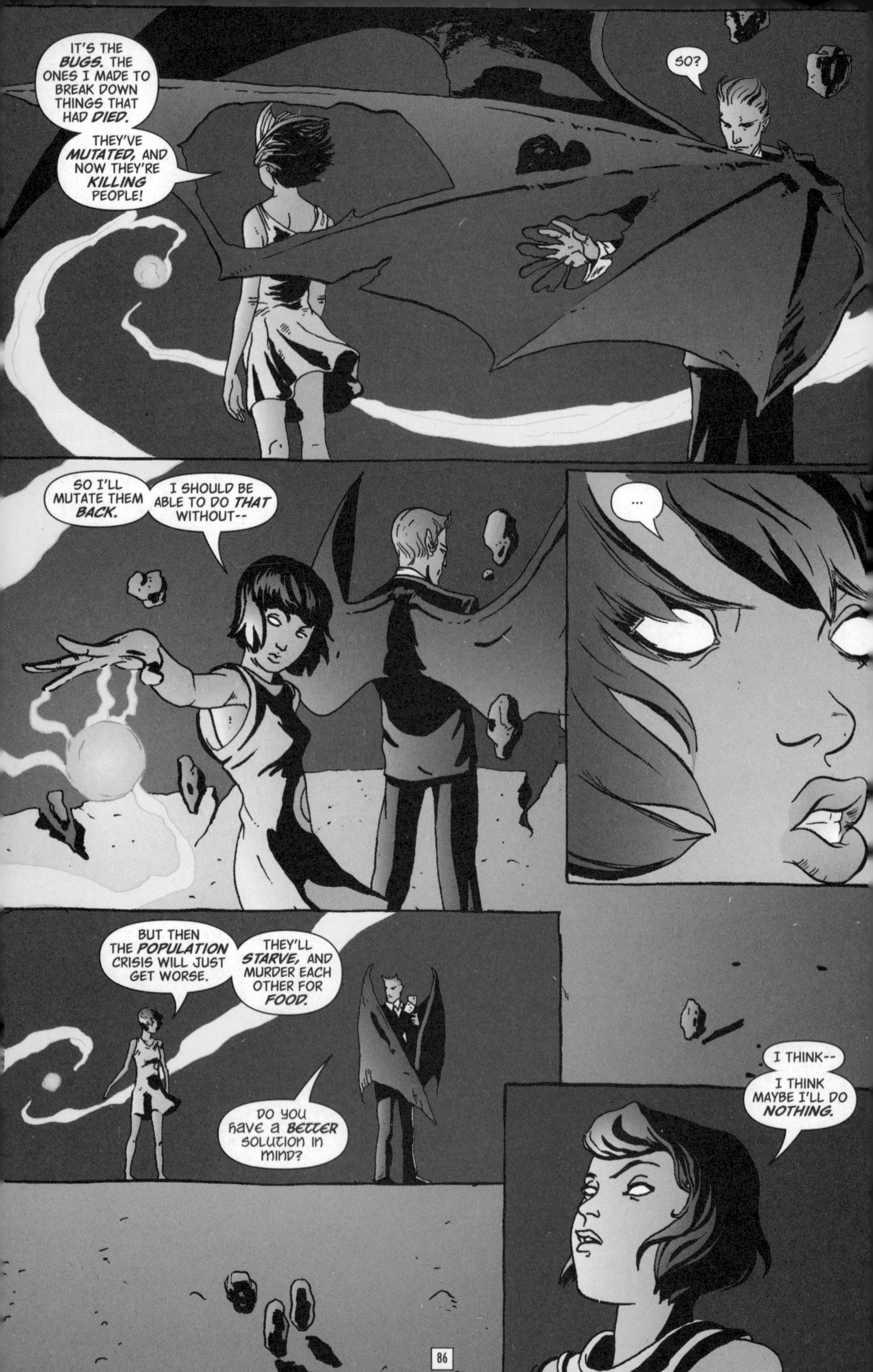
IT'S THE BUGS. THE ONES I MADE TO BREAK DOWN THINGS THAT HAD DIED.
THEY'VE MUTATED, AND NOW THEY'RE KILLING PEOPLE!
SO?
SO I'LL MUTATE THEM BACK.
I SHOULD BE ABLE TO DO THAT WITHOUT--
...
BUT THEN THE POPULATION CRISIS WILL JUST GET WORSE.
THEY'LL STARVE, AND MURDER EACH OTHER FOR FOOD.
DO YOU HAVE A BETTER SOLUTION IN MIND?
I THINK--
I THINK MAYBE I'LL DO NOTHING.

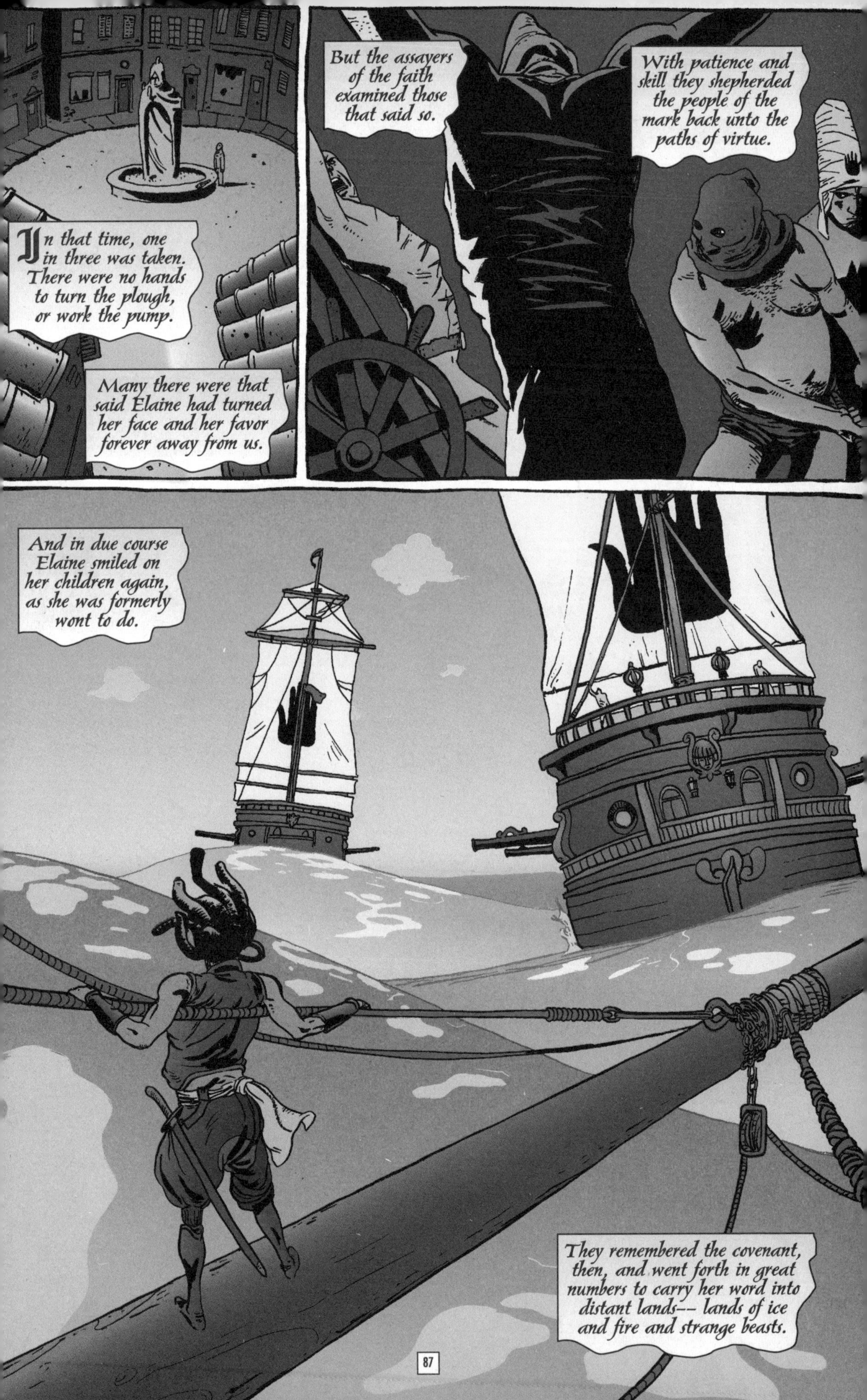
In that time, one in three was taken. There were no hands to turn the plough, or work the pump.
Many there were that said Elaine had turned her face and her favor forever away from us.
But the assayers of the faith examined those that said so.
With patience and skill they shepherded the people of the mark back unto the paths of virtue.
And in due course Elaine smiled on her children again, as she was formerly wont to do.
They remembered the covenant, then, and went forth in great numbers to carry her word into distant lands-- lands of ice and fire and strange beasts.

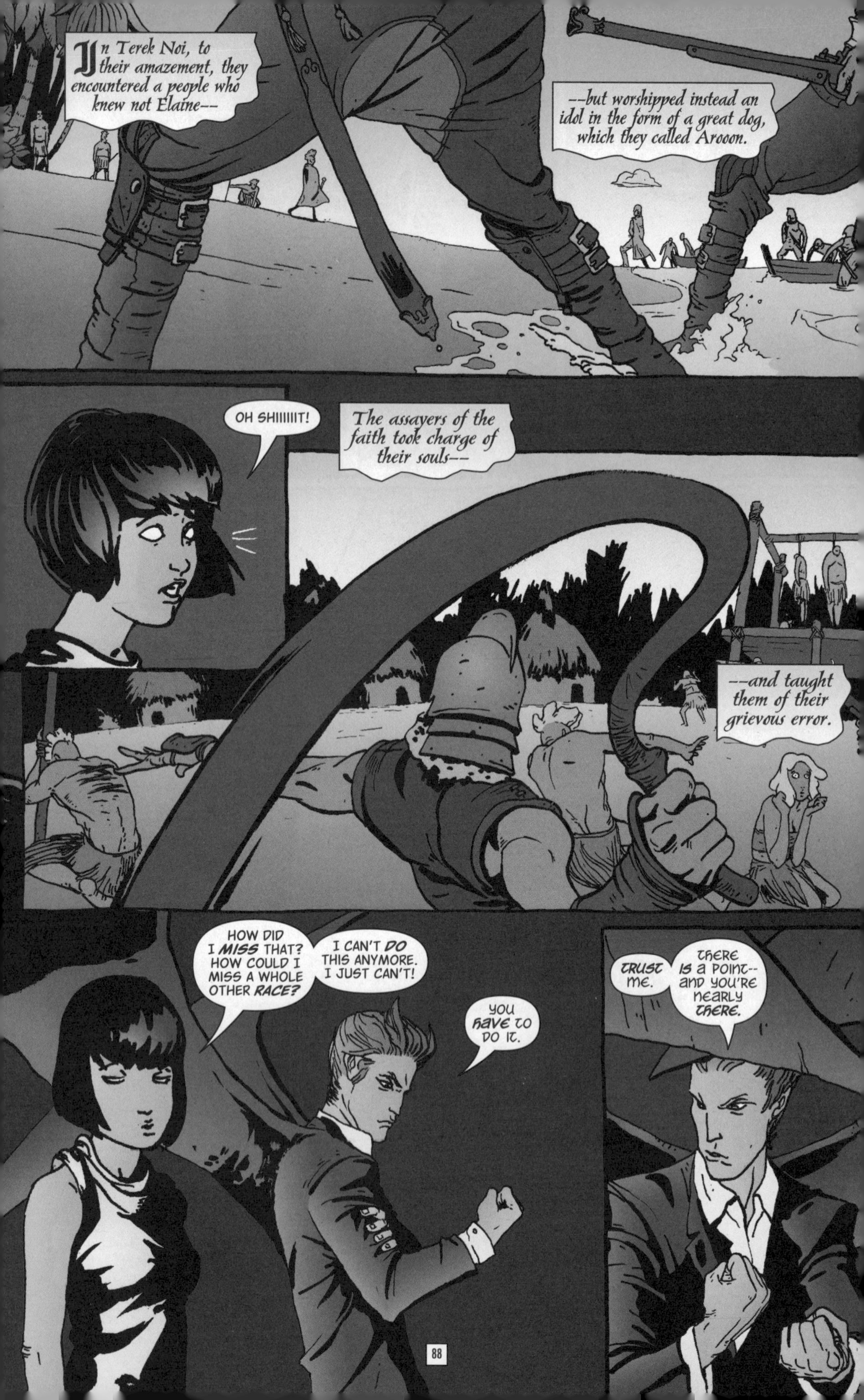
In Terek Noi, to their amazement, they encountered a people who knew not Elaine--
--but worshipped instead an idol in the form of a great dog, which they called Arooon.
OH SHIIIIIIT!
The assayers of the faith took charge of their souls--
--and taught them of their grievous error.
HOW DID I MISS THAT? HOW COULD I MISS A WHOLE OTHER RACE?
I CAN'T DO THIS ANYMORE. I JUST CAN'T!
YOU HAVE TO DO IT.
TRUST ME.
THERE IS A POINT-- AND YOU'RE NEARLY THERE.

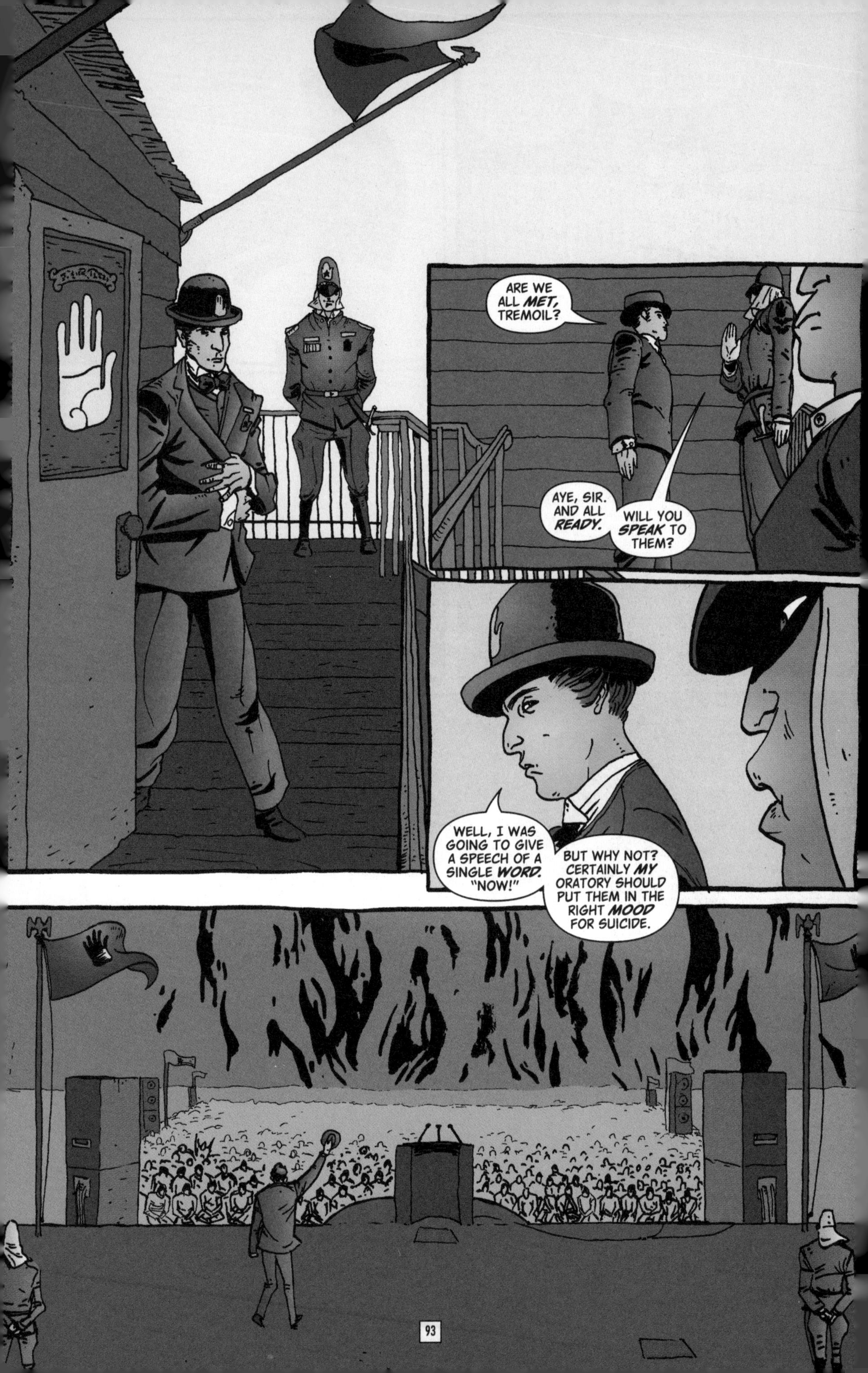
ARE WE ALL MET, TREMOIL?
AYE, SIR. AND ALL READY.
WILL YOU SPEAK TO THEM?
WELL, I WAS GOING TO GIVE A SPEECH OF A SINGLE WORD. "NOW!"
BUT WHY NOT? CERTAINLY MY ORATORY SHOULD PUT THEM IN THE RIGHT MOOD FOR SUICIDE.

MY FRIENDS, YOU HAVE **COME** HERE TO TAKE PART IN A GREAT **VENTURE.**

TO **KILL** YOURSELVES-- AND AS YOU DIE, TO THROW THE **PAIN** OF YOUR DEATHS AGAINST THE WALL.

A HUNDRED **THOUSAND** MORTAL WOUNDS ARE A GREAT FORCE **INDEED.**

AND I-- YOUR **LENS**-- WILL MAGNIFY THEM SO THAT THEY ARE EVEN **GREATER.**

BUT STILL, THE WALL **MIGHT** ENDURE.

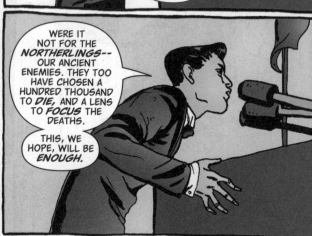

WERE IT NOT FOR THE **NORTHERLINGS**-- OUR ANCIENT ENEMIES. THEY TOO HAVE CHOSEN A HUNDRED THOUSAND TO **DIE,** AND A LENS TO **FOCUS** THE DEATHS.

THIS, WE HOPE, WILL BE **ENOUGH.**

I DON'T KNOW **ANYTHING** ABOUT ANY OF YOU. YOU MAY BE GREAT HEROES, OR GREAT **ROGUES.**

BUT FOR WHAT YOU DO HERE TODAY, YOU WILL BE **REMEMBERED** UNTIL THE WORLD ENDS.

RAISE YOUR **DAGGERS,** NOW. INTONE THE WORDS OF YOUR **CHOOSING.**

FIX YOUR **MINDS** UPON THE WALL.

AND STR--

TCHANG

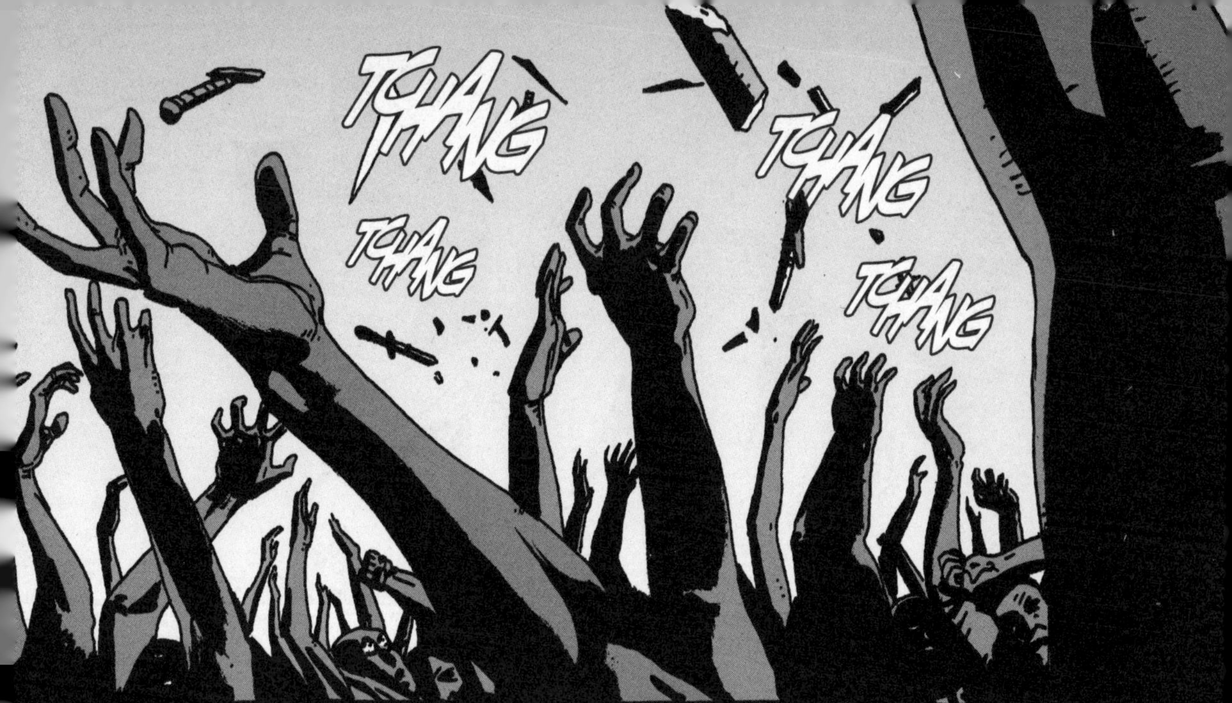
TCHANG
TCHANG
TCHANG
TCHANG

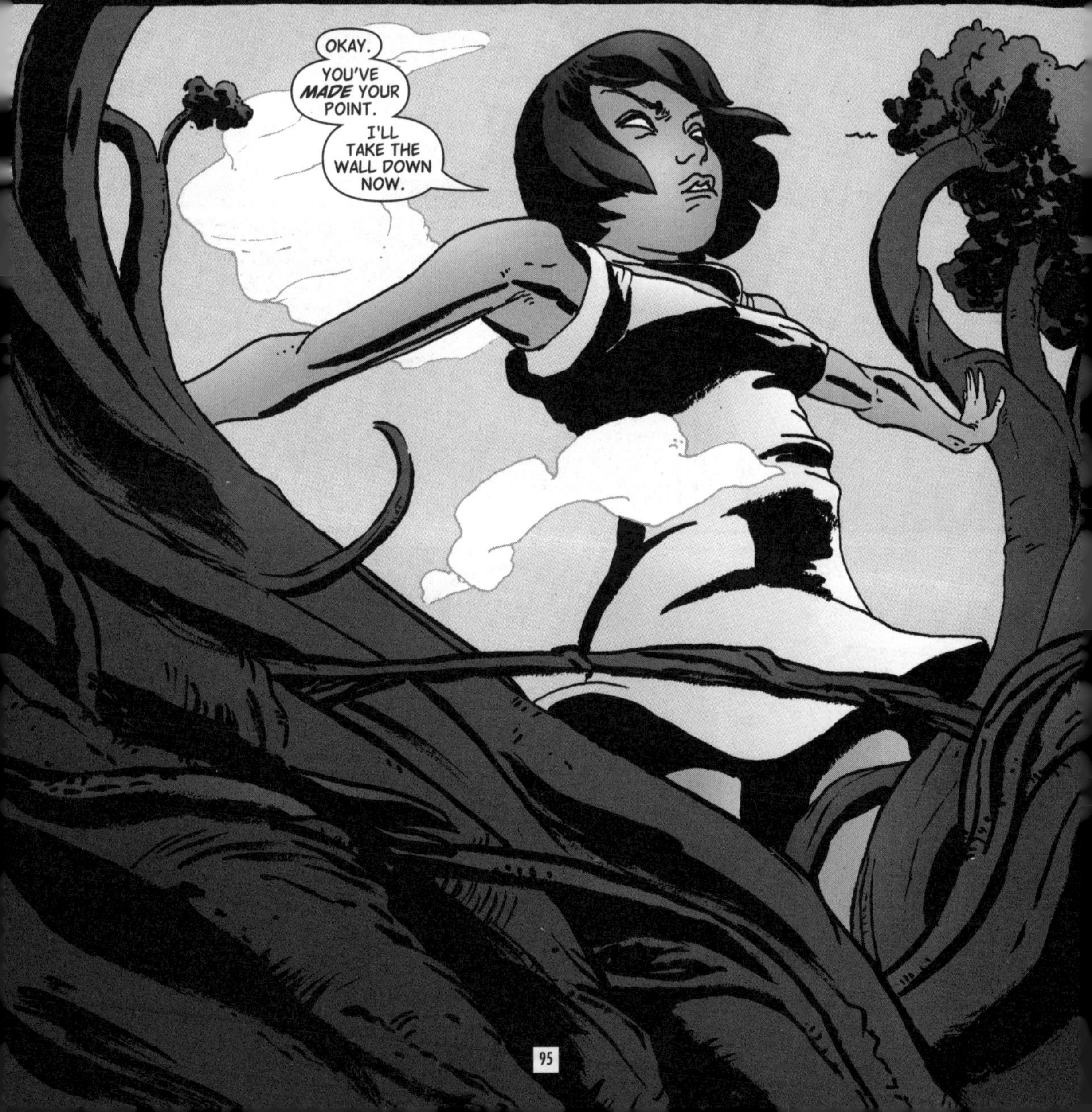
OKAY.
YOU'VE *MADE* YOUR POINT.
I'LL TAKE THE WALL DOWN NOW.

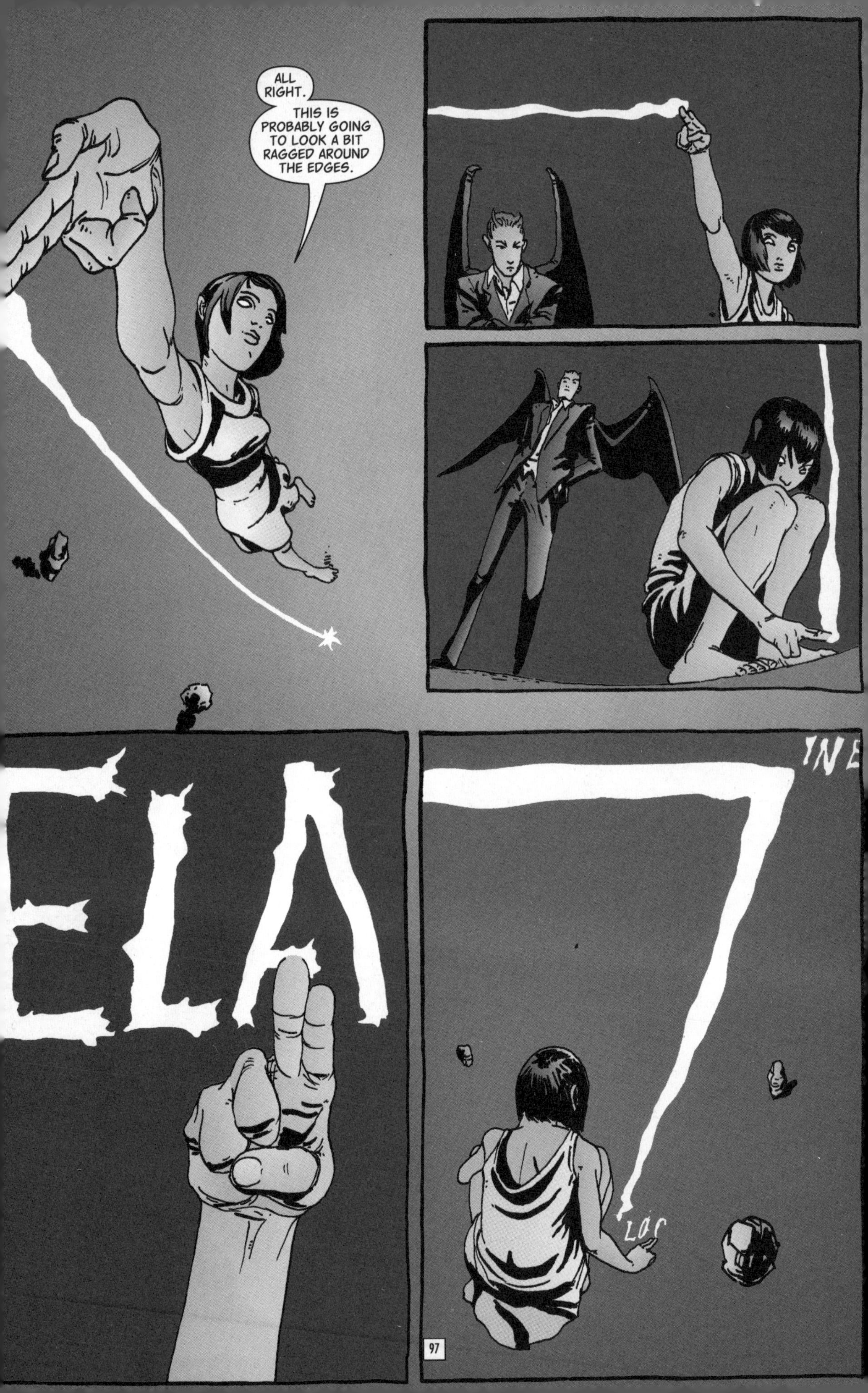
ALL RIGHT.
THIS IS PROBABLY GOING TO LOOK A BIT RAGGED AROUND THE EDGES.

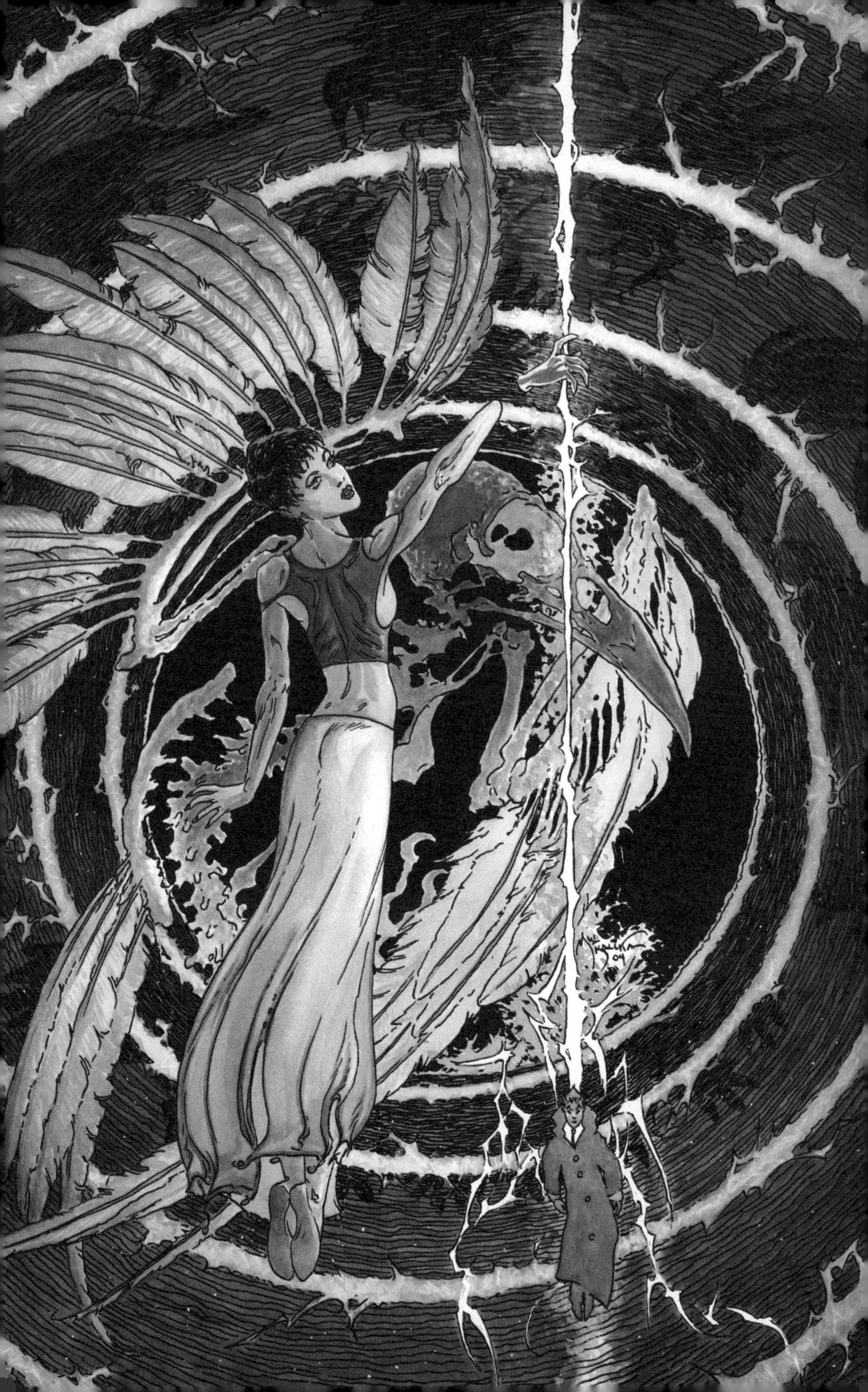

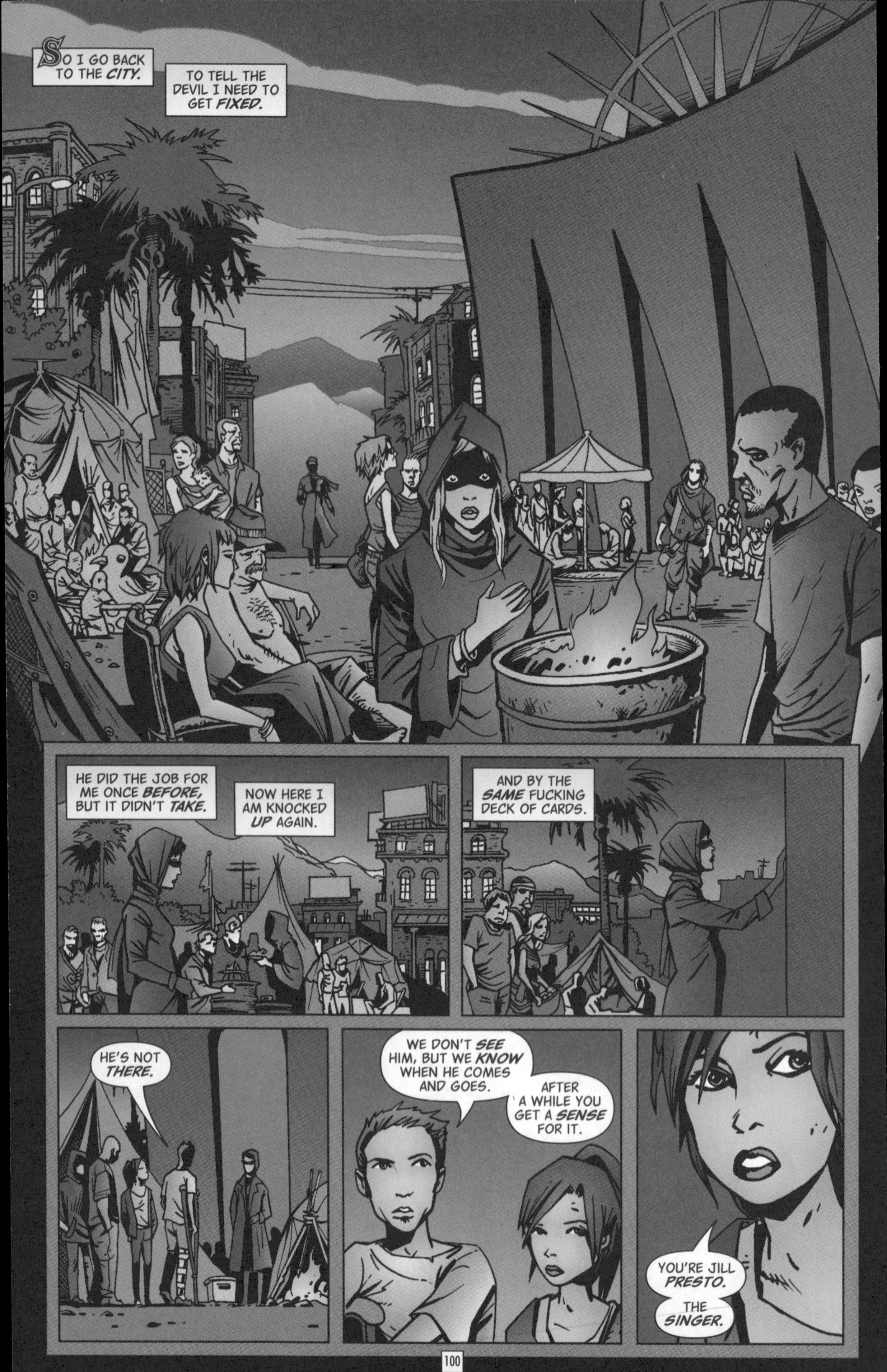
So I go back to the *city*.
To tell the devil I need to get *fixed*.
He did the job for me once *before*, but it didn't *take*.
Now here I am knocked *up* again.
And by the *same* fucking deck of cards.
He's not *there*.
We don't *see* him, but we *know* when he comes and goes.
After a while you get a *sense* for it.
You're Jill *Presto*.
The *singer*.

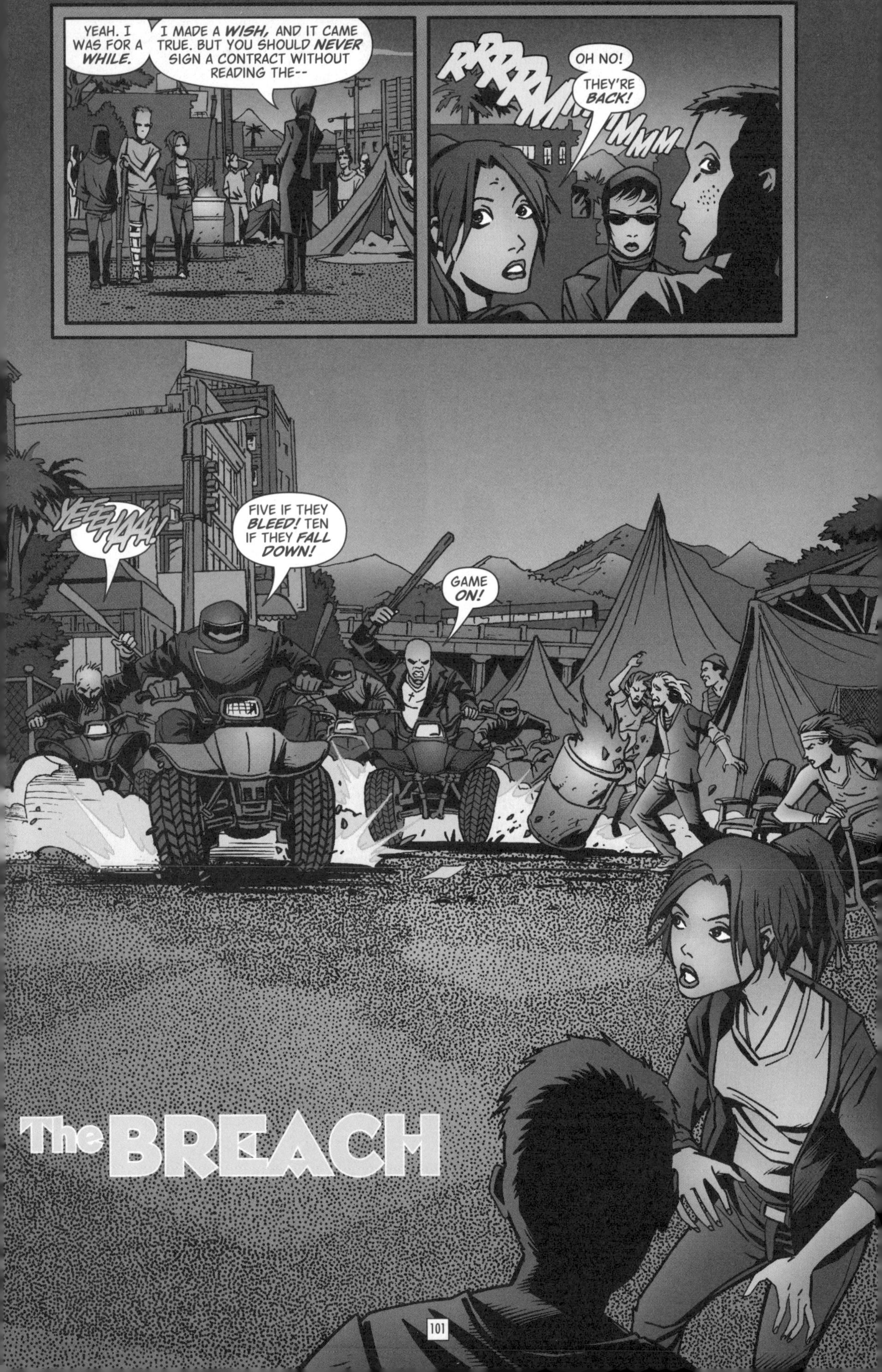
YEAH. I WAS FOR A WHILE.
I MADE A WISH, AND IT CAME TRUE. BUT YOU SHOULD NEVER SIGN A CONTRACT WITHOUT READING THE--
RRRRRMMMMMMM
OH NO!
THEY'RE BACK!
YEEEHAAA!
FIVE IF THEY BLEED! TEN IF THEY FALL DOWN!
GAME ON!
The BREACH

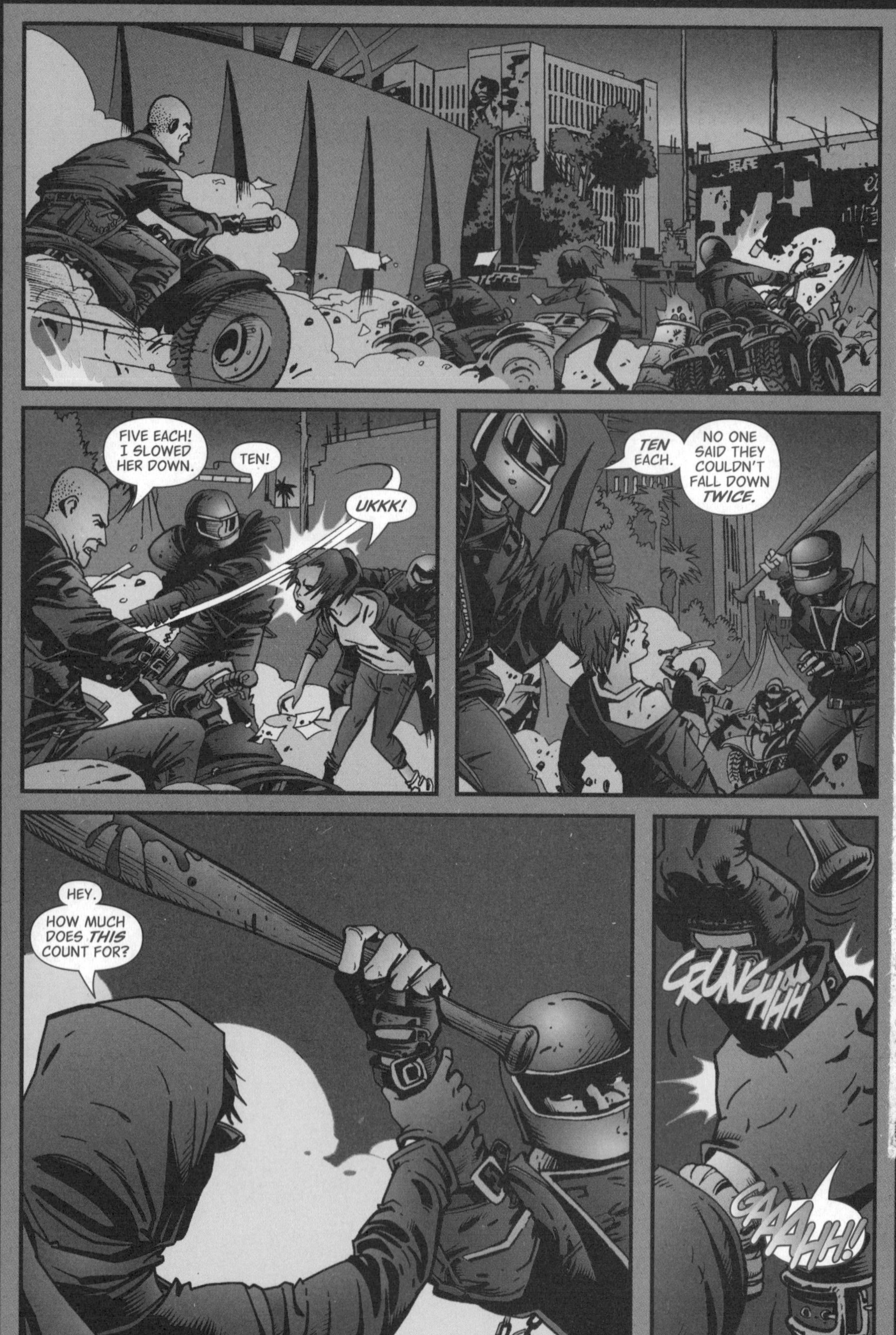
FIVE EACH! I SLOWED HER DOWN.
TEN!
UKKK!
TEN EACH.
NO ONE SAID THEY COULDN'T FALL DOWN TWICE.
HEY.
HOW MUCH DOES THIS COUNT FOR?
CRUNCHHH
GAAAHH!

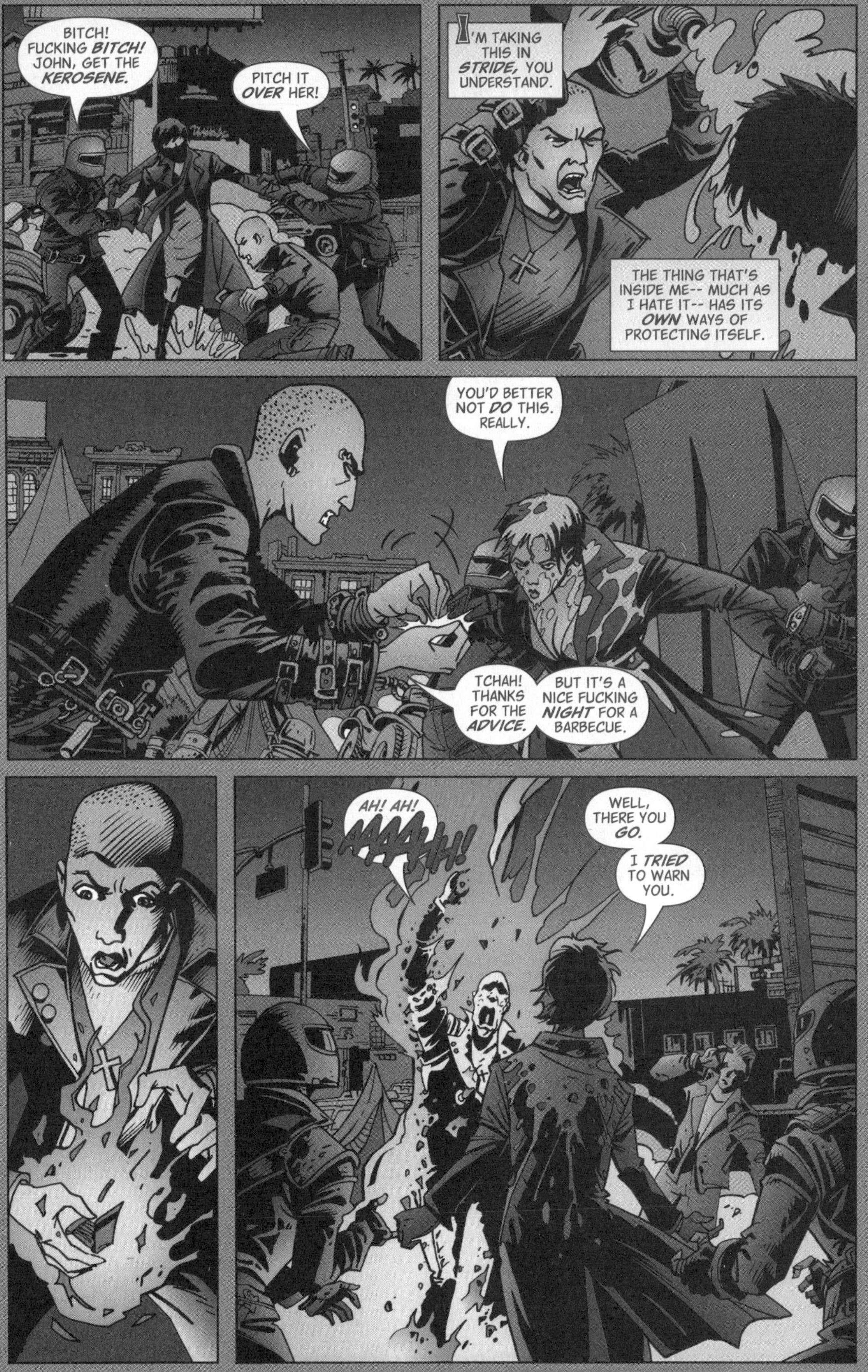
BITCH! FUCKING BITCH! JOHN, GET THE KEROSENE.
PITCH IT OVER HER!
I'M TAKING THIS IN STRIDE, YOU UNDERSTAND.
THE THING THAT'S INSIDE ME-- MUCH AS I HATE IT-- HAS ITS OWN WAYS OF PROTECTING ITSELF.
YOU'D BETTER NOT DO THIS. REALLY.
TCHAH! THANKS FOR THE ADVICE.
BUT IT'S A NICE FUCKING NIGHT FOR A BARBECUE.
AH! AH! AAAAHH!
WELL, THERE YOU GO.
I TRIED TO WARN YOU.

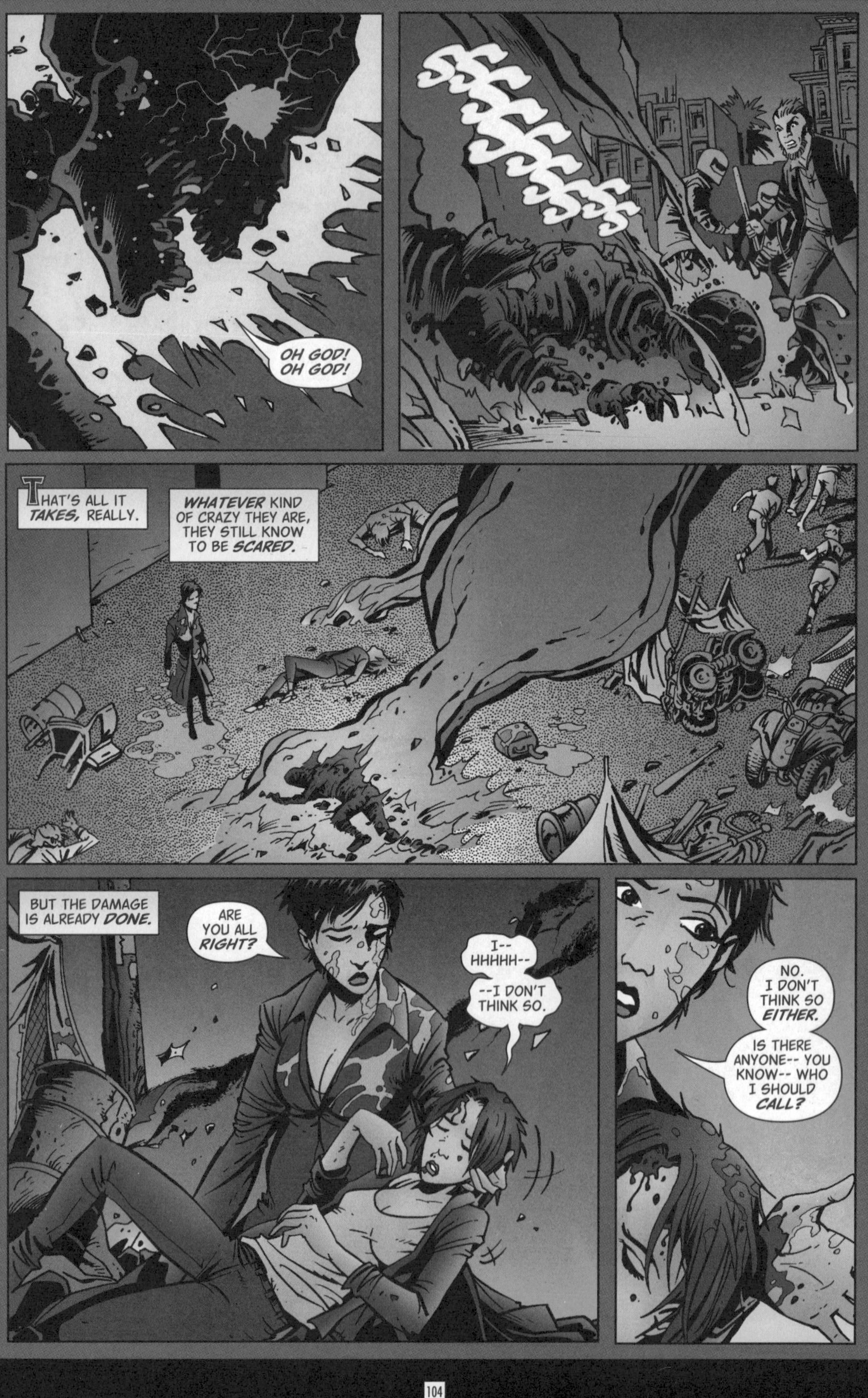
OH GOD! OH GOD!
SSSSSSSSSS
THAT'S ALL IT TAKES, REALLY.
WHATEVER KIND OF CRAZY THEY ARE, THEY STILL KNOW TO BE SCARED.
BUT THE DAMAGE IS ALREADY DONE.
ARE YOU ALL RIGHT?
I-- HHHHH--
--I DON'T THINK SO.
NO. I DON'T THINK SO EITHER.
IS THERE ANYONE-- YOU KNOW-- WHO I SHOULD CALL?

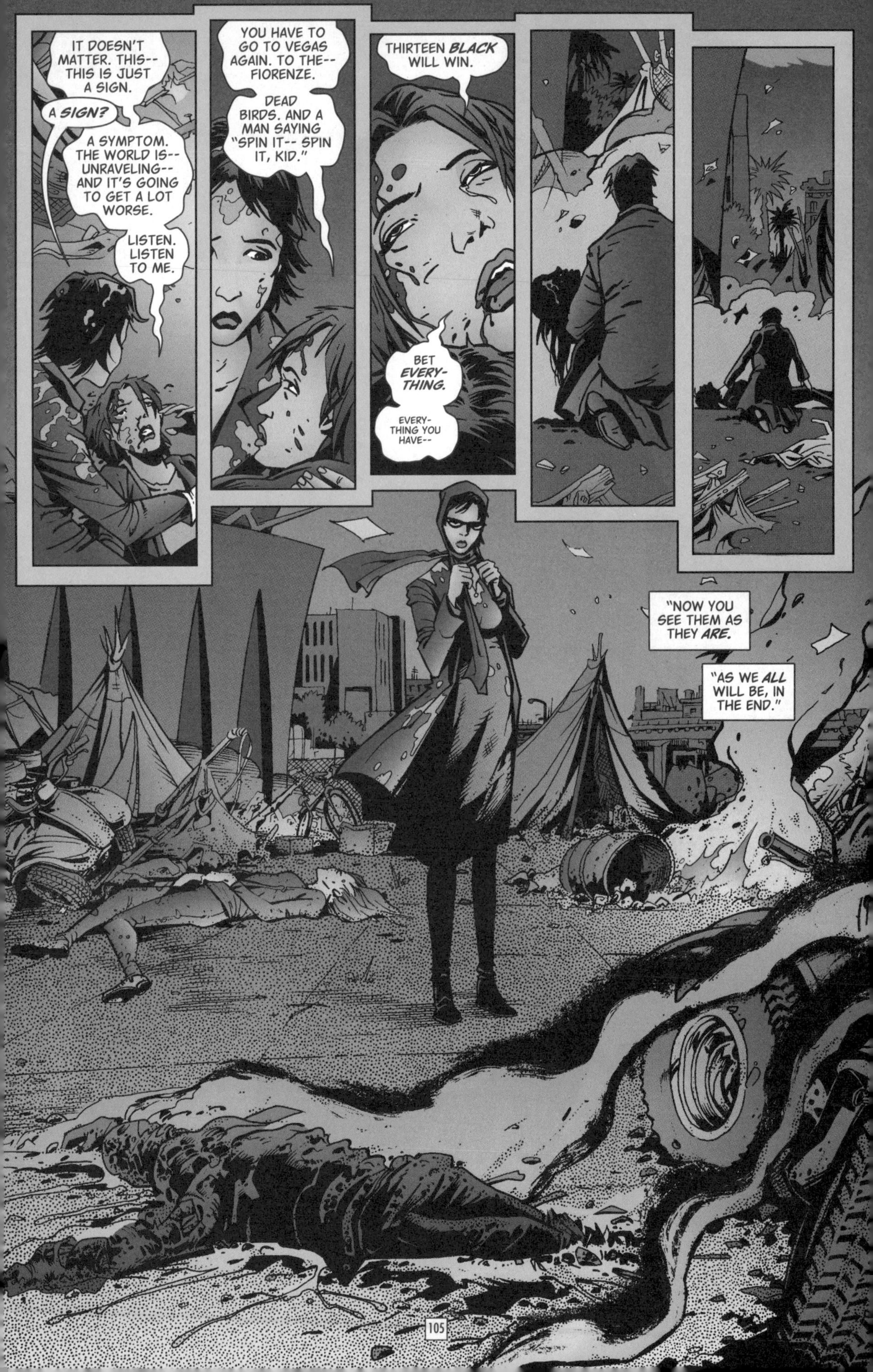
IT DOESN'T MATTER. THIS-- THIS IS JUST A SIGN.
A SIGN?
A SYMPTOM. THE WORLD IS-- UNRAVELING-- AND IT'S GOING TO GET A LOT WORSE.
LISTEN. LISTEN TO ME.
YOU HAVE TO GO TO VEGAS AGAIN. TO THE-- FIORENZE.
DEAD BIRDS. AND A MAN SAYING "SPIN IT-- SPIN IT, KID."
THIRTEEN BLACK WILL WIN.
BET EVERYTHING.
EVERYTHING YOU HAVE--
"NOW YOU SEE THEM AS THEY ARE.
"AS WE ALL WILL BE, IN THE END."

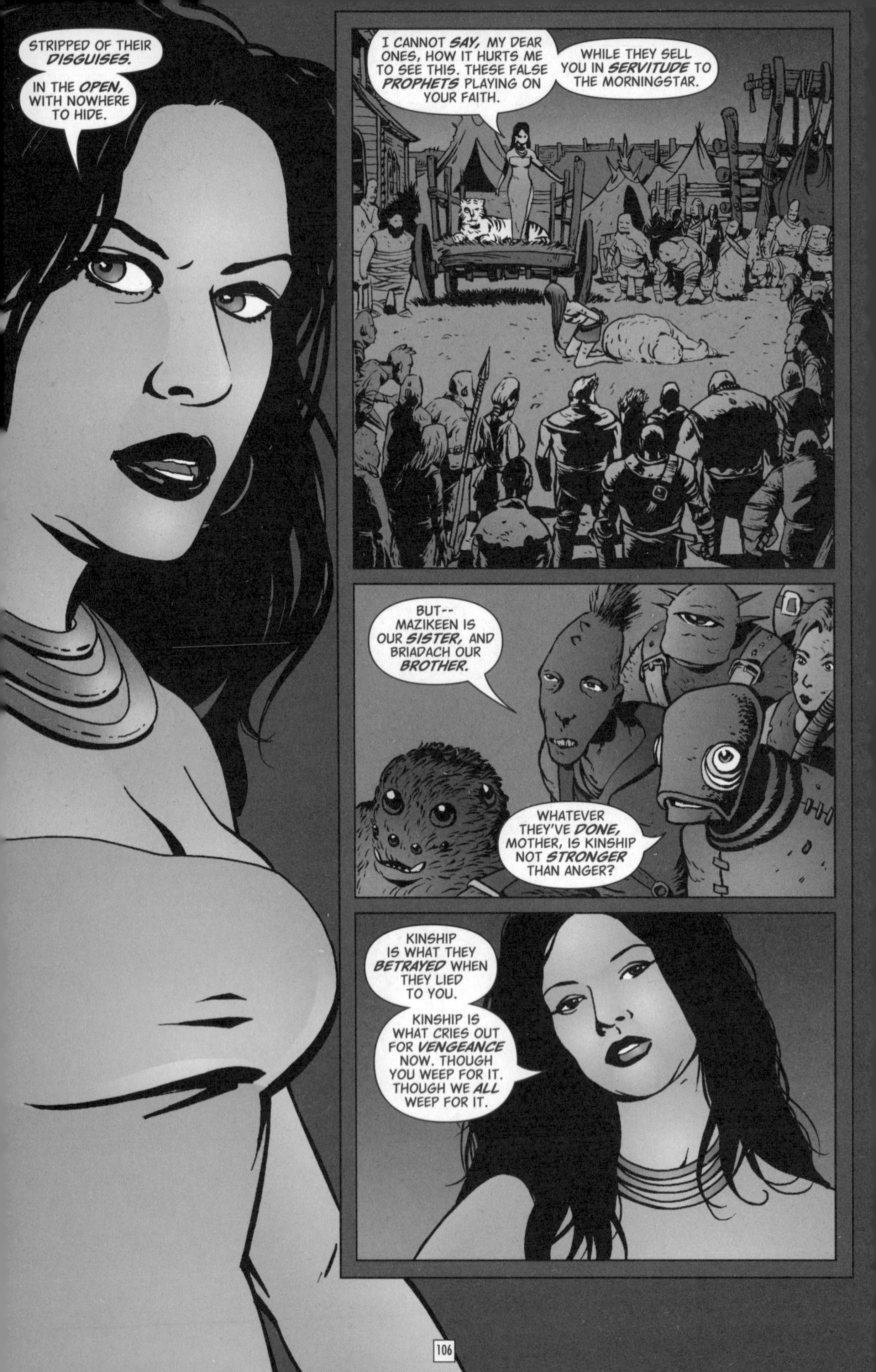
STRIPPED OF THEIR DISGUISES.
IN THE OPEN, WITH NOWHERE TO HIDE.
I CANNOT SAY, MY DEAR ONES, HOW IT HURTS ME TO SEE THIS. THESE FALSE PROPHETS PLAYING ON YOUR FAITH.
WHILE THEY SELL YOU IN SERVITUDE TO THE MORNINGSTAR.
BUT-- MAZIKEEN IS OUR SISTER, AND BRIADACH OUR BROTHER.
WHATEVER THEY'VE DONE, MOTHER, IS KINSHIP NOT STRONGER THAN ANGER?
KINSHIP IS WHAT THEY BETRAYED WHEN THEY LIED TO YOU.
KINSHIP IS WHAT CRIES OUT FOR VENGEANCE NOW. THOUGH YOU WEEP FOR IT. THOUGH WE ALL WEEP FOR IT.

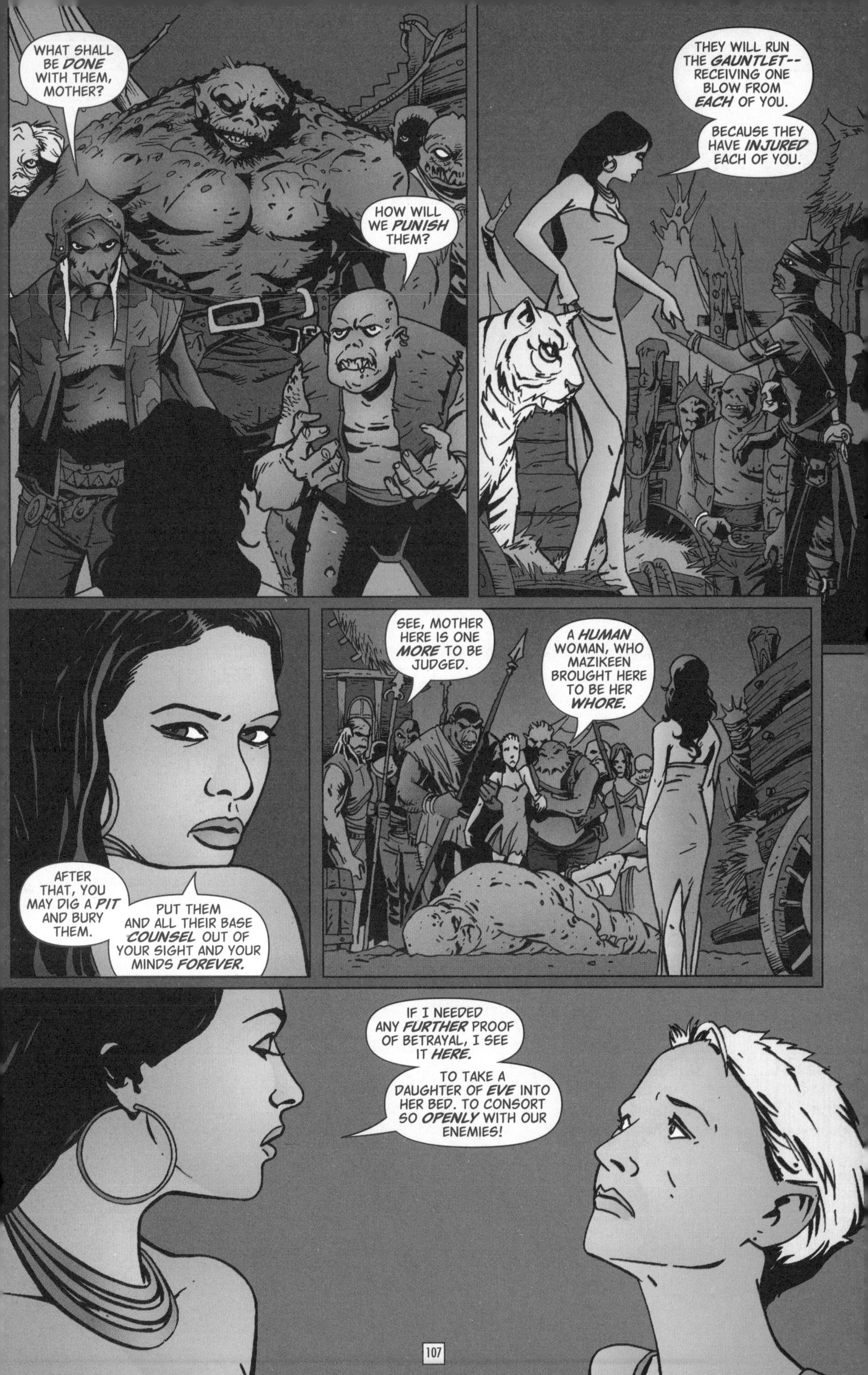
WHAT SHALL BE DONE WITH THEM, MOTHER?
HOW WILL WE PUNISH THEM?
THEY WILL RUN THE GAUNTLET-- RECEIVING ONE BLOW FROM EACH OF YOU.
BECAUSE THEY HAVE INJURED EACH OF YOU.
AFTER THAT, YOU MAY DIG A PIT AND BURY THEM.
PUT THEM AND ALL THEIR BASE COUNSEL OUT OF YOUR SIGHT AND YOUR MINDS FOREVER.
SEE, MOTHER HERE IS ONE MORE TO BE JUDGED.
A HUMAN WOMAN, WHO MAZIKEEN BROUGHT HERE TO BE HER WHORE.
IF I NEEDED ANY FURTHER PROOF OF BETRAYAL, I SEE IT HERE.
TO TAKE A DAUGHTER OF EVE INTO HER BED. TO CONSORT SO OPENLY WITH OUR ENEMIES!

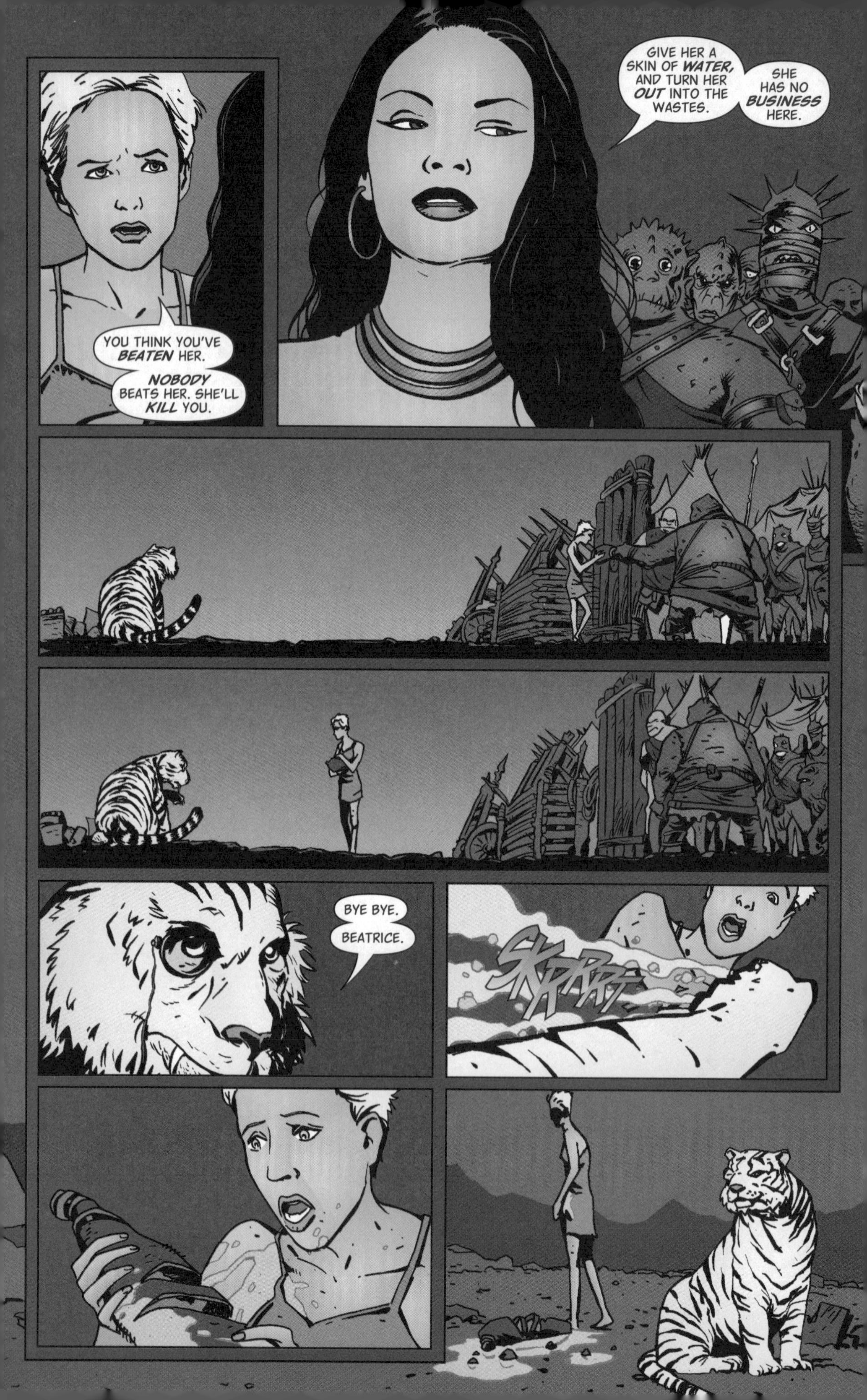
YOU THINK YOU'VE BEATEN HER.
NOBODY BEATS HER. SHE'LL KILL YOU.
GIVE HER A SKIN OF WATER, AND TURN HER OUT INTO THE WASTES.
SHE HAS NO BUSINESS HERE.
BYE BYE.
BEATRICE.
SKRRRT

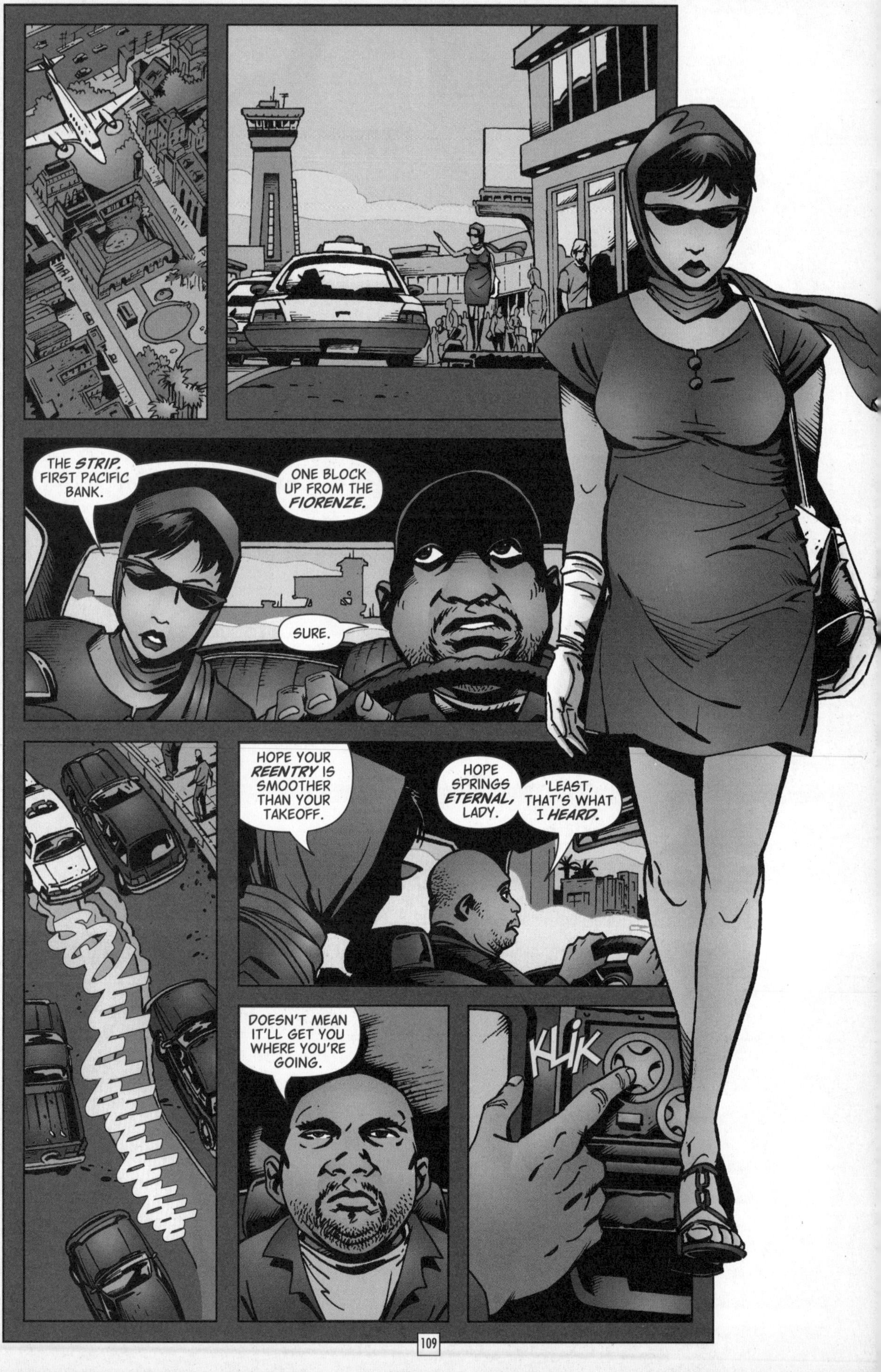
THE STRIP. FIRST PACIFIC BANK.
ONE BLOCK UP FROM THE FIORENZE.
SURE.
HOPE YOUR REENTRY IS SMOOTHER THAN YOUR TAKEOFF.
HOPE SPRINGS ETERNAL, LADY.
'LEAST, THAT'S WHAT I HEARD.
DOESN'T MEAN IT'LL GET YOU WHERE YOU'RE GOING.
KLIK

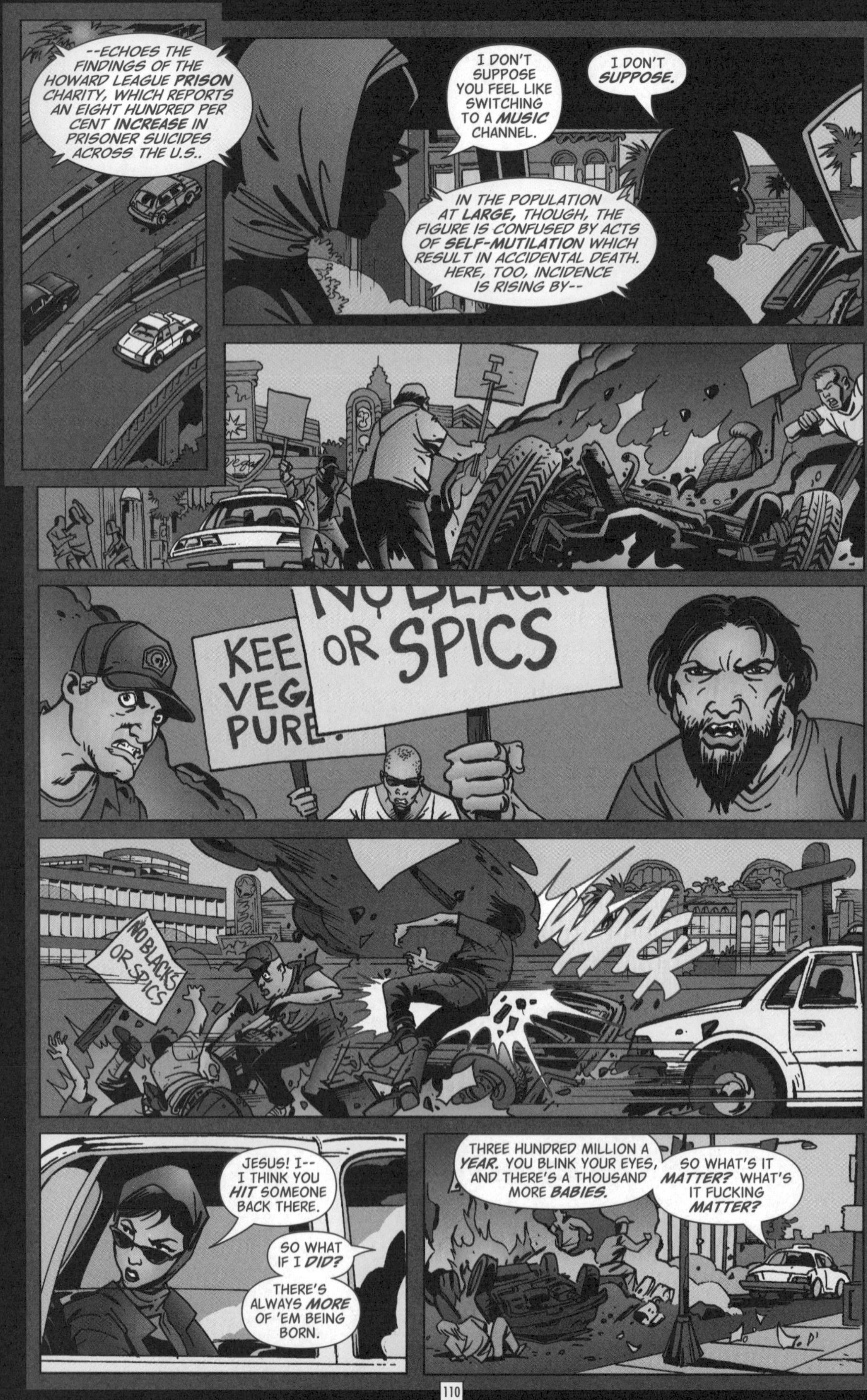
--ECHOES THE FINDINGS OF THE HOWARD LEAGUE PRISON CHARITY, WHICH REPORTS AN EIGHT HUNDRED PER CENT INCREASE IN PRISONER SUICIDES ACROSS THE U.S..
I DON'T SUPPOSE YOU FEEL LIKE SWITCHING TO A MUSIC CHANNEL.
I DON'T SUPPOSE.
IN THE POPULATION AT LARGE, THOUGH, THE FIGURE IS CONFUSED BY ACTS OF SELF-MUTILATION WHICH RESULT IN ACCIDENTAL DEATH. HERE, TOO, INCIDENCE IS RISING BY--
NO BLACKS OR SPICS
JESUS! I-- I THINK YOU HIT SOMEONE BACK THERE.
SO WHAT IF I DID?
THERE'S ALWAYS MORE OF 'EM BEING BORN.
THREE HUNDRED MILLION A YEAR. YOU BLINK YOUR EYES, AND THERE'S A THOUSAND MORE BABIES.
SO WHAT'S IT MATTER? WHAT'S IT FUCKING MATTER?

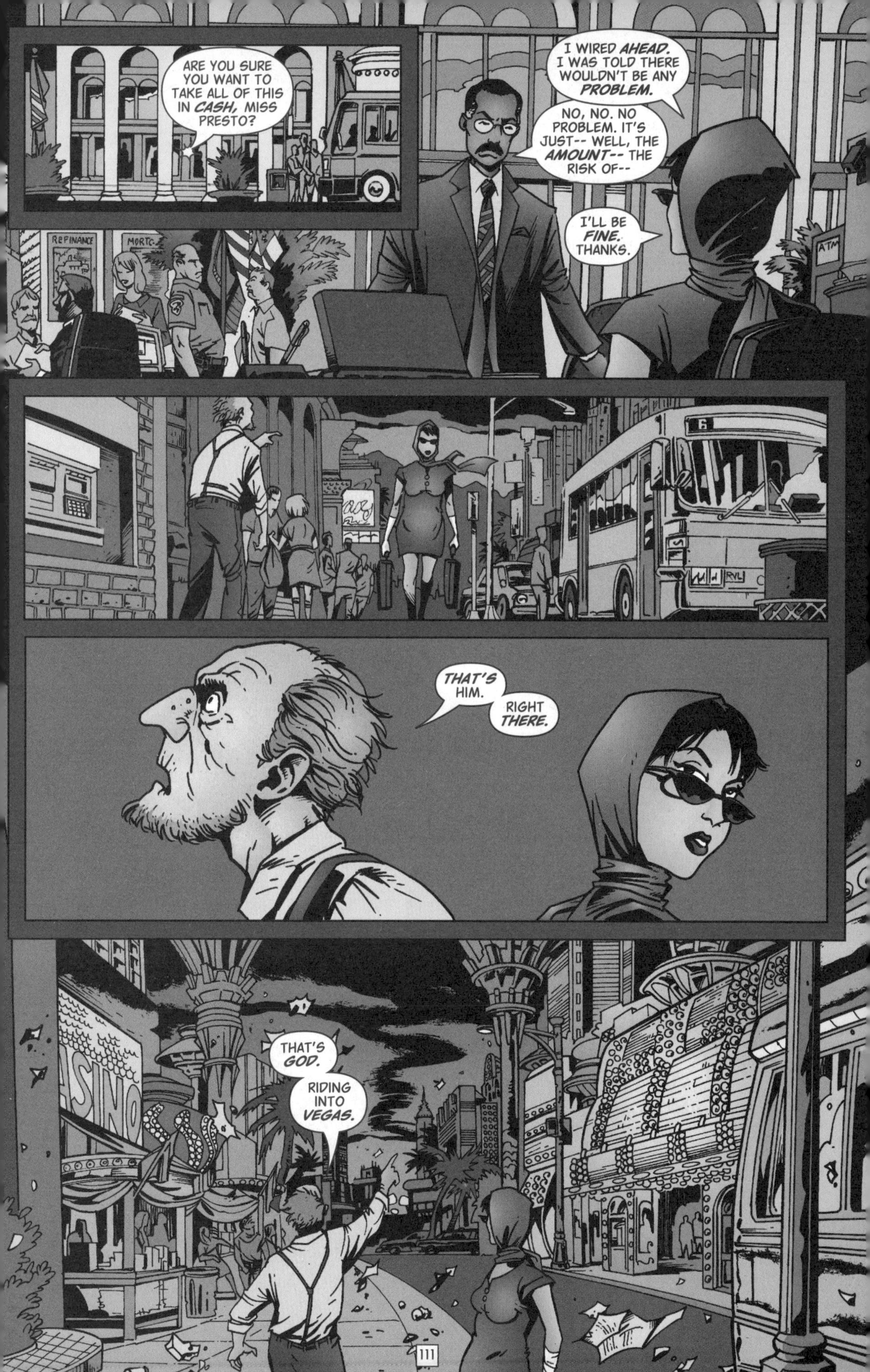
ARE YOU SURE YOU WANT TO TAKE ALL OF THIS IN CASH, MISS PRESTO?
I WIRED AHEAD. I WAS TOLD THERE WOULDN'T BE ANY PROBLEM.
NO, NO. NO PROBLEM. IT'S JUST-- WELL, THE AMOUNT-- THE RISK OF--
I'LL BE FINE. THANKS.
REFINANCE
MORTG
ATM
6
THAT'S HIM.
RIGHT THERE.
THAT'S GOD.
RIDING INTO VEGAS.
ASINO

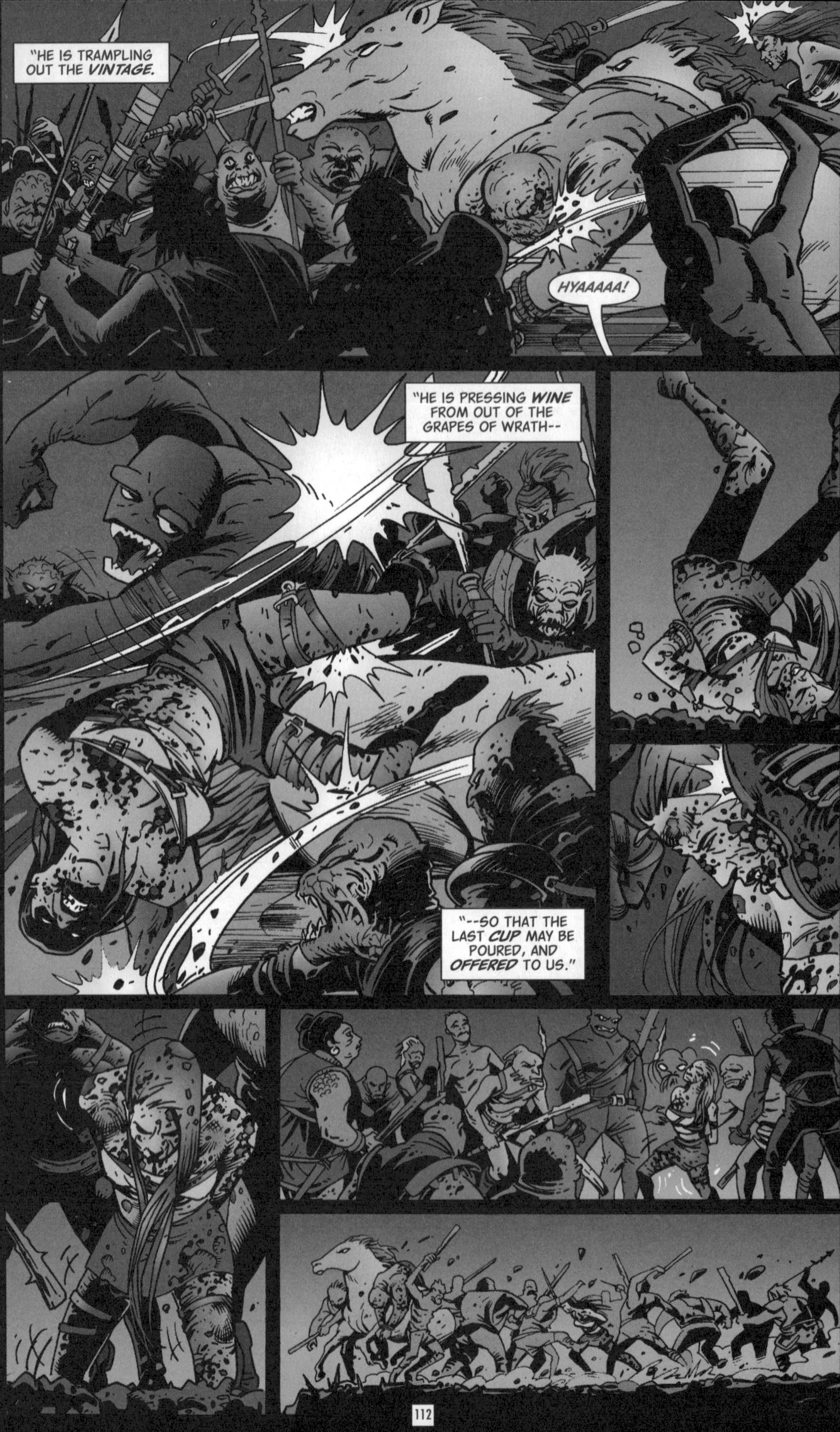
"HE IS TRAMPLING OUT THE *VINTAGE.*
HYAAAAA!
"HE IS PRESSING *WINE* FROM OUT OF THE GRAPES OF WRATH--
"--SO THAT THE LAST *CUP* MAY BE POURED, AND *OFFERED* TO US."

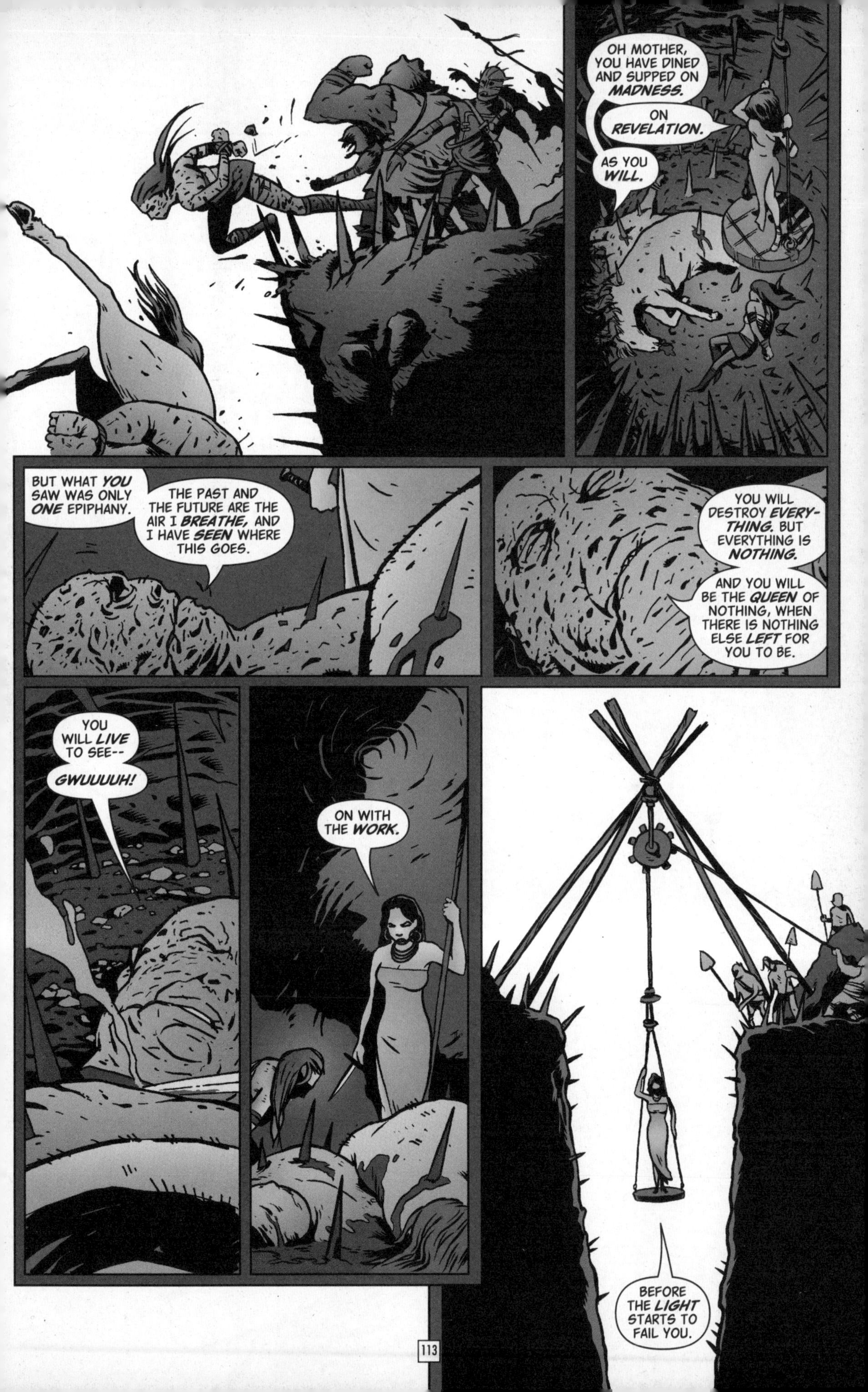
OH MOTHER, YOU HAVE DINED AND SUPPED ON MADNESS.
ON REVELATION.
AS YOU WILL.
BUT WHAT YOU SAW WAS ONLY ONE EPIPHANY.
THE PAST AND THE FUTURE ARE THE AIR I BREATHE, AND I HAVE SEEN WHERE THIS GOES.
YOU WILL DESTROY EVERY-THING. BUT EVERYTHING IS NOTHING.
AND YOU WILL BE THE QUEEN OF NOTHING, WHEN THERE IS NOTHING ELSE LEFT FOR YOU TO BE.
YOU WILL LIVE TO SEE--
GWUUUUH!
ON WITH THE WORK.
BEFORE THE LIGHT STARTS TO FAIL YOU.

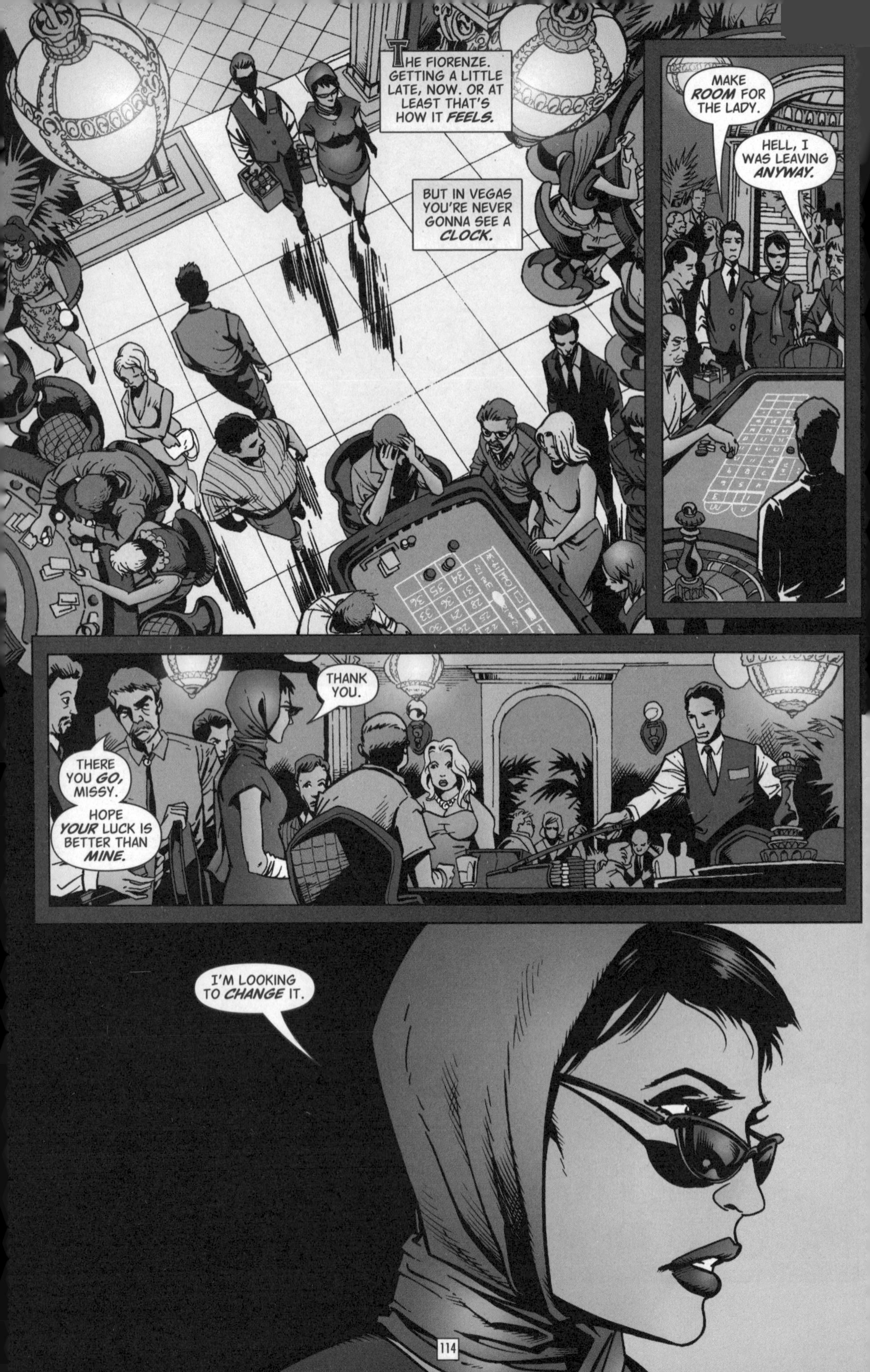
THE FIORENZE. GETTING A LITTLE LATE, NOW. OR AT LEAST THAT'S HOW IT FEELS.
BUT IN VEGAS YOU'RE NEVER GONNA SEE A CLOCK.
MAKE ROOM FOR THE LADY.
HELL, I WAS LEAVING ANYWAY.
THERE YOU GO, MISSY.
HOPE YOUR LUCK IS BETTER THAN MINE.
THANK YOU.
I'M LOOKING TO CHANGE IT.

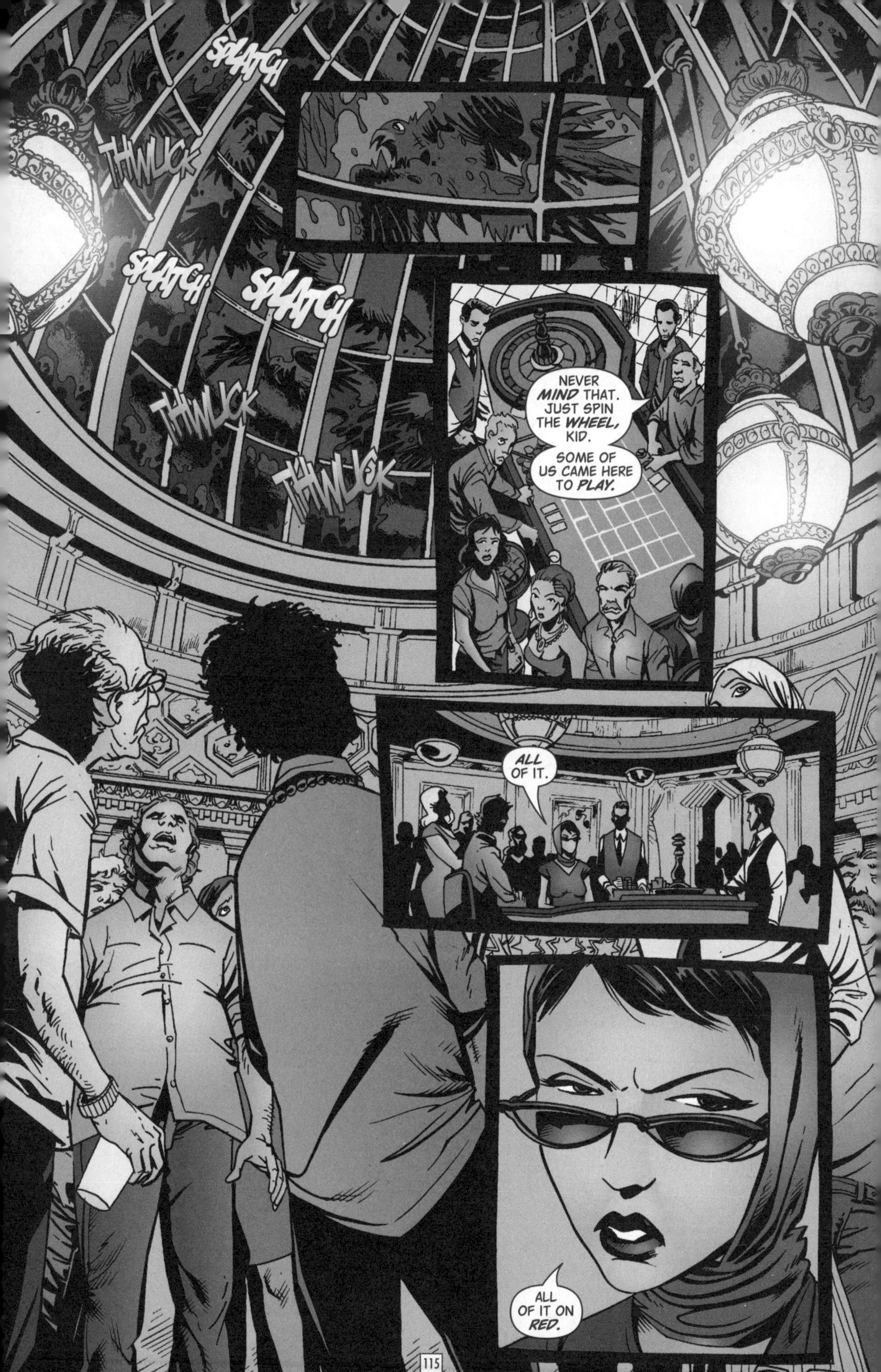
SPLATCH
THWUCK
SPLATCH
SPLATCH
THWUCK
THWUCK
NEVER MIND THAT. JUST SPIN THE WHEEL, KID.
SOME OF US CAME HERE TO PLAY.
ALL OF IT.
ALL OF IT ON RED.

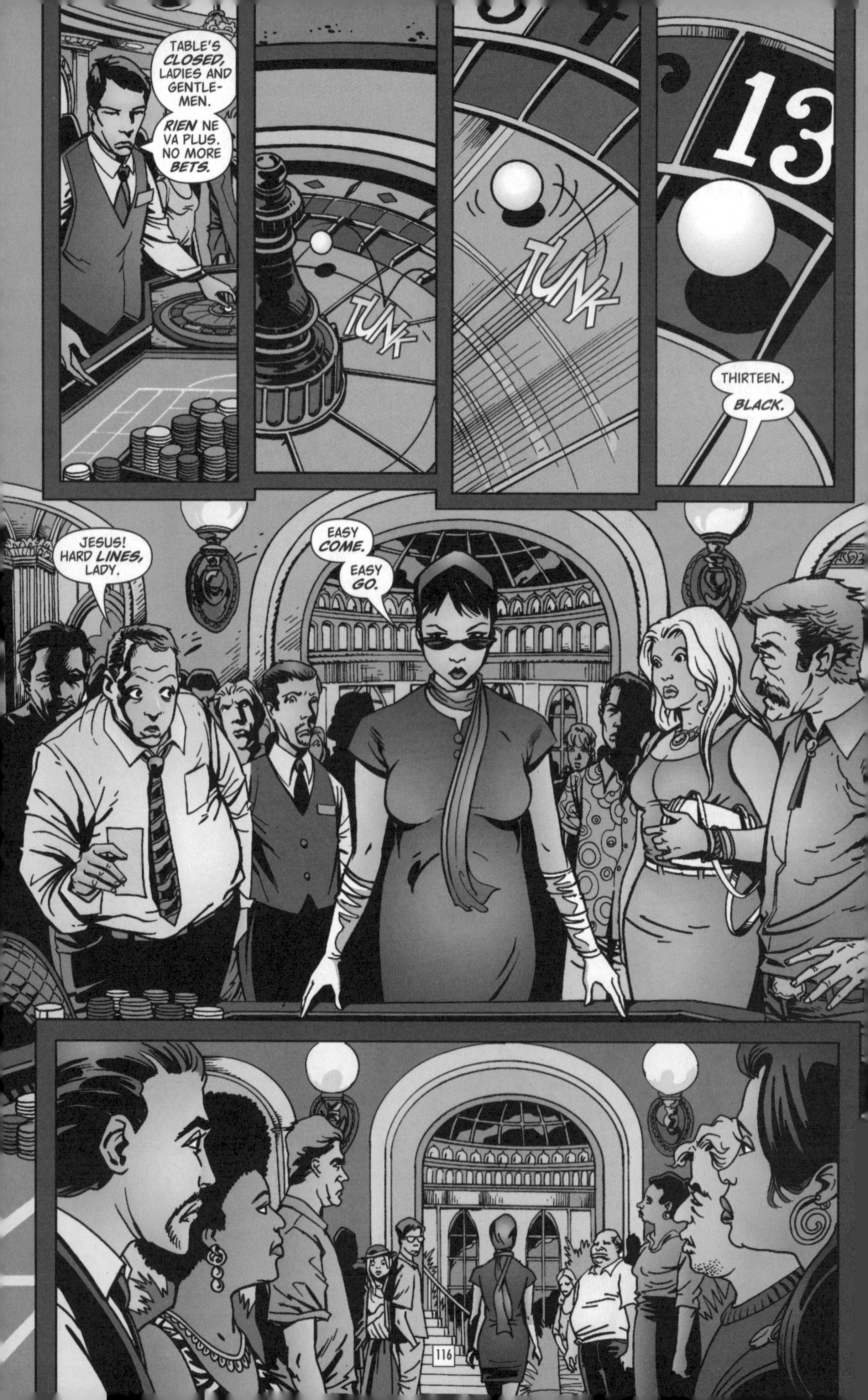
TABLE'S CLOSED, LADIES AND GENTLEMEN.
RIEN NE VA PLUS. NO MORE BETS.
TUNK
TUNK
13
THIRTEEN. BLACK.
JESUS! HARD LINES, LADY.
EASY COME.
EASY GO.

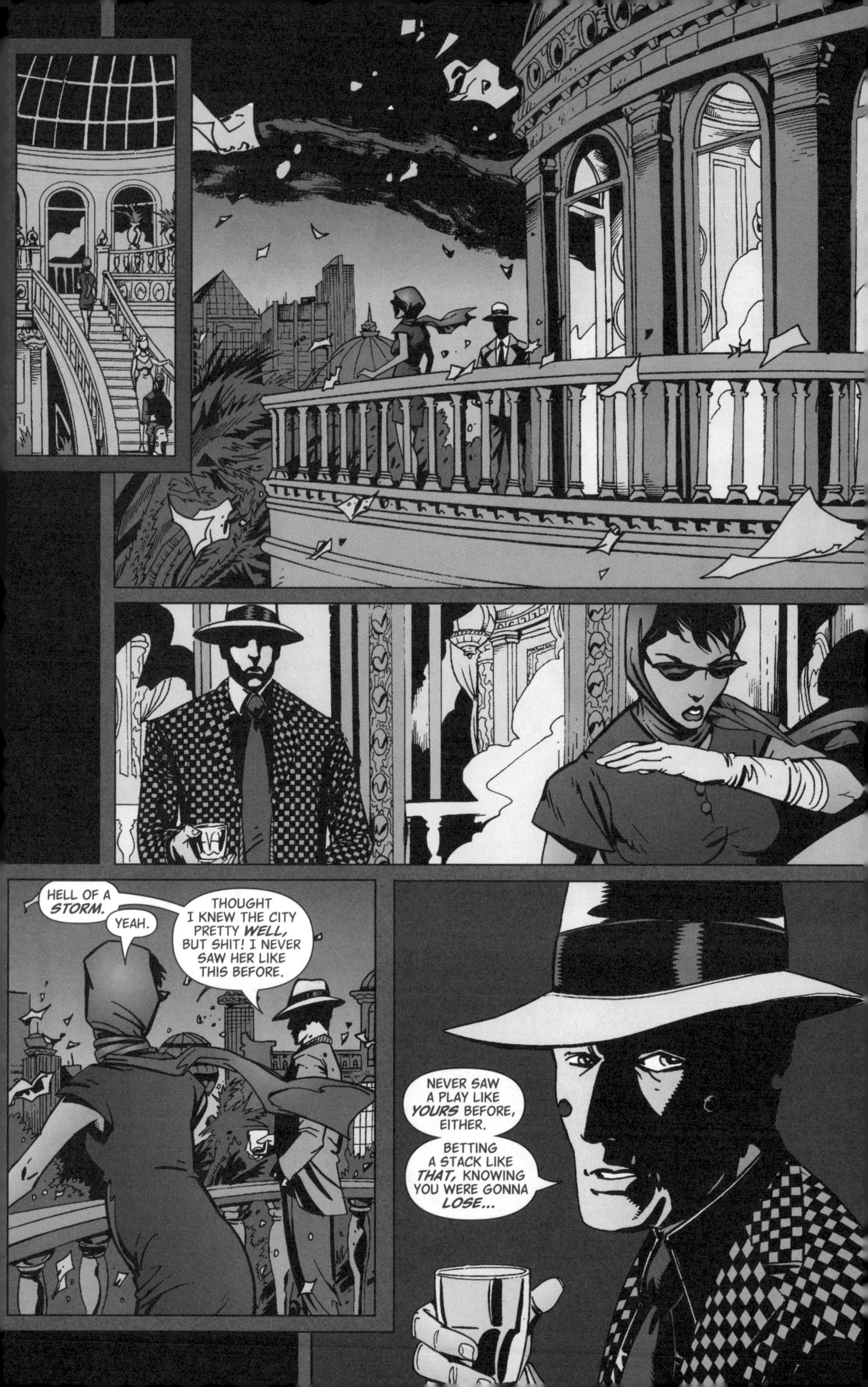
HELL OF A STORM.
YEAH.
THOUGHT I KNEW THE CITY PRETTY WELL, BUT SHIT! I NEVER SAW HER LIKE THIS BEFORE.
NEVER SAW A PLAY LIKE YOURS BEFORE, EITHER.
BETTING A STACK LIKE THAT, KNOWING YOU WERE GONNA LOSE...

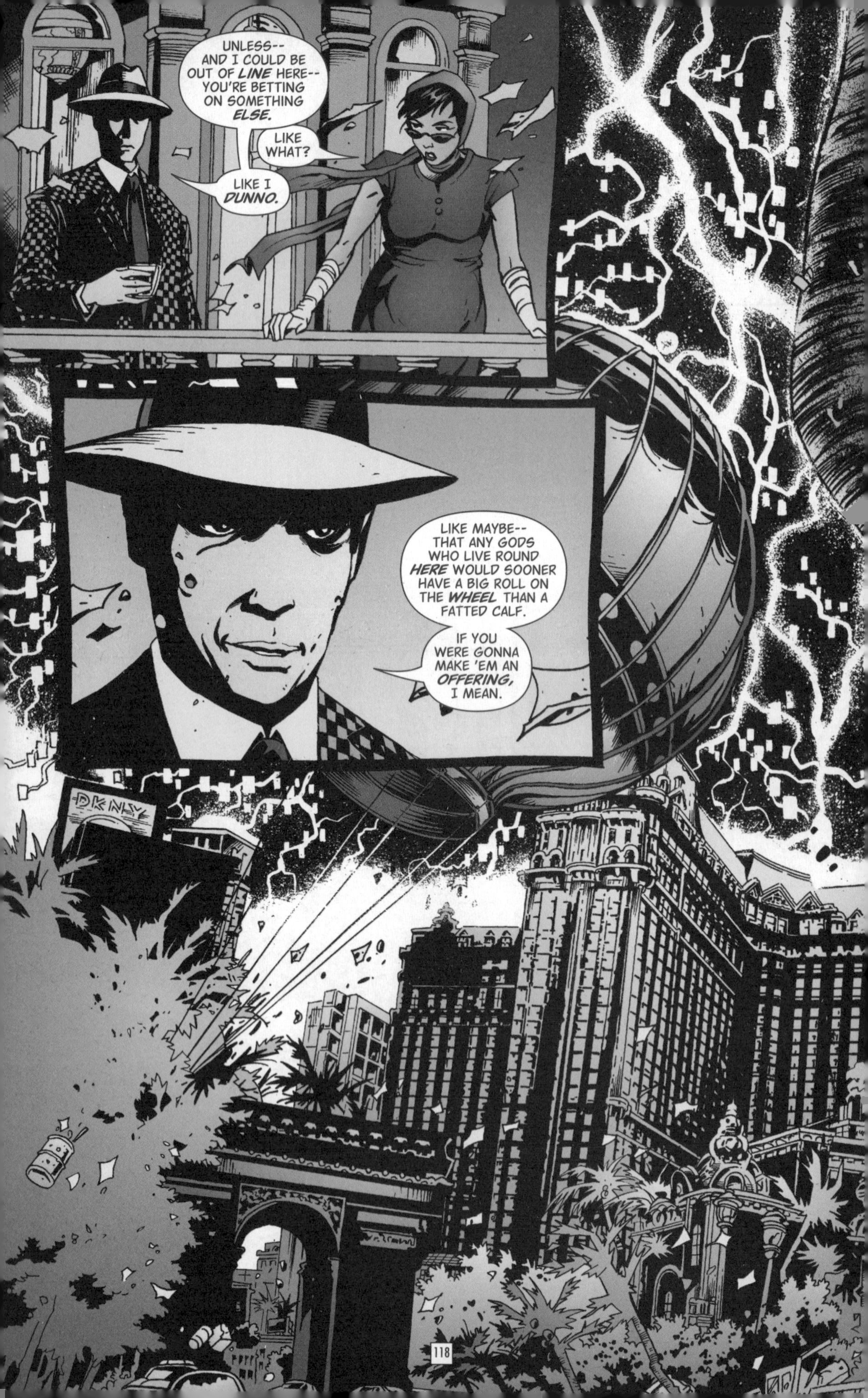
UNLESS-- AND I COULD BE OUT OF LINE HERE-- YOU'RE BETTING ON SOMETHING ELSE.
LIKE WHAT?
LIKE I DUNNO.
LIKE MAYBE-- THAT ANY GODS WHO LIVE ROUND HERE WOULD SOONER HAVE A BIG ROLL ON THE WHEEL THAN A FATTED CALF.
IF YOU WERE GONNA MAKE 'EM AN OFFERING, I MEAN.
DKNY

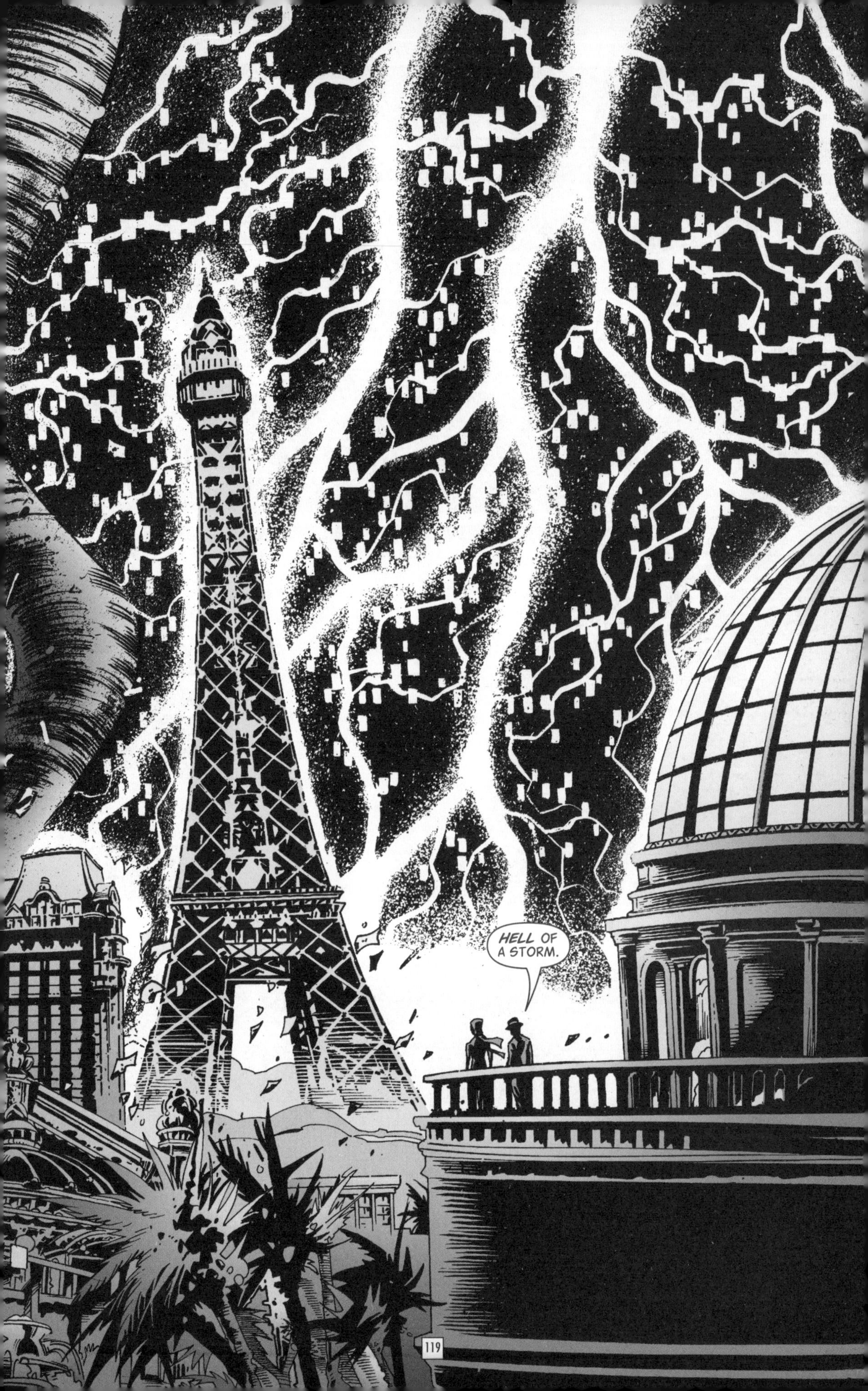
HELL OF A STORM.

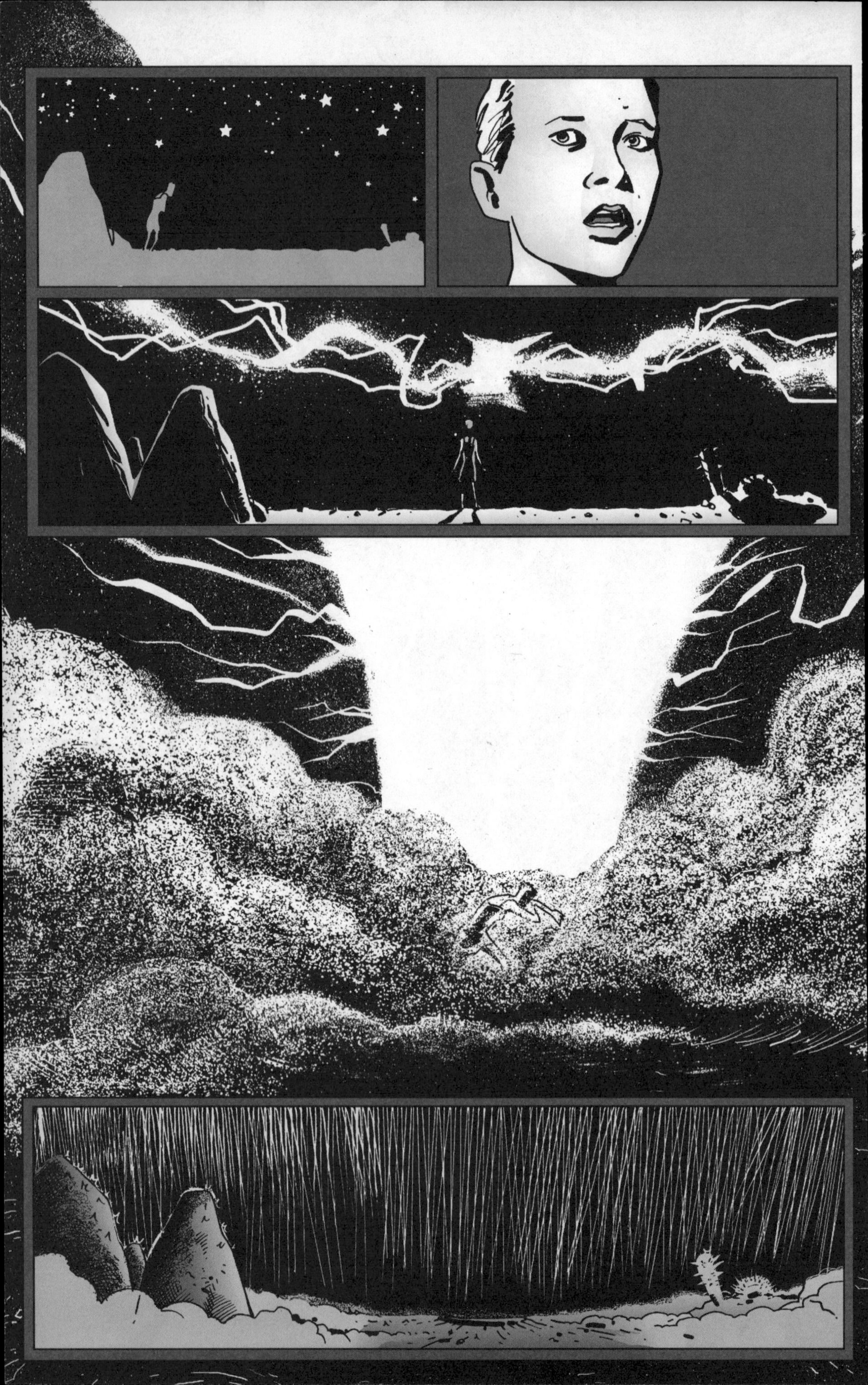

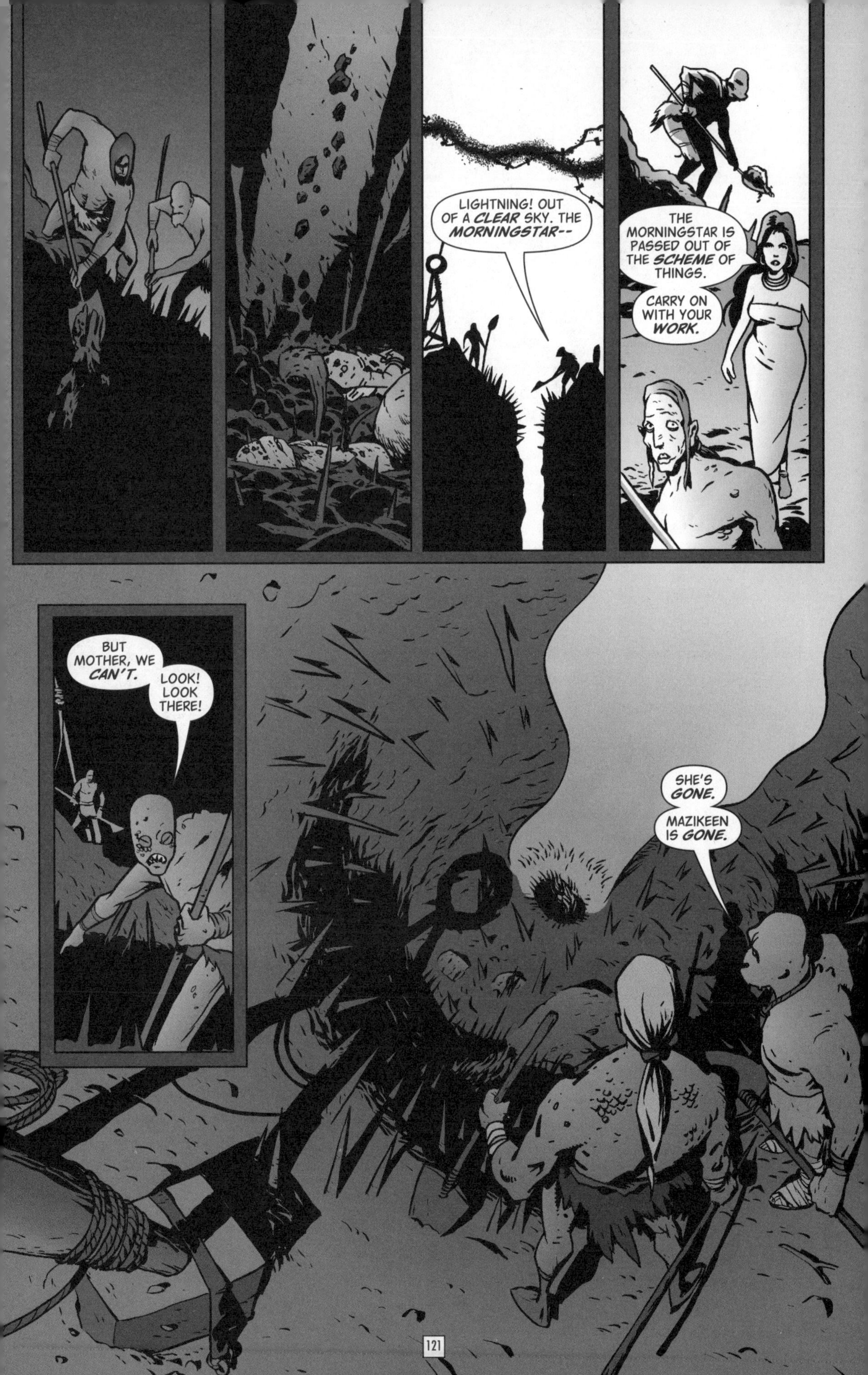
LIGHTNING! OUT OF A CLEAR SKY. THE MORNINGSTAR--
THE MORNINGSTAR IS PASSED OUT OF THE SCHEME OF THINGS.
CARRY ON WITH YOUR WORK.
BUT MOTHER, WE CAN'T.
LOOK! LOOK THERE!
SHE'S GONE.
MAZIKEEN IS GONE.

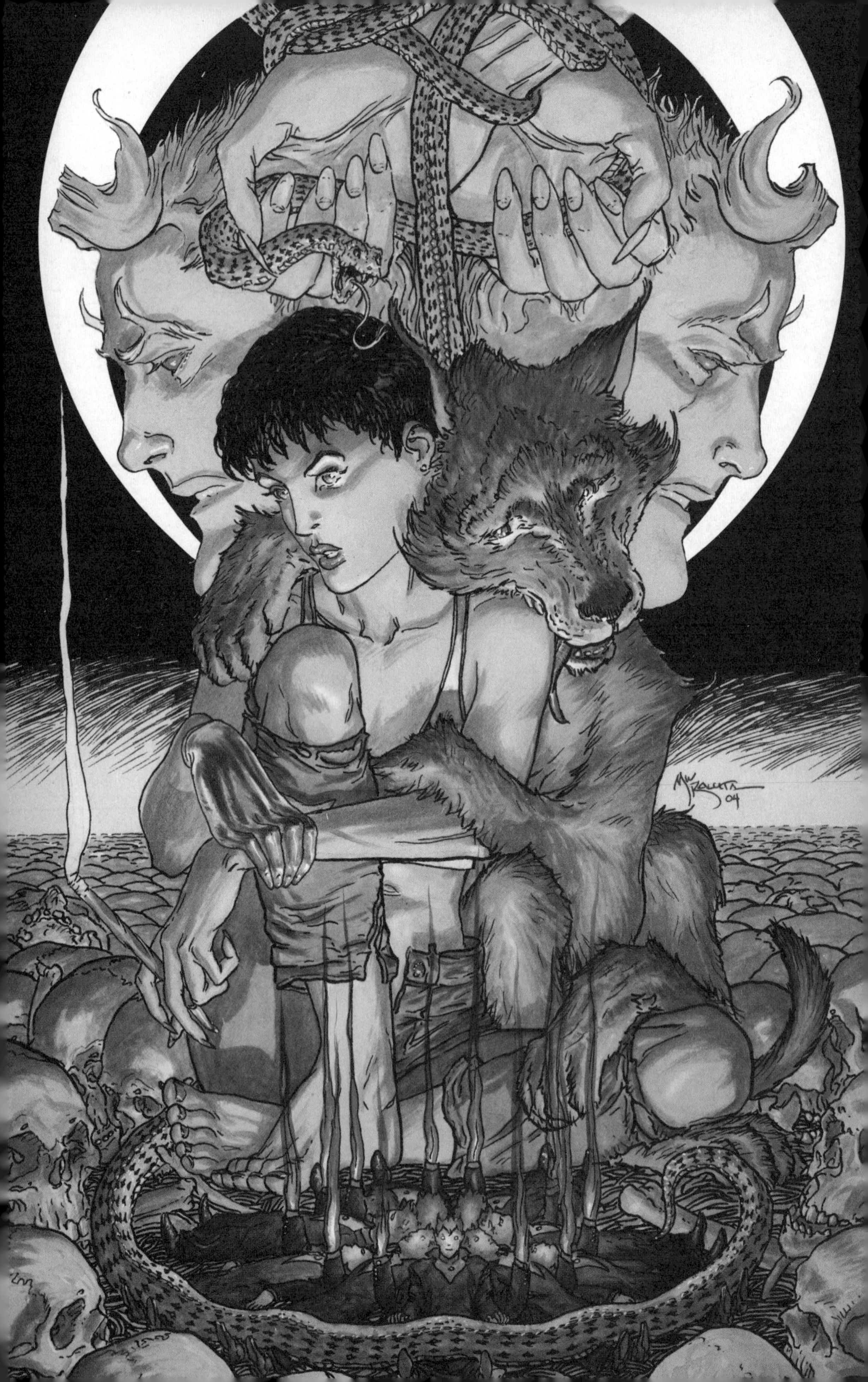

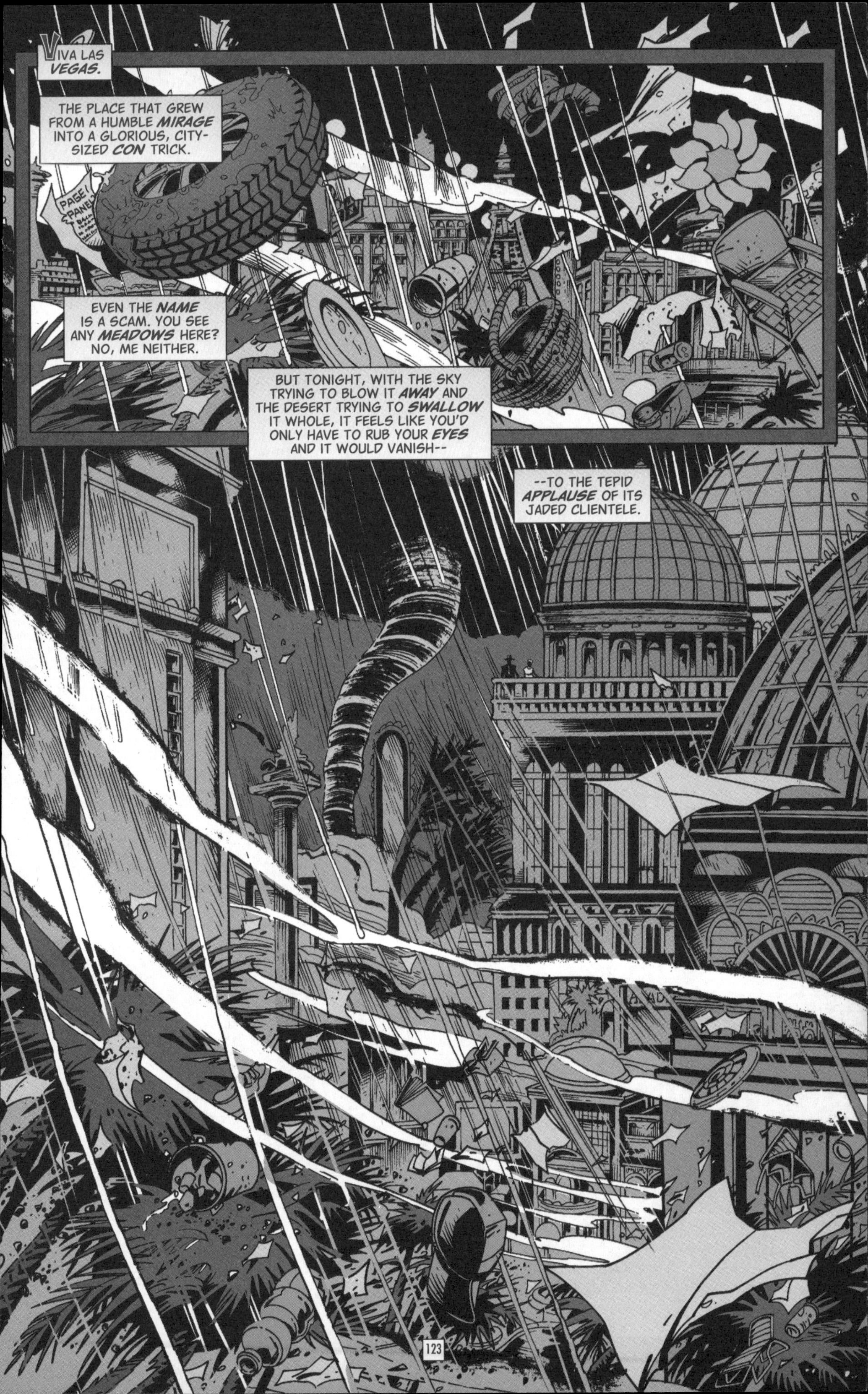
VIVA LAS VEGAS.
THE PLACE THAT GREW FROM A HUMBLE MIRAGE INTO A GLORIOUS, CITY-SIZED CON TRICK.
EVEN THE NAME IS A SCAM. YOU SEE ANY MEADOWS HERE? NO, ME NEITHER.
BUT TONIGHT, WITH THE SKY TRYING TO BLOW IT AWAY AND THE DESERT TRYING TO SWALLOW IT WHOLE, IT FEELS LIKE YOU'D ONLY HAVE TO RUB YOUR EYES AND IT WOULD VANISH--
--TO THE TEPID APPLAUSE OF ITS JADED CLIENTELE.

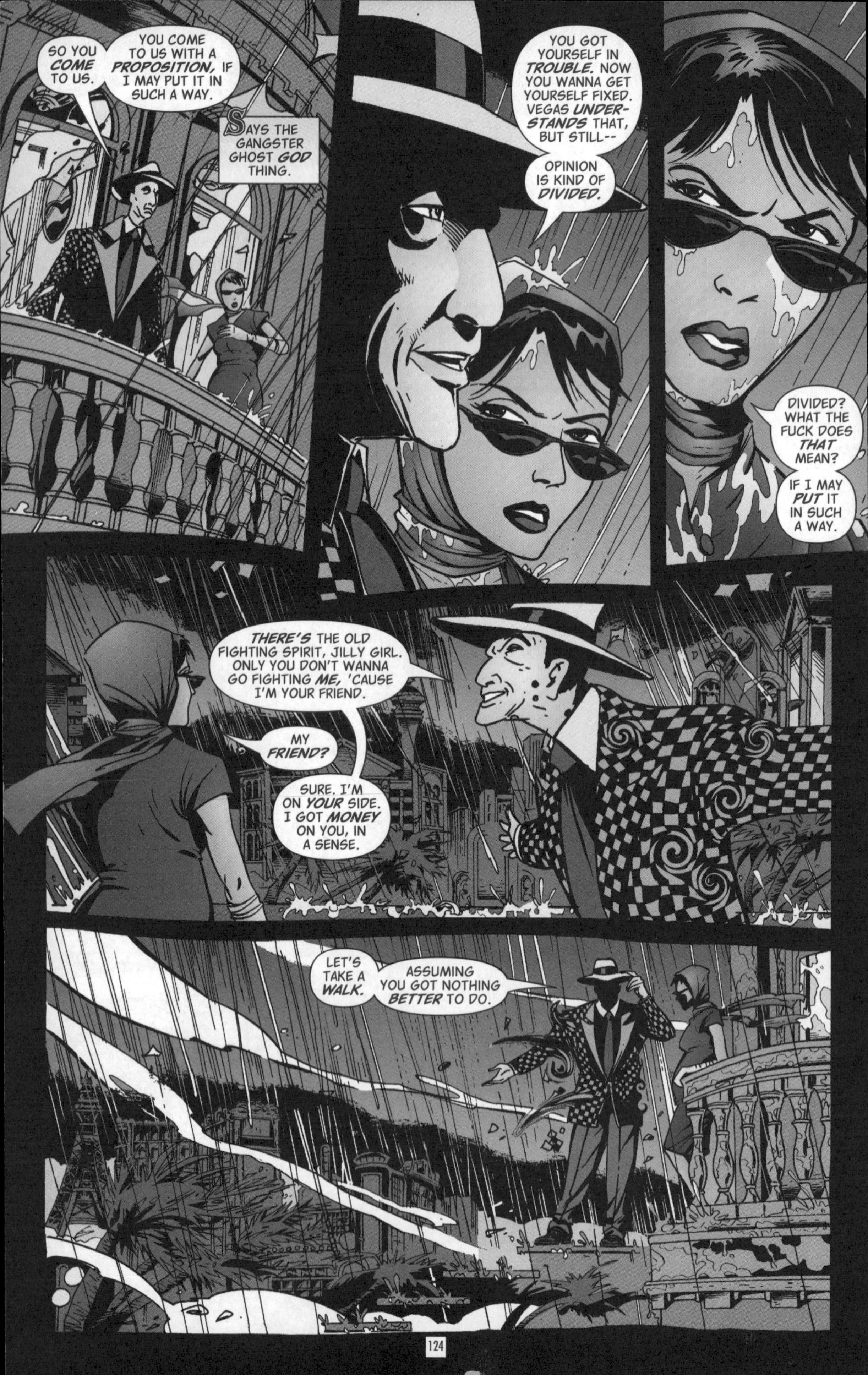
SO YOU COME TO US.
YOU COME TO US WITH A PROPOSITION, IF I MAY PUT IT IN SUCH A WAY.
SAYS THE GANGSTER GHOST GOD THING.
YOU GOT YOURSELF IN TROUBLE. NOW YOU WANNA GET YOURSELF FIXED. VEGAS UNDERSTANDS THAT, BUT STILL--
OPINION IS KIND OF DIVIDED.
DIVIDED? WHAT THE FUCK DOES THAT MEAN?
IF I MAY PUT IT IN SUCH A WAY.
THERE'S THE OLD FIGHTING SPIRIT, JILLY GIRL. ONLY YOU DON'T WANNA GO FIGHTING ME, 'CAUSE I'M YOUR FRIEND.
MY FRIEND?
SURE. I'M ON YOUR SIDE. I GOT MONEY ON YOU, IN A SENSE.
LET'S TAKE A WALK.
ASSUMING YOU GOT NOTHING BETTER TO DO.

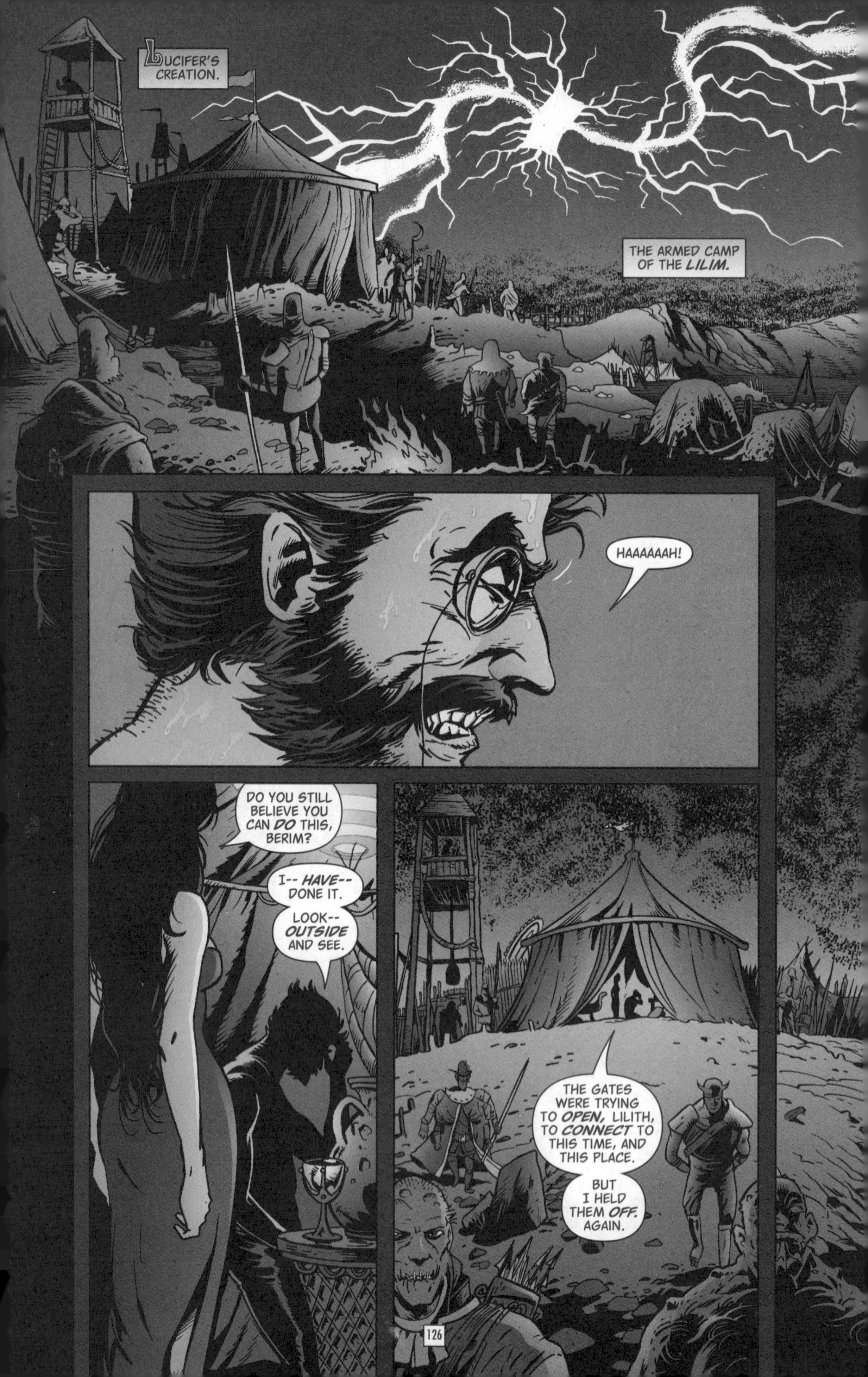
LUCIFER'S CREATION.
THE ARMED CAMP OF THE LILIM.
HAAAAAAH!
DO YOU STILL BELIEVE YOU CAN DO THIS, BERIM?
I-- HAVE-- DONE IT.
LOOK-- OUTSIDE AND SEE.
THE GATES WERE TRYING TO OPEN, LILITH, TO CONNECT TO THIS TIME, AND THIS PLACE.
BUT I HELD THEM OFF. AGAIN.

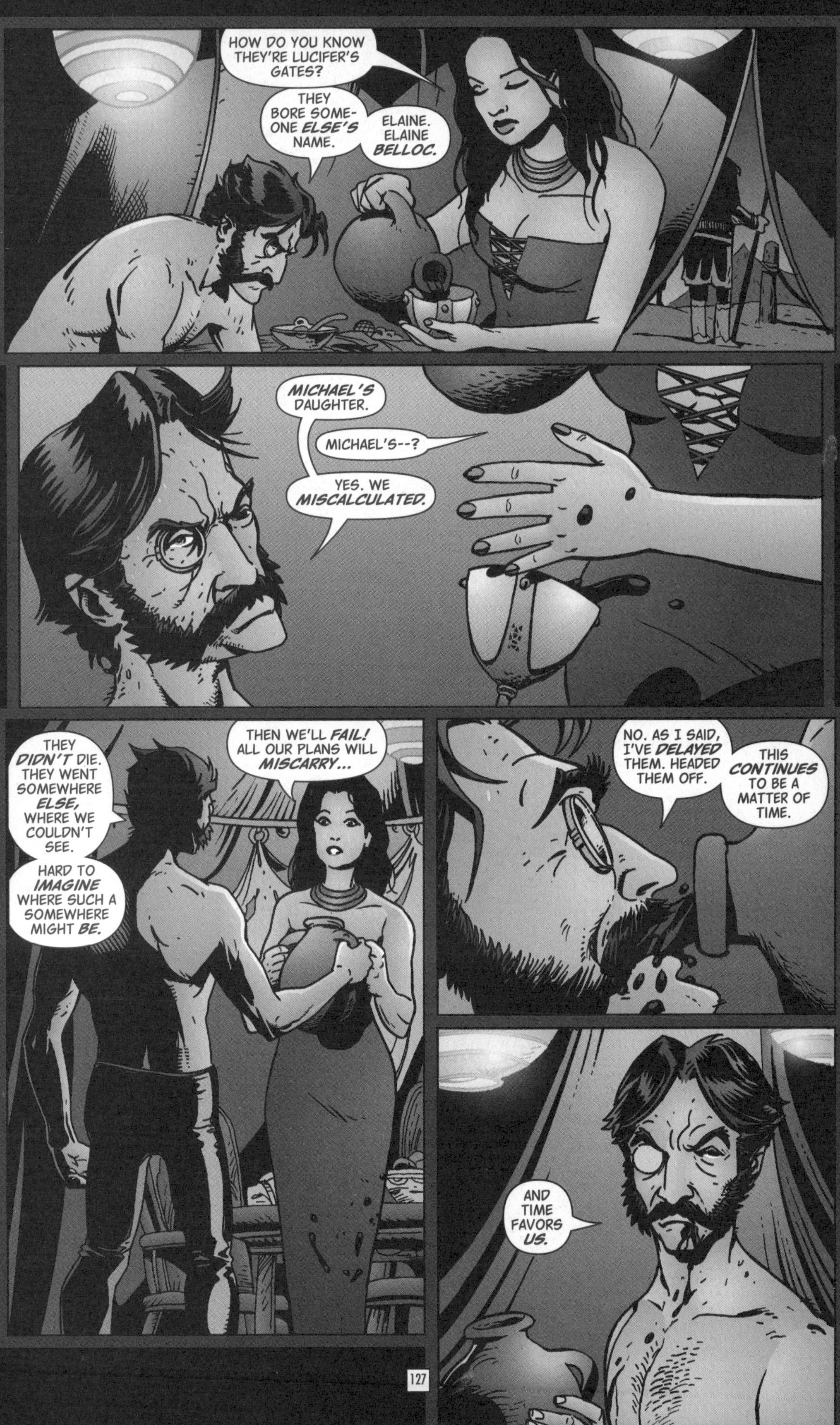
HOW DO YOU KNOW THEY'RE LUCIFER'S GATES?
THEY BORE SOME-ONE *ELSE'S* NAME.
ELAINE. ELAINE *BELLOC.*
MICHAEL'S DAUGHTER.
MICHAEL'S--?
YES. WE *MISCALCULATED.*
THEN WE'LL *FAIL!* ALL OUR PLANS WILL *MISCARRY...*
THEY *DIDN'T* DIE. THEY WENT SOMEWHERE *ELSE,* WHERE WE COULDN'T SEE.
HARD TO *IMAGINE* WHERE SUCH A SOMEWHERE MIGHT *BE.*
NO. AS I SAID, I'VE *DELAYED* THEM. HEADED THEM OFF.
THIS *CONTINUES* TO BE A MATTER OF TIME.
AND TIME FAVORS *US.*

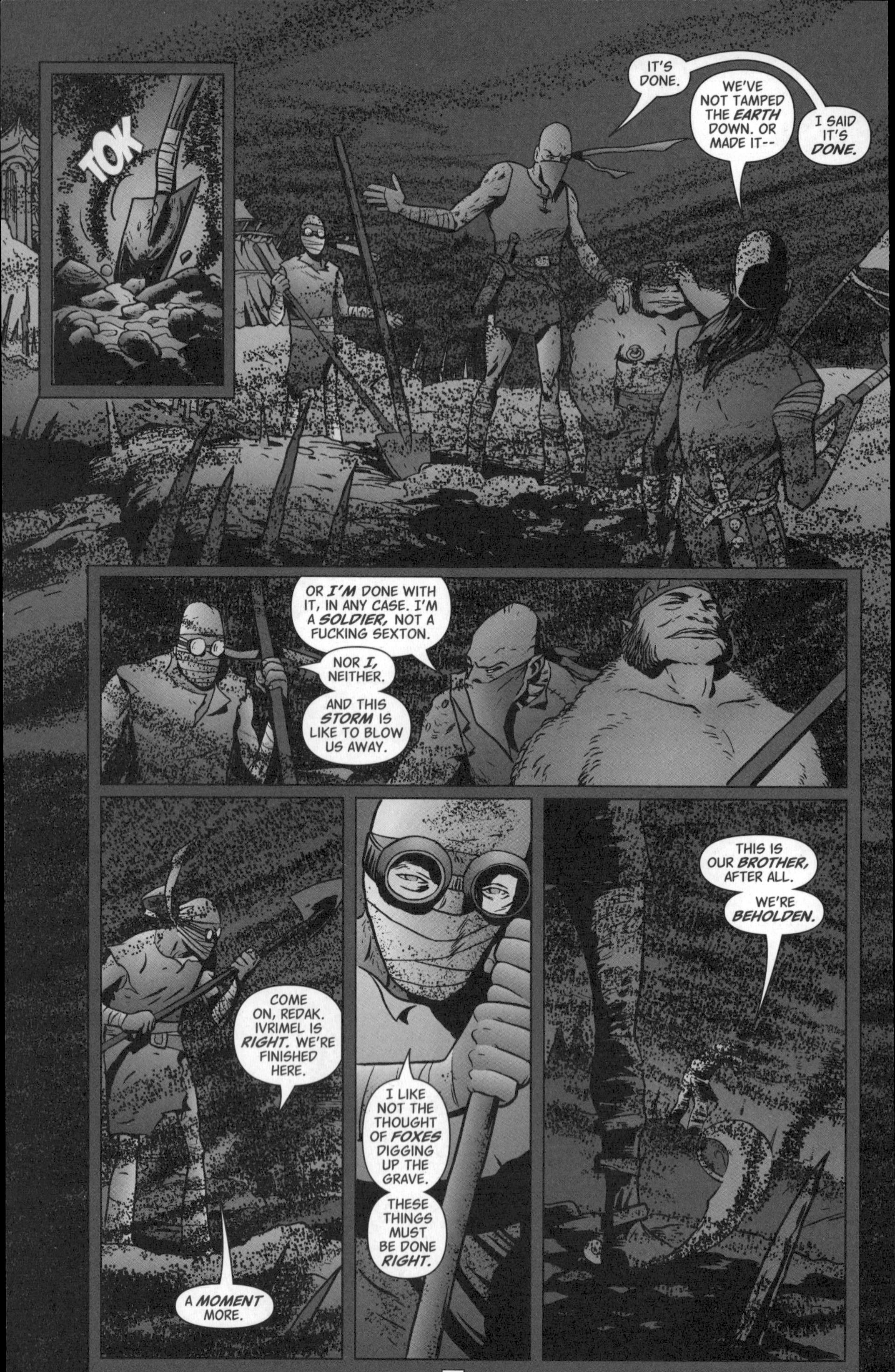
TOK
IT'S DONE.
WE'VE NOT TAMPED THE EARTH DOWN. OR MADE IT--
I SAID IT'S DONE.
OR I'M DONE WITH IT, IN ANY CASE. I'M A SOLDIER, NOT A FUCKING SEXTON.
NOR I, NEITHER.
AND THIS STORM IS LIKE TO BLOW US AWAY.
COME ON, REDAK. IVRIMEL IS RIGHT. WE'RE FINISHED HERE.
A MOMENT MORE.
I LIKE NOT THE THOUGHT OF FOXES DIGGING UP THE GRAVE.
THESE THINGS MUST BE DONE RIGHT.
THIS IS OUR BROTHER, AFTER ALL.
WE'RE BEHOLDEN.

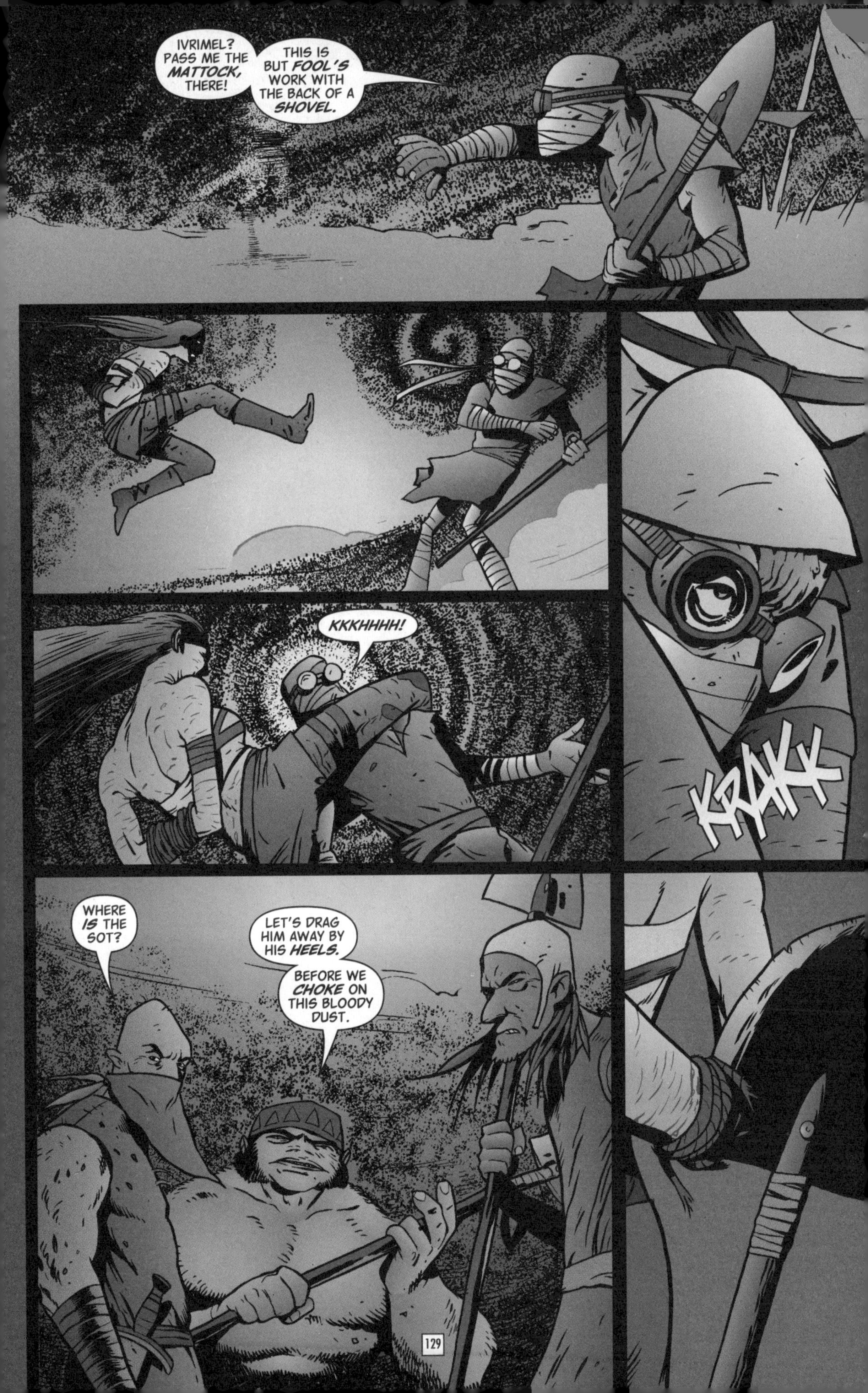
IVRIMEL? PASS ME THE MATTOCK, THERE!
THIS IS BUT FOOL'S WORK WITH THE BACK OF A SHOVEL.
KKKHHHH!
KRAKK
WHERE IS THE SOT?
LET'S DRAG HIM AWAY BY HIS HEELS.
BEFORE WE CHOKE ON THIS BLOODY DUST.

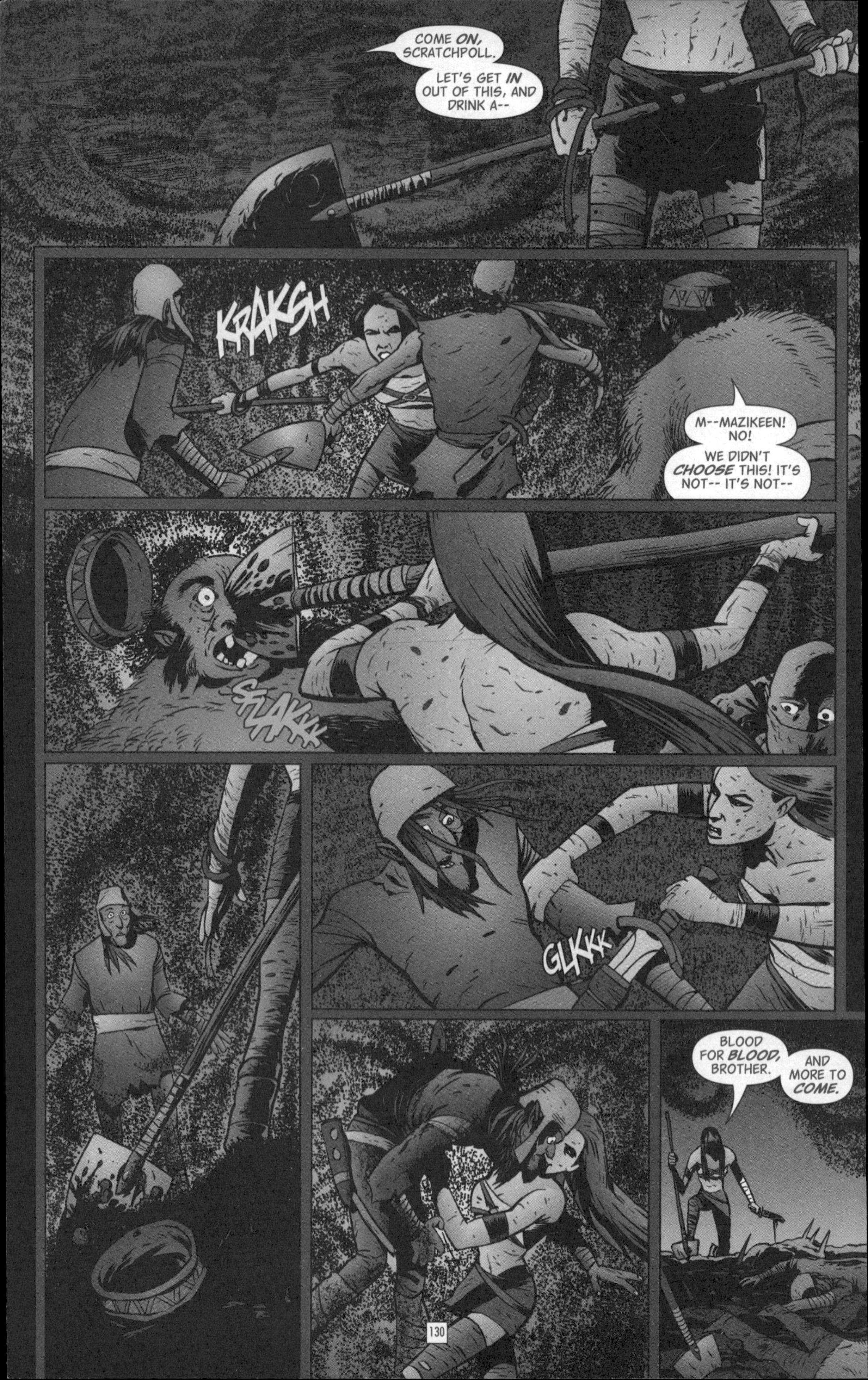
COME *ON*, SCRATCHPOLL.
LET'S GET *IN* OUT OF THIS, AND DRINK A--
KRAKSH
M--MAZIKEEN! NO!
WE DIDN'T *CHOOSE* THIS! IT'S NOT-- IT'S NOT--
SFLAKKK
GLKKK
BLOOD FOR *BLOOD*, BROTHER.
AND MORE TO *COME*.

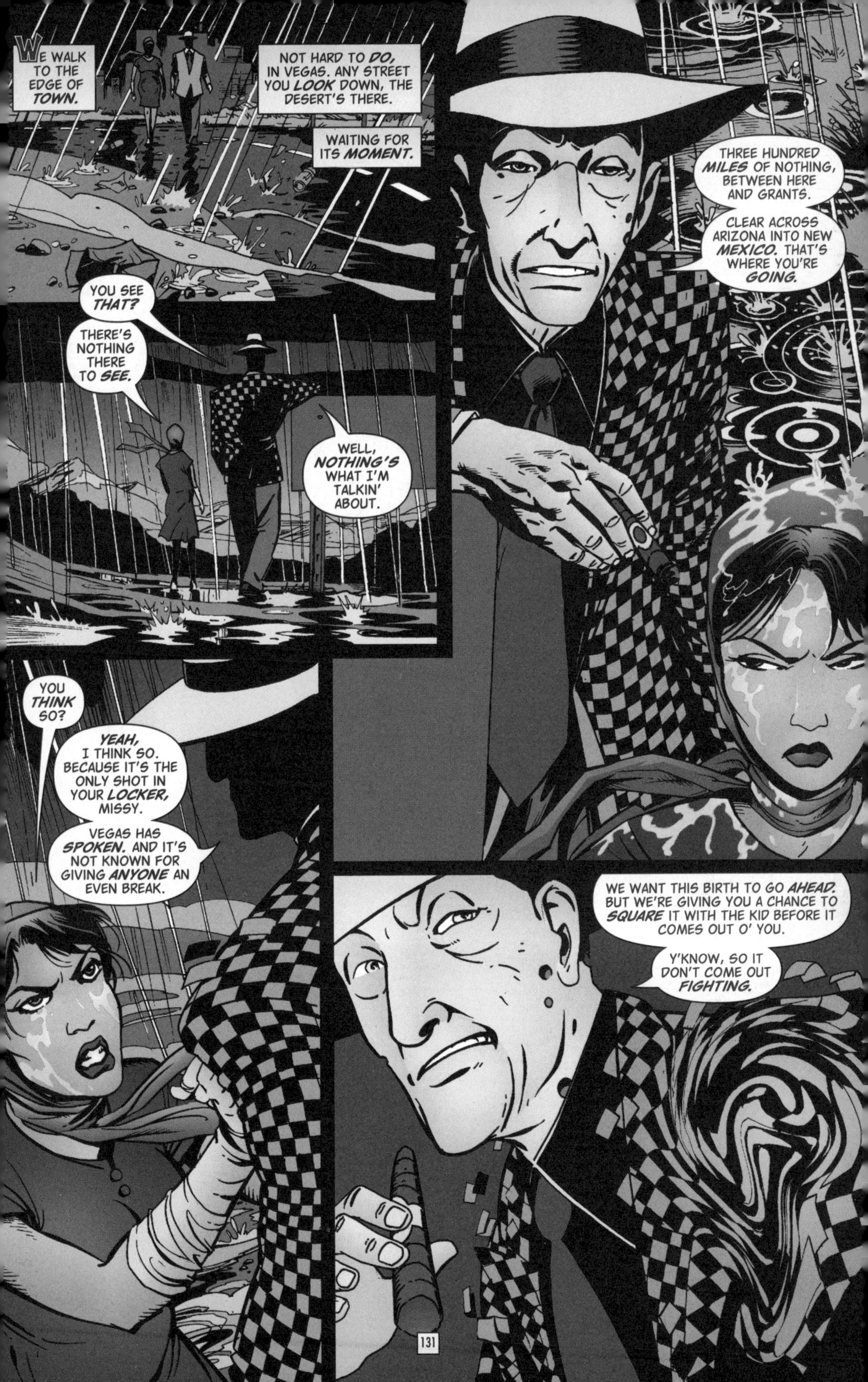
WE WALK TO THE EDGE OF TOWN.
NOT HARD TO DO, IN VEGAS. ANY STREET YOU LOOK DOWN, THE DESERT'S THERE.
WAITING FOR ITS MOMENT.
YOU SEE THAT?
THERE'S NOTHING THERE TO SEE.
WELL, NOTHING'S WHAT I'M TALKIN' ABOUT.
THREE HUNDRED MILES OF NOTHING, BETWEEN HERE AND GRANTS.
CLEAR ACROSS ARIZONA INTO NEW MEXICO. THAT'S WHERE YOU'RE GOING.
YOU THINK SO?
YEAH, I THINK SO. BECAUSE IT'S THE ONLY SHOT IN YOUR LOCKER, MISSY.
VEGAS HAS SPOKEN. AND IT'S NOT KNOWN FOR GIVING ANYONE AN EVEN BREAK.
WE WANT THIS BIRTH TO GO AHEAD. BUT WE'RE GIVING YOU A CHANCE TO SQUARE IT WITH THE KID BEFORE IT COMES OUT O' YOU.
Y'KNOW, SO IT DON'T COME OUT FIGHTING.

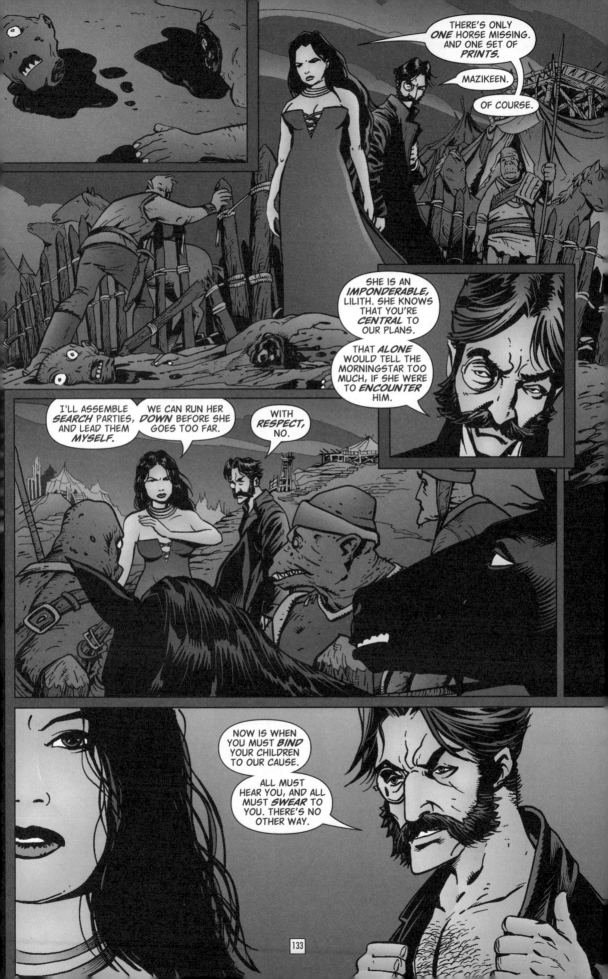

133

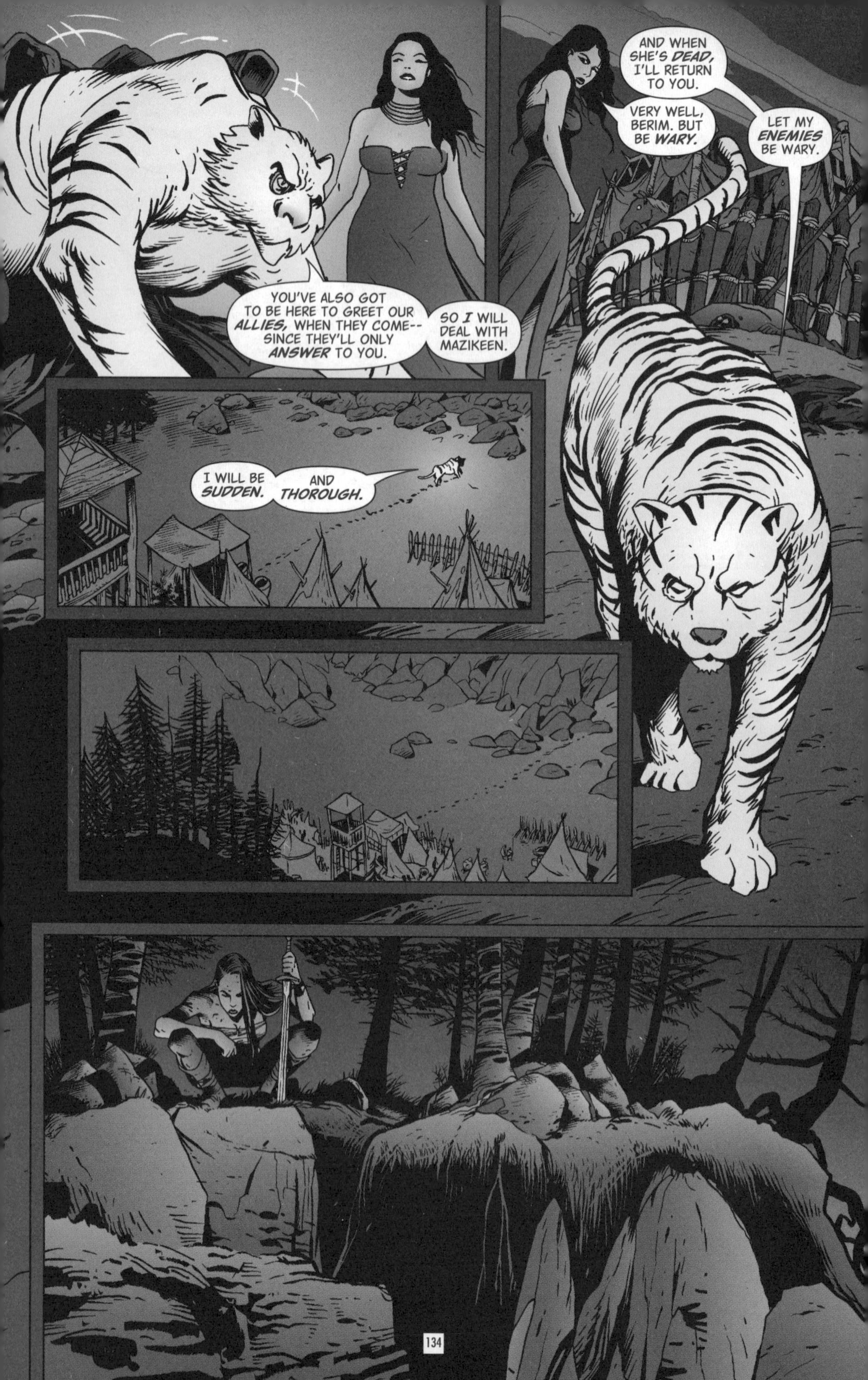
YOU'VE ALSO GOT TO BE HERE TO GREET OUR ALLIES, WHEN THEY COME-- SINCE THEY'LL ONLY ANSWER TO YOU.
SO I WILL DEAL WITH MAZIKEEN.
VERY WELL, BERIM. BUT BE WARY.
AND WHEN SHE'S DEAD, I'LL RETURN TO YOU.
LET MY ENEMIES BE WARY.
I WILL BE SUDDEN.
AND THOROUGH.

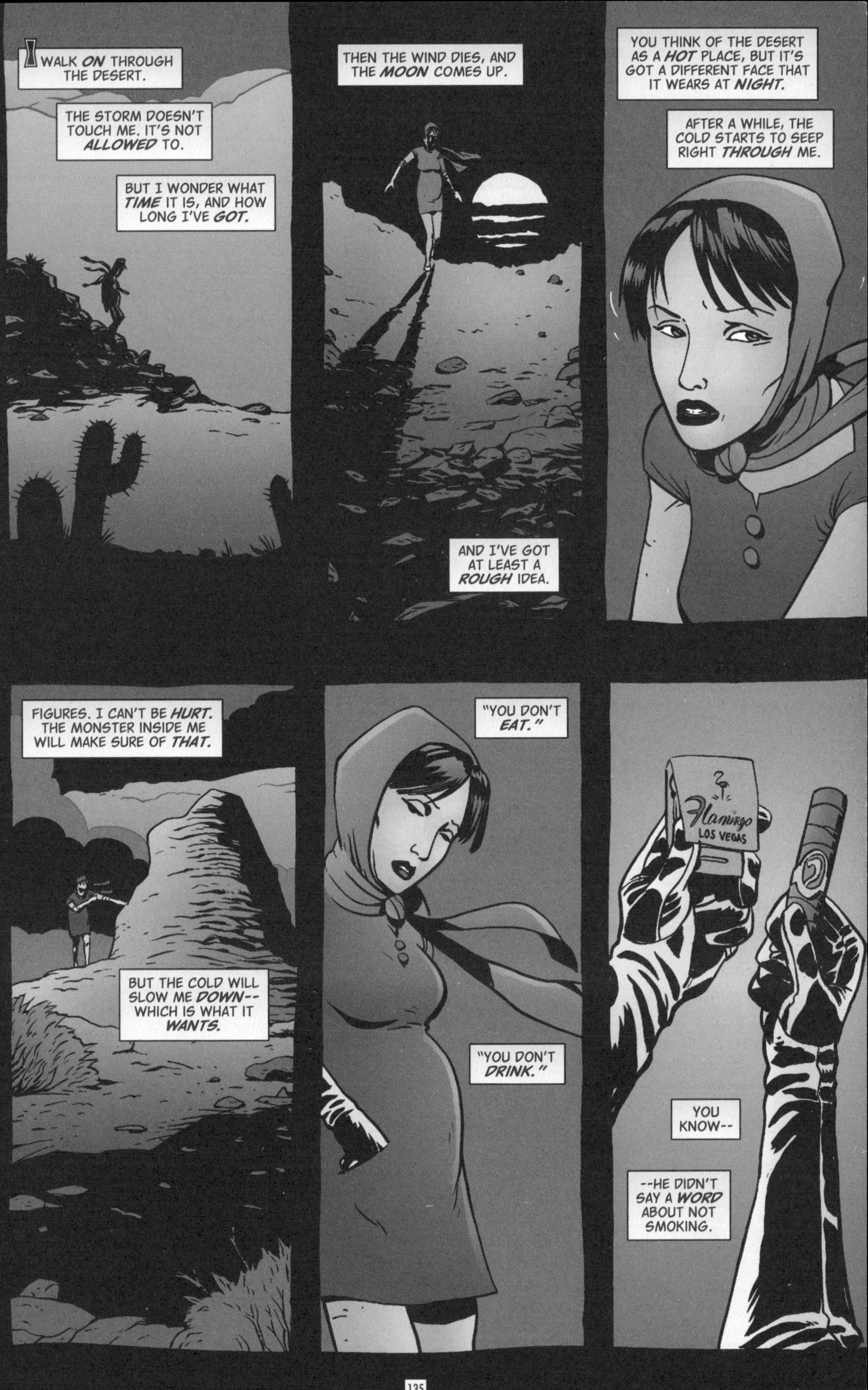
I WALK ON THROUGH THE DESERT.
THE STORM DOESN'T TOUCH ME. IT'S NOT ALLOWED TO.
BUT I WONDER WHAT TIME IT IS, AND HOW LONG I'VE GOT.
THEN THE WIND DIES, AND THE MOON COMES UP.
AND I'VE GOT AT LEAST A ROUGH IDEA.
YOU THINK OF THE DESERT AS A HOT PLACE, BUT IT'S GOT A DIFFERENT FACE THAT IT WEARS AT NIGHT.
AFTER A WHILE, THE COLD STARTS TO SEEP RIGHT THROUGH ME.
FIGURES. I CAN'T BE HURT. THE MONSTER INSIDE ME WILL MAKE SURE OF THAT.
BUT THE COLD WILL SLOW ME DOWN-- WHICH IS WHAT IT WANTS.
"YOU DON'T EAT."
"YOU DON'T DRINK."
Flamingo
LOS VEGAS
YOU KNOW--
--HE DIDN'T SAY A WORD ABOUT NOT SMOKING.

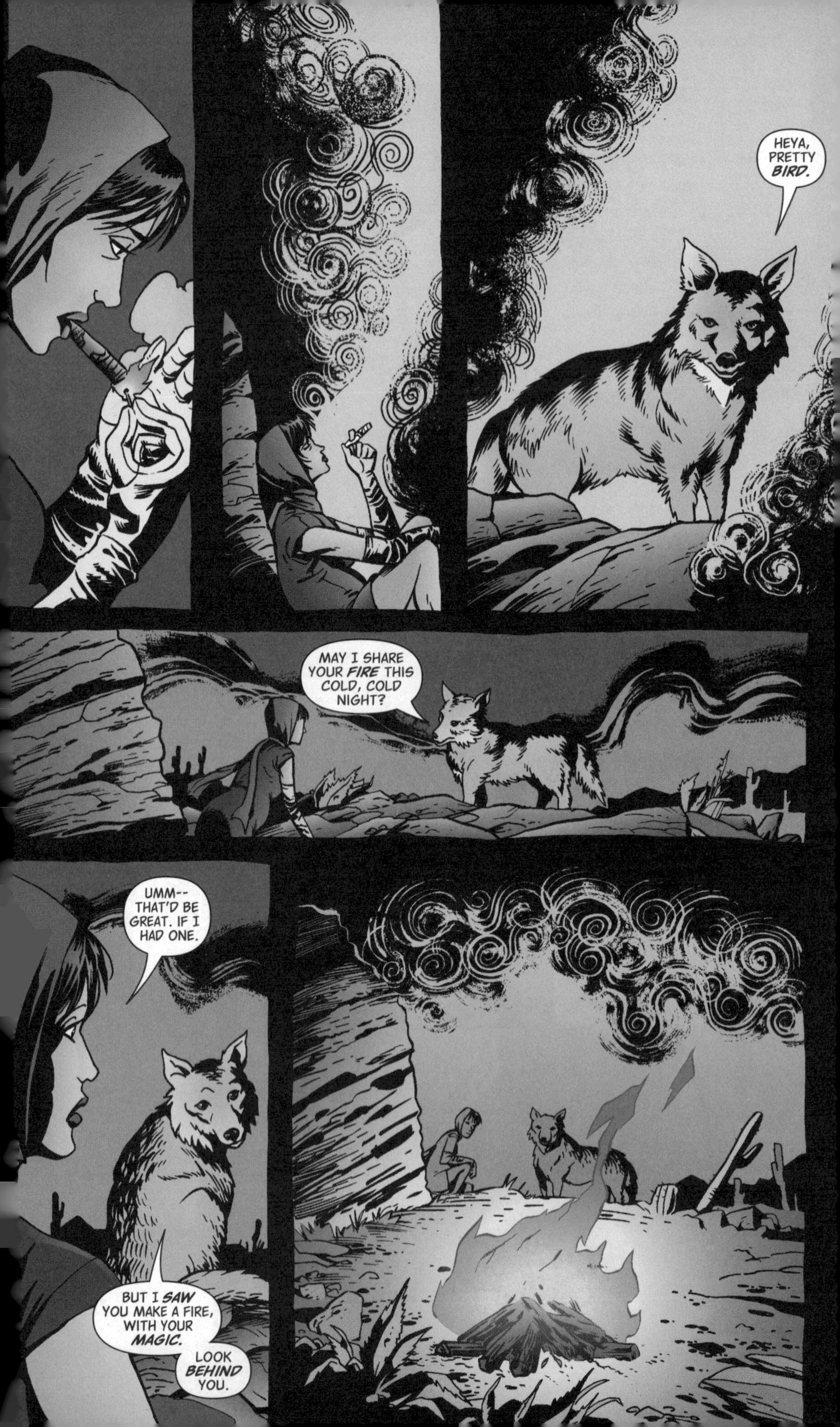
HEYA, PRETTY BIRD.
MAY I SHARE YOUR FIRE THIS COLD, COLD NIGHT?
UMM-- THAT'D BE GREAT. IF I HAD ONE.
BUT I SAW YOU MAKE A FIRE, WITH YOUR MAGIC.
LOOK BEHIND YOU.

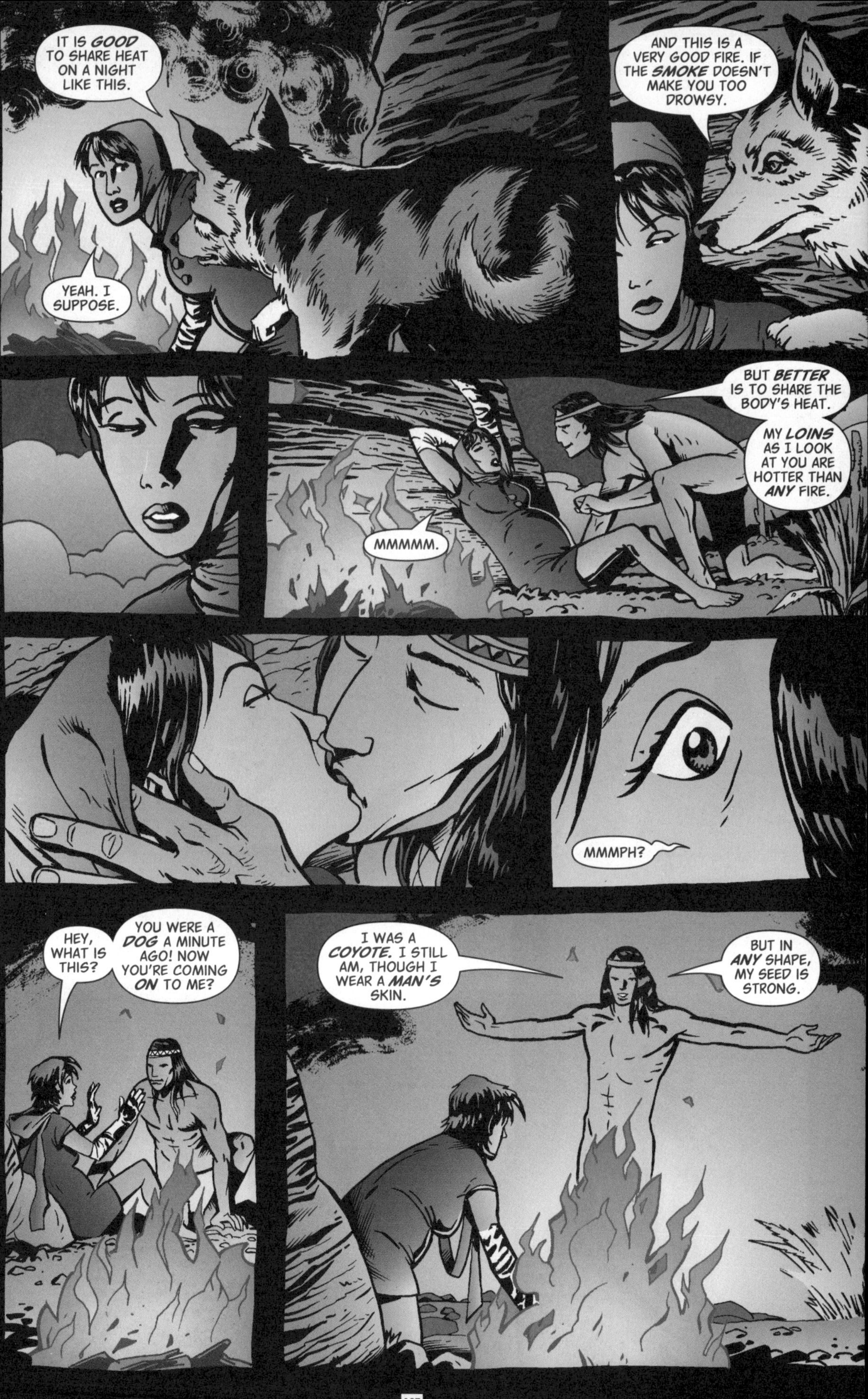
IT IS GOOD TO SHARE HEAT ON A NIGHT LIKE THIS.
YEAH. I SUPPOSE.
AND THIS IS A VERY GOOD FIRE. IF THE SMOKE DOESN'T MAKE YOU TOO DROWSY.
BUT BETTER IS TO SHARE THE BODY'S HEAT.
MY LOINS AS I LOOK AT YOU ARE HOTTER THAN ANY FIRE.
MMMMM.
MMMPH?
HEY, WHAT IS THIS?
YOU WERE A DOG A MINUTE AGO! NOW YOU'RE COMING ON TO ME?
I WAS A COYOTE. I STILL AM, THOUGH I WEAR A MAN'S SKIN.
BUT IN ANY SHAPE, MY SEED IS STRONG.

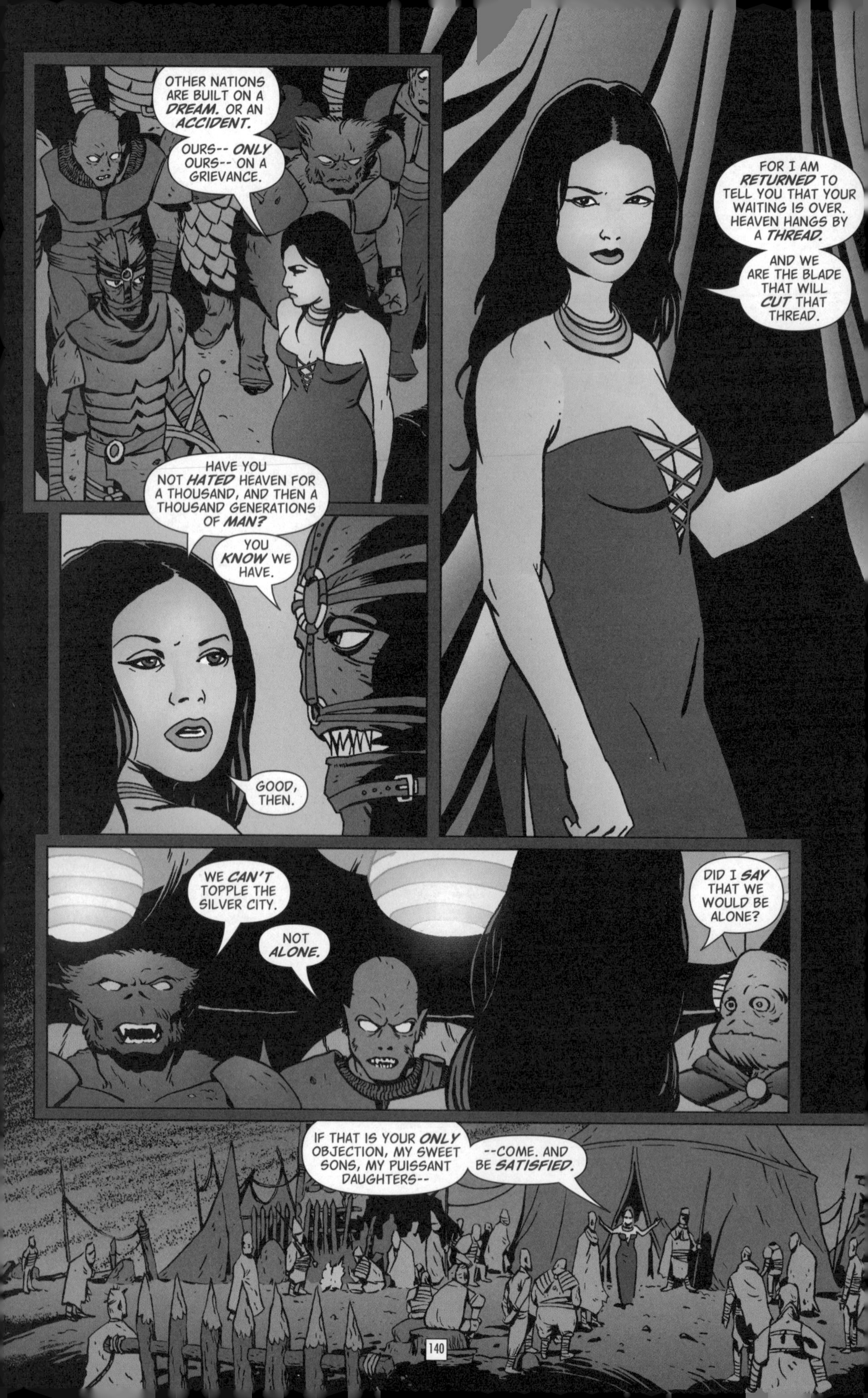
OTHER NATIONS ARE BUILT ON A DREAM. OR AN ACCIDENT.
OURS-- ONLY OURS-- ON A GRIEVANCE.
FOR I AM RETURNED TO TELL YOU THAT YOUR WAITING IS OVER. HEAVEN HANGS BY A THREAD.
AND WE ARE THE BLADE THAT WILL CUT THAT THREAD.
HAVE YOU NOT HATED HEAVEN FOR A THOUSAND, AND THEN A THOUSAND GENERATIONS OF MAN?
YOU KNOW WE HAVE.
GOOD, THEN.
WE CAN'T TOPPLE THE SILVER CITY.
NOT ALONE.
DID I SAY THAT WE WOULD BE ALONE?
IF THAT IS YOUR ONLY OBJECTION, MY SWEET SONS, MY PUISSANT DAUGHTERS--
--COME. AND BE SATISFIED.

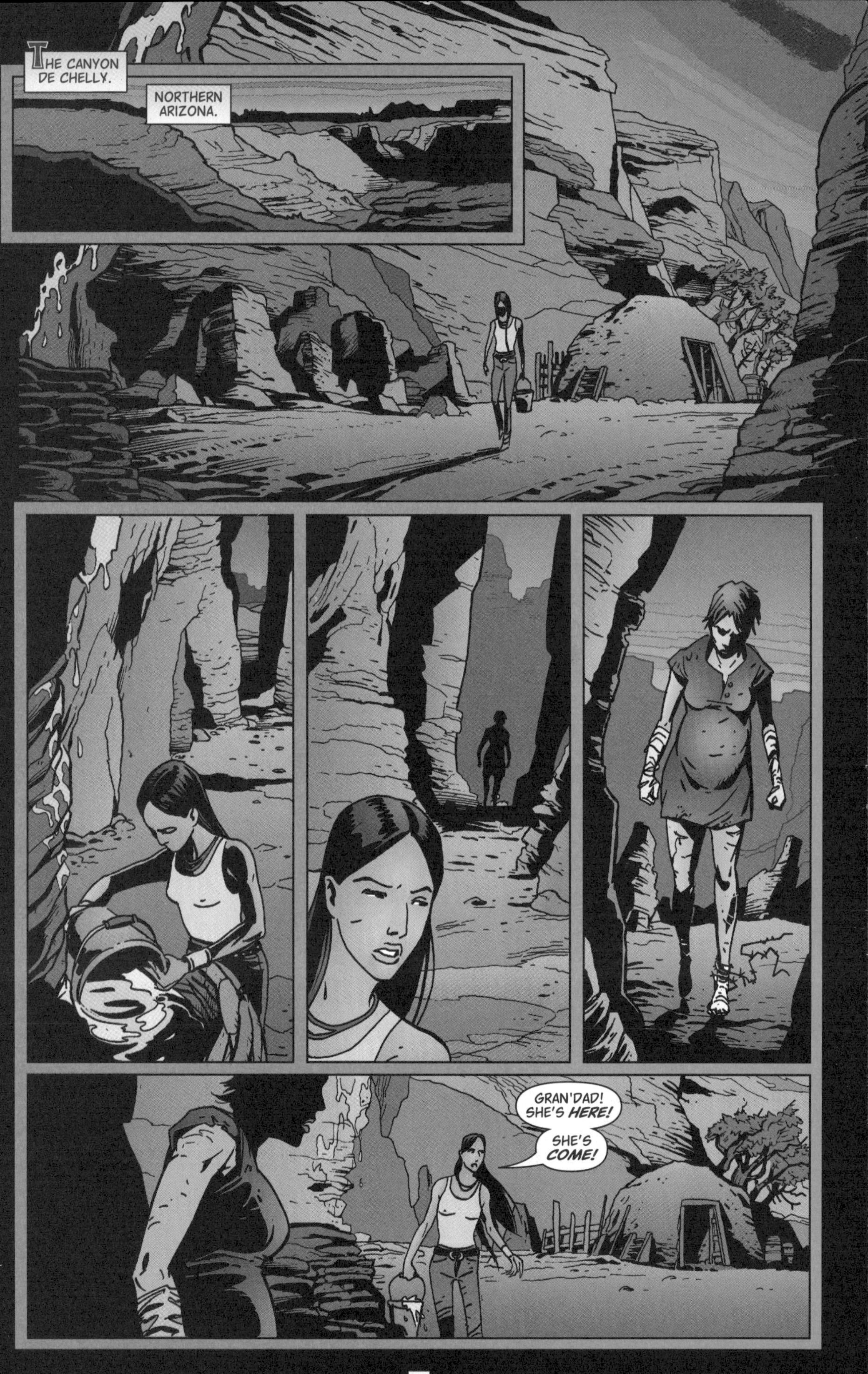
THE CANYON DE CHELLY.
NORTHERN ARIZONA.
GRAN'DAD! SHE'S *HERE!*
SHE'S *COME!*

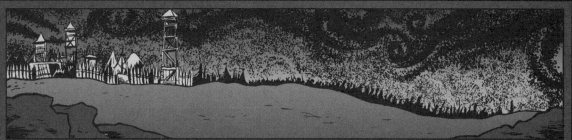

WHERE ARE WE *GOING?*

MOTHER SPOKE OF *ALLIES.* STRONG ONES, WHO'LL HELP US *STRIKE* AT HEAVEN.

MADNESS! *WHAT* ALLIES?

MY CHILDREN, I SAW A *VISION* A LONG TIME AGO.

I WAS IN THIS PLACE, AND A *HOST* DESCENDED TO MEET ME.

AN *ANGEL?*

BUT ANGELS *CANNOT--*

SO I SET ABOUT TO *FORGE* THIS HOST. *ANGELS,* BUT NOT OF HEAVEN.

I MET THEIR FATHER-- A *SON* OF HEAVEN-- IN THE SOFT PLACES. WE *COUPLED* THERE, AND I CONCEIVED.

NOT ONCE, BUT *MANY* TIMES.

THEY CANNOT, BUT *I* CAN. EVEN A *BREATH* MAKES MY WOMB QUICKEN.

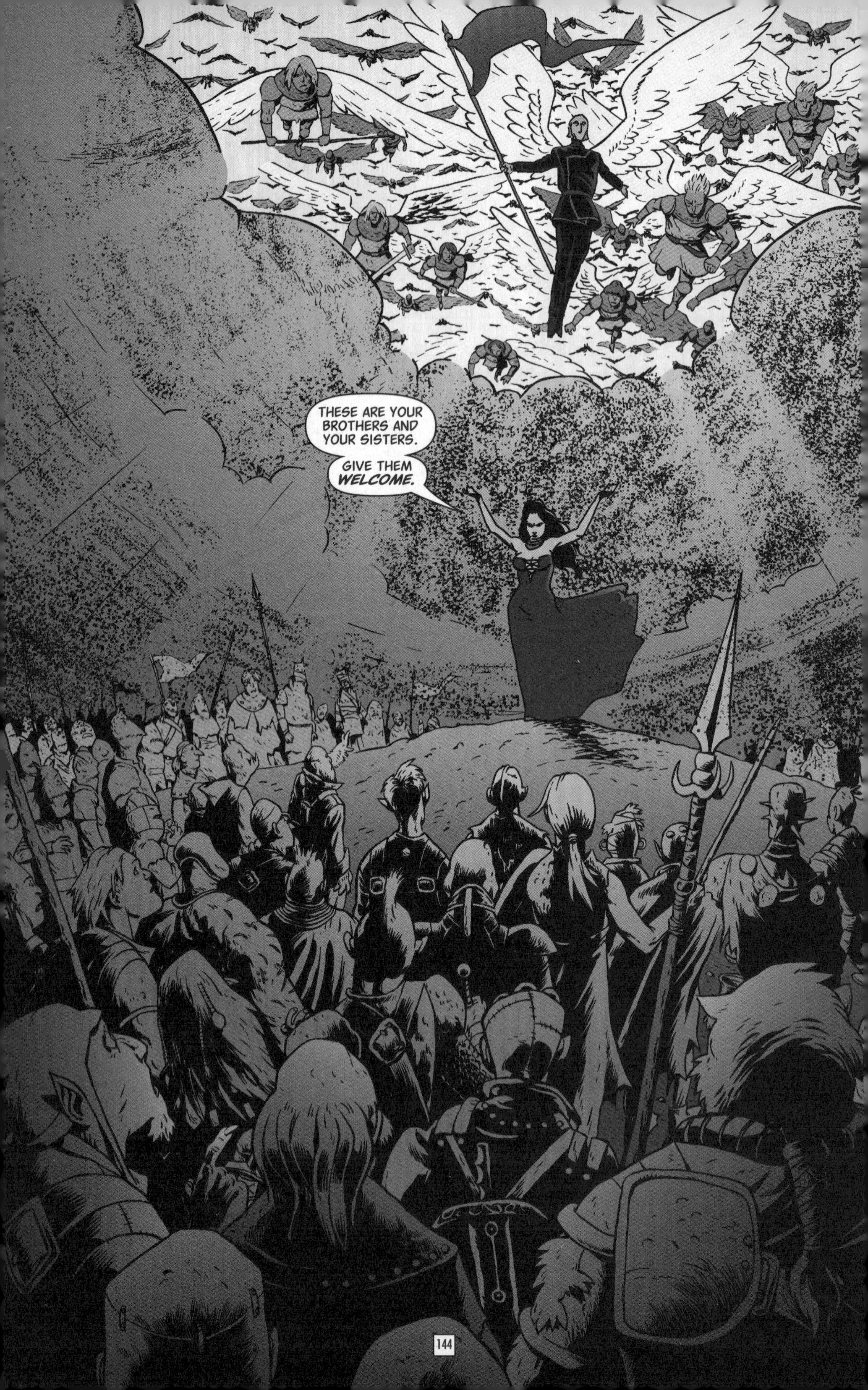
THESE ARE YOUR BROTHERS AND YOUR SISTERS.
GIVE THEM *WELCOME.*

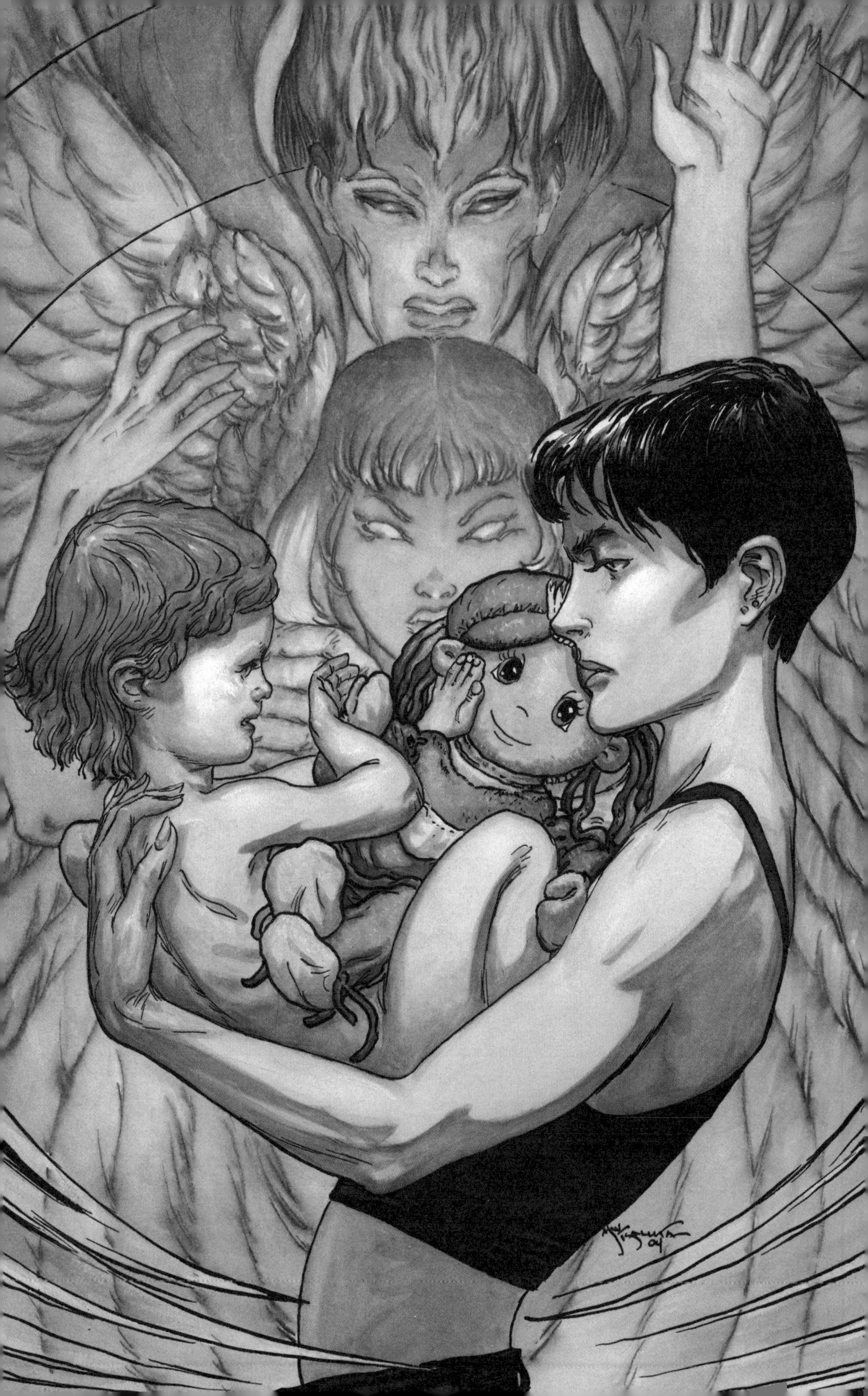

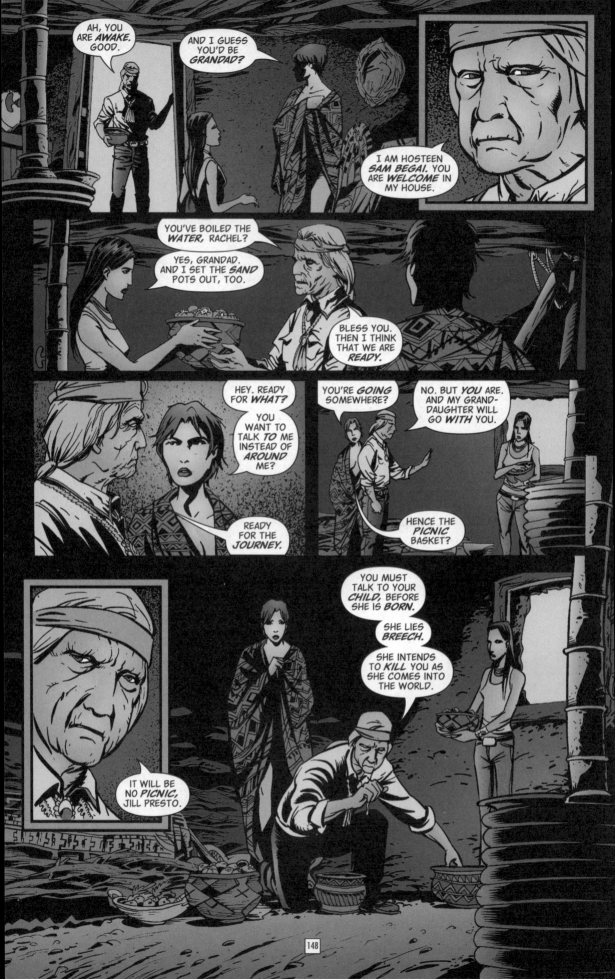

148

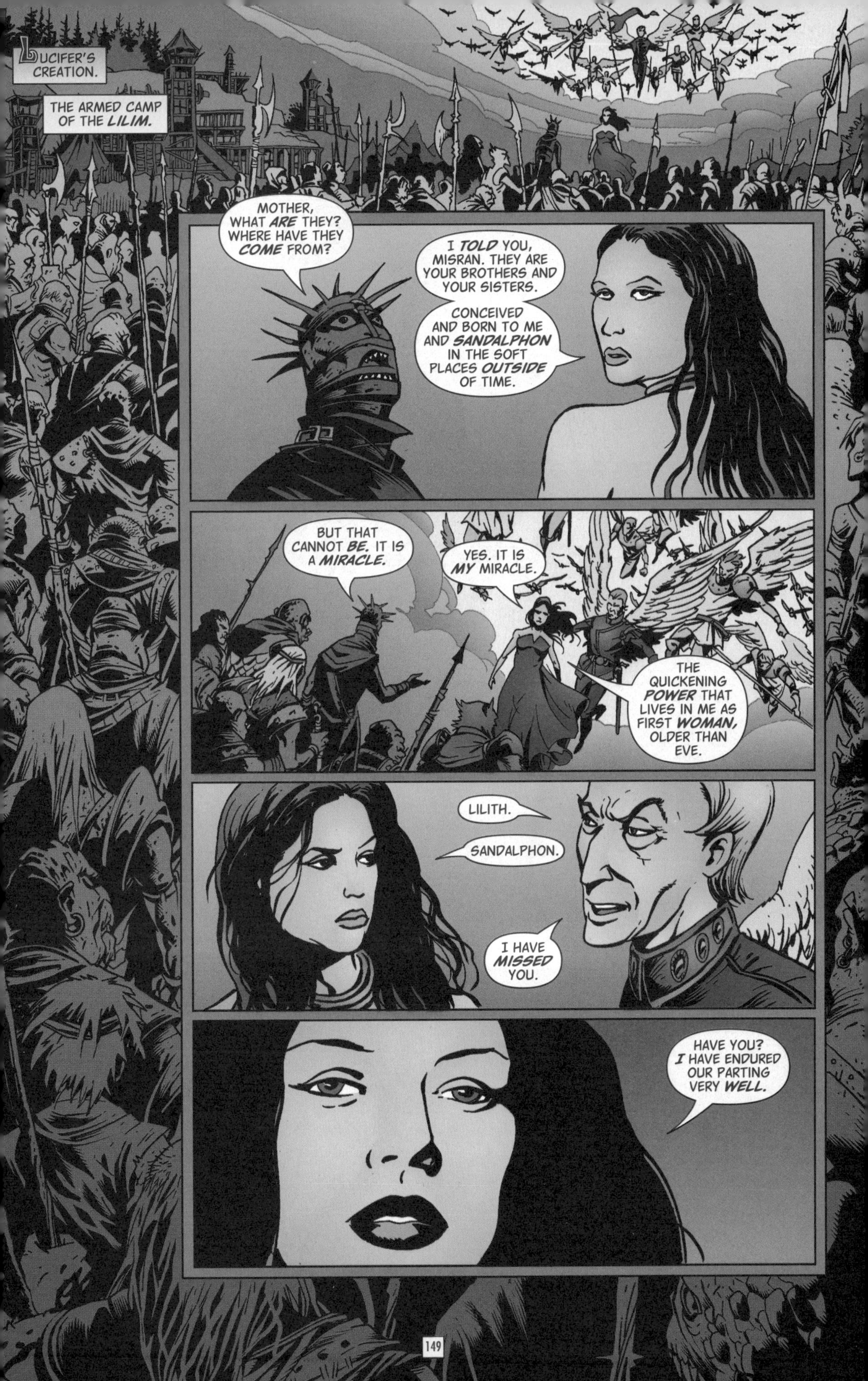
LUCIFER'S CREATION.
THE ARMED CAMP OF THE LILIM.
MOTHER, WHAT ARE THEY? WHERE HAVE THEY COME FROM?
I TOLD YOU, MISRAN. THEY ARE YOUR BROTHERS AND YOUR SISTERS.
CONCEIVED AND BORN TO ME AND SANDALPHON IN THE SOFT PLACES OUTSIDE OF TIME.
BUT THAT CANNOT BE. IT IS A MIRACLE.
YES. IT IS MY MIRACLE.
THE QUICKENING POWER THAT LIVES IN ME AS FIRST WOMAN, OLDER THAN EVE.
LILITH.
SANDALPHON.
I HAVE MISSED YOU.
HAVE YOU? I HAVE ENDURED OUR PARTING VERY WELL.

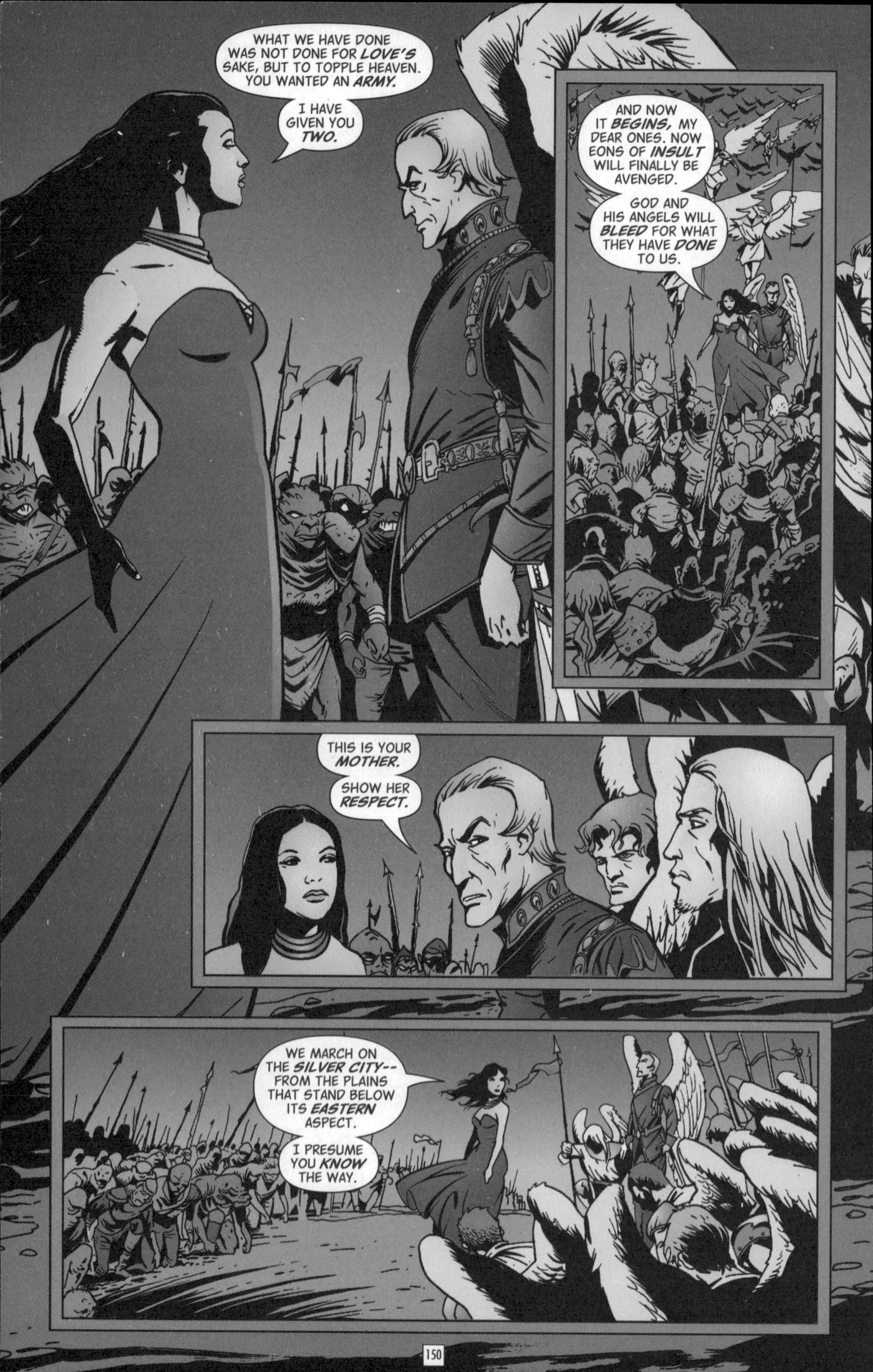
WHAT WE HAVE DONE WAS NOT DONE FOR LOVE'S SAKE, BUT TO TOPPLE HEAVEN. YOU WANTED AN ARMY.
I HAVE GIVEN YOU TWO.
AND NOW IT BEGINS, MY DEAR ONES. NOW EONS OF INSULT WILL FINALLY BE AVENGED.
GOD AND HIS ANGELS WILL BLEED FOR WHAT THEY HAVE DONE TO US.
THIS IS YOUR MOTHER.
SHOW HER RESPECT.
WE MARCH ON THE SILVER CITY-- FROM THE PLAINS THAT STAND BELOW ITS EASTERN ASPECT.
I PRESUME YOU KNOW THE WAY.

RIGHT. *WHAT* DOES SHE EAT, EXACTLY?

IT'S LOPHOPHORA. *PEYOTE.*

OH, FUCKING *WONDERFUL.*

SHE FACES THE *EAST.*

HEYA! SHE FACES THE *EAST.*

SHE FACES THE EAST AND SHE *EATS.*

MY FETUS WANTS TO LAUNCH A *COMMANDO* RAID AGAINST ME FROM THE INSIDE.

YOU REALLY THINK GETTING *HIGH* IS AN ADEQUATE *RESPONSE?*

NO *OTHER* WAY FOR YOU TO GO WHERE YOU *MUST* GO.

IT IS HARD TO PASS A *NEEDLE* THROUGH ITS OWN *EYE,* JILL PRESTO.

YOU *TOO,* RACHEL.

THANKS, GRANDAD.

EUGH! DOES SHE WASH IT DOWN WITH A SHOT OF *TEQUILA,* BY ANY CHANCE?

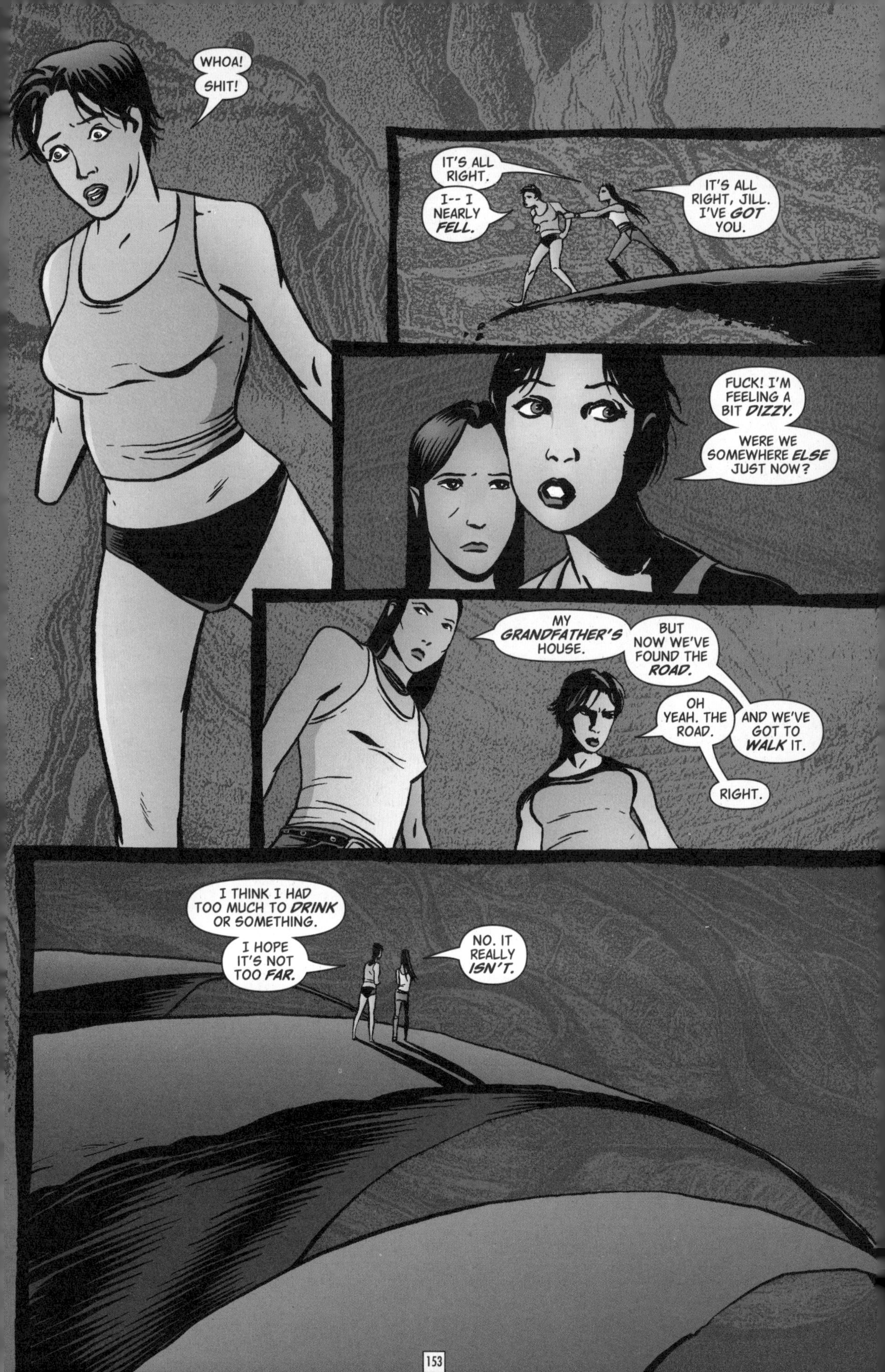
WHOA! SHIT!
IT'S ALL RIGHT.
I-- I NEARLY FELL.
IT'S ALL RIGHT, JILL. I'VE GOT YOU.
FUCK! I'M FEELING A BIT DIZZY.
WERE WE SOMEWHERE ELSE JUST NOW?
MY GRANDFATHER'S HOUSE.
BUT NOW WE'VE FOUND THE ROAD.
OH YEAH. THE ROAD.
AND WE'VE GOT TO WALK IT.
RIGHT.
I THINK I HAD TOO MUCH TO DRINK OR SOMETHING.
I HOPE IT'S NOT TOO FAR.
NO. IT REALLY ISN'T.

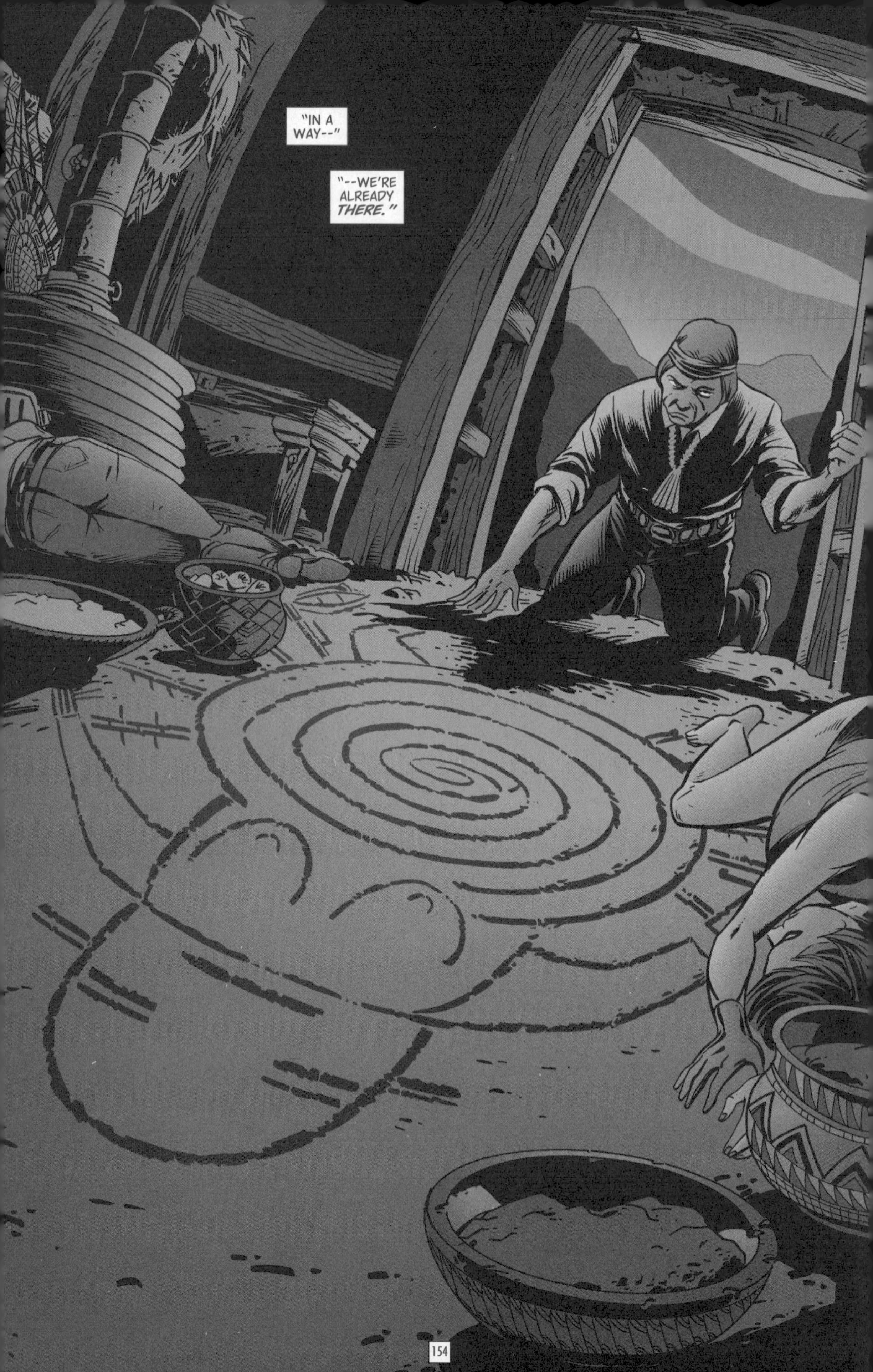
"IN A WAY--"
"--WE'RE ALREADY *THERE.*"

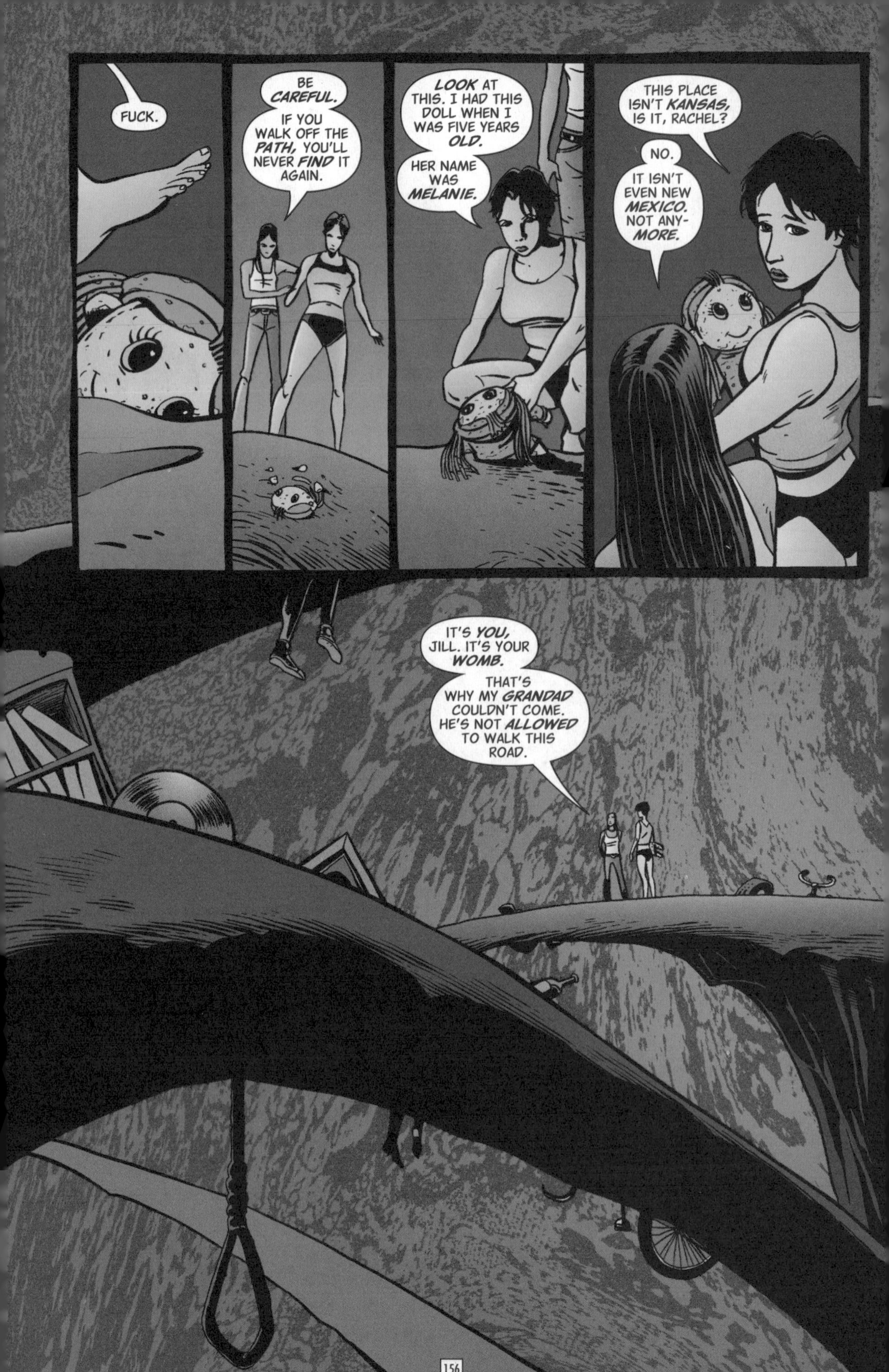
FUCK.
BE CAREFUL.
IF YOU WALK OFF THE PATH, YOU'LL NEVER FIND IT AGAIN.
LOOK AT THIS. I HAD THIS DOLL WHEN I WAS FIVE YEARS OLD.
HER NAME WAS MELANIE.
THIS PLACE ISN'T KANSAS, IS IT, RACHEL?
NO.
IT ISN'T EVEN NEW MEXICO. NOT ANY-MORE.
IT'S YOU, JILL. IT'S YOUR WOMB.
THAT'S WHY MY GRANDAD COULDN'T COME. HE'S NOT ALLOWED TO WALK THIS ROAD.

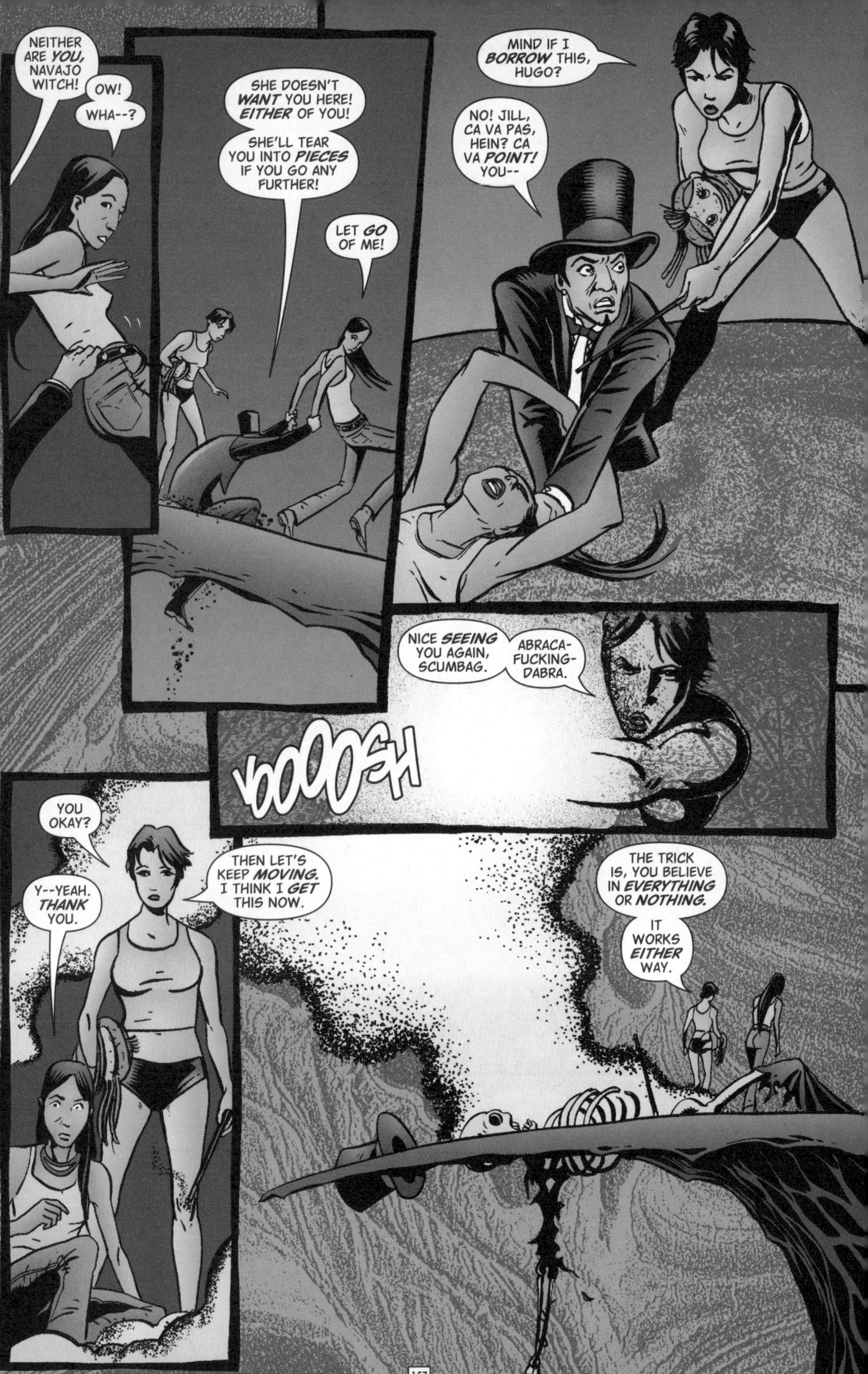
NEITHER ARE YOU, NAVAJO WITCH!
OW!
WHA--?
SHE DOESN'T WANT YOU HERE! EITHER OF YOU!
SHE'LL TEAR YOU INTO PIECES IF YOU GO ANY FURTHER!
LET GO OF ME!
MIND IF I BORROW THIS, HUGO?
NO! JILL, CA VA PAS, HEIN? CA VA POINT! YOU--
NICE SEEING YOU AGAIN, SCUMBAG.
ABRACA-FUCKING-DABRA.
VOOOOSH
YOU OKAY?
Y--YEAH. THANK YOU.
THEN LET'S KEEP MOVING. I THINK I GET THIS NOW.
THE TRICK IS, YOU BELIEVE IN EVERYTHING OR NOTHING.
IT WORKS EITHER WAY.

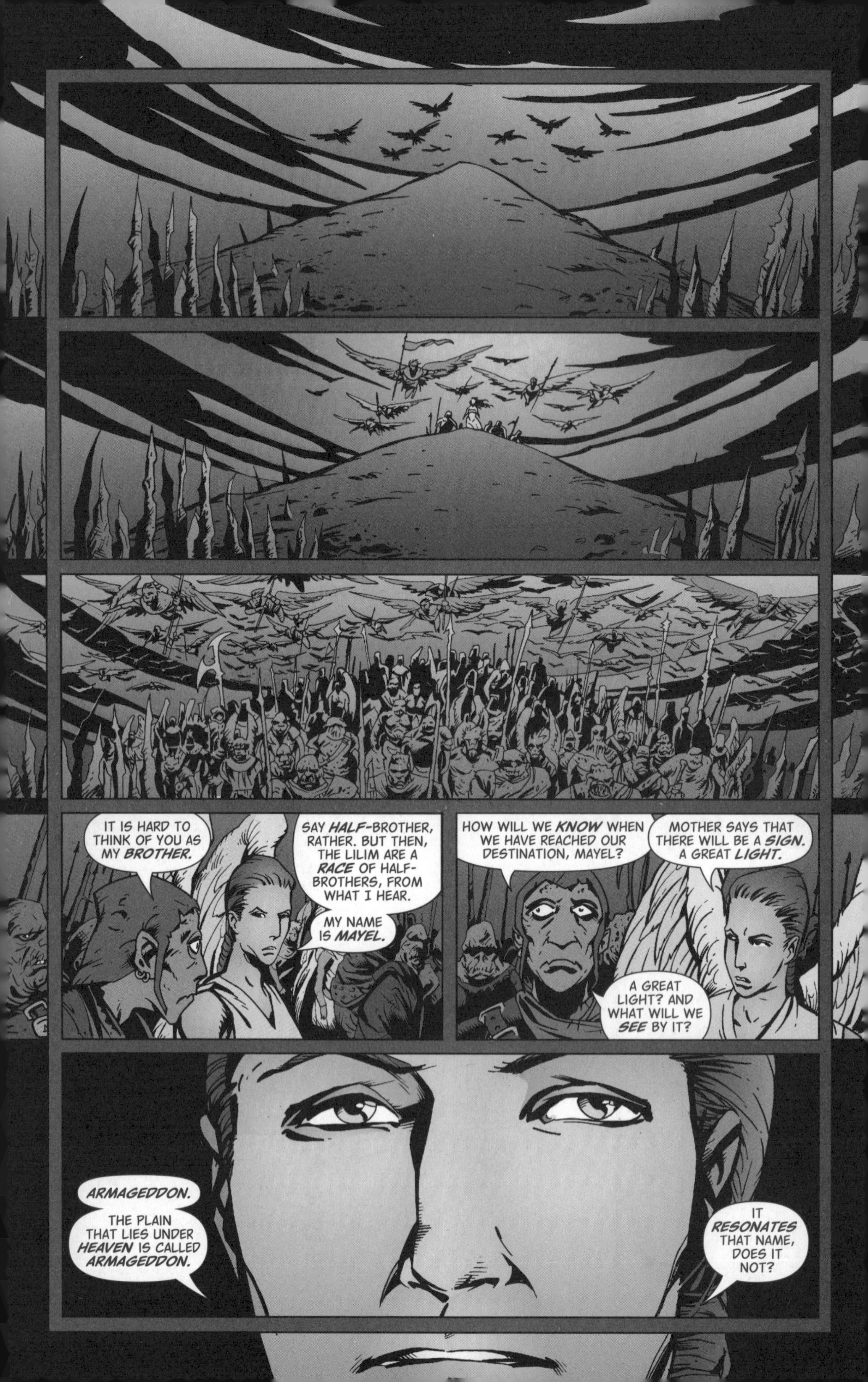

IT IS HARD TO THINK OF YOU AS MY BROTHER.
SAY HALF-BROTHER, RATHER. BUT THEN, THE LILIM ARE A RACE OF HALF-BROTHERS, FROM WHAT I HEAR.
MY NAME IS MAYEL.
HOW WILL WE KNOW WHEN WE HAVE REACHED OUR DESTINATION, MAYEL?
MOTHER SAYS THAT THERE WILL BE A SIGN. A GREAT LIGHT.
A GREAT LIGHT? AND WHAT WILL WE SEE BY IT?
ARMAGEDDON.
THE PLAIN THAT LIES UNDER HEAVEN IS CALLED ARMAGEDDON.
IT RESONATES THAT NAME, DOES IT NOT?

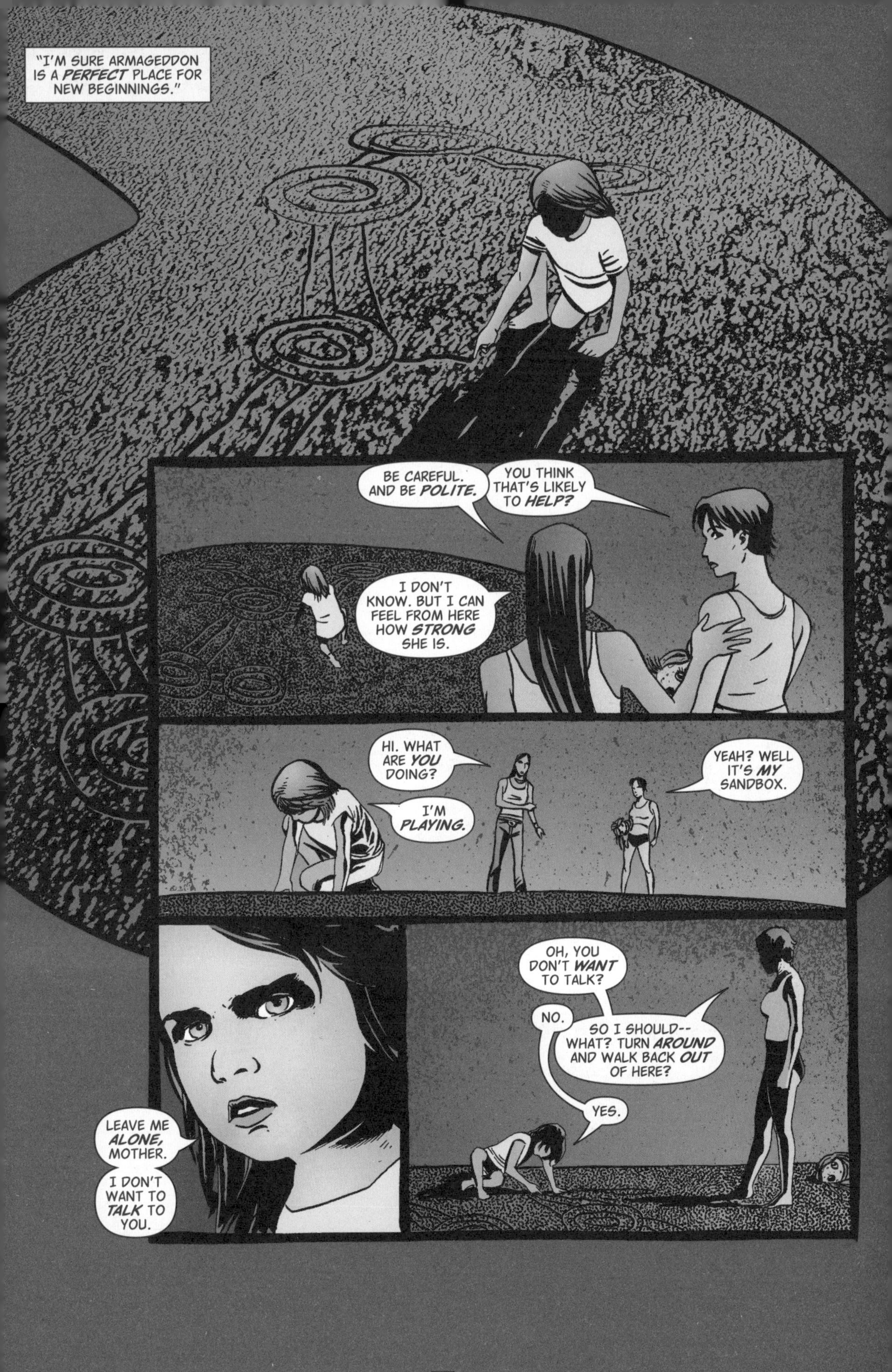
"I'M SURE ARMAGEDDON IS A PERFECT PLACE FOR NEW BEGINNINGS."
BE CAREFUL. AND BE POLITE.
YOU THINK THAT'S LIKELY TO HELP?
I DON'T KNOW. BUT I CAN FEEL FROM HERE HOW STRONG SHE IS.
HI. WHAT ARE YOU DOING?
I'M PLAYING.
YEAH? WELL IT'S MY SANDBOX.
LEAVE ME ALONE, MOTHER.
I DON'T WANT TO TALK TO YOU.
OH, YOU DON'T WANT TO TALK?
NO.
SO I SHOULD-- WHAT? TURN AROUND AND WALK BACK OUT OF HERE?
YES.

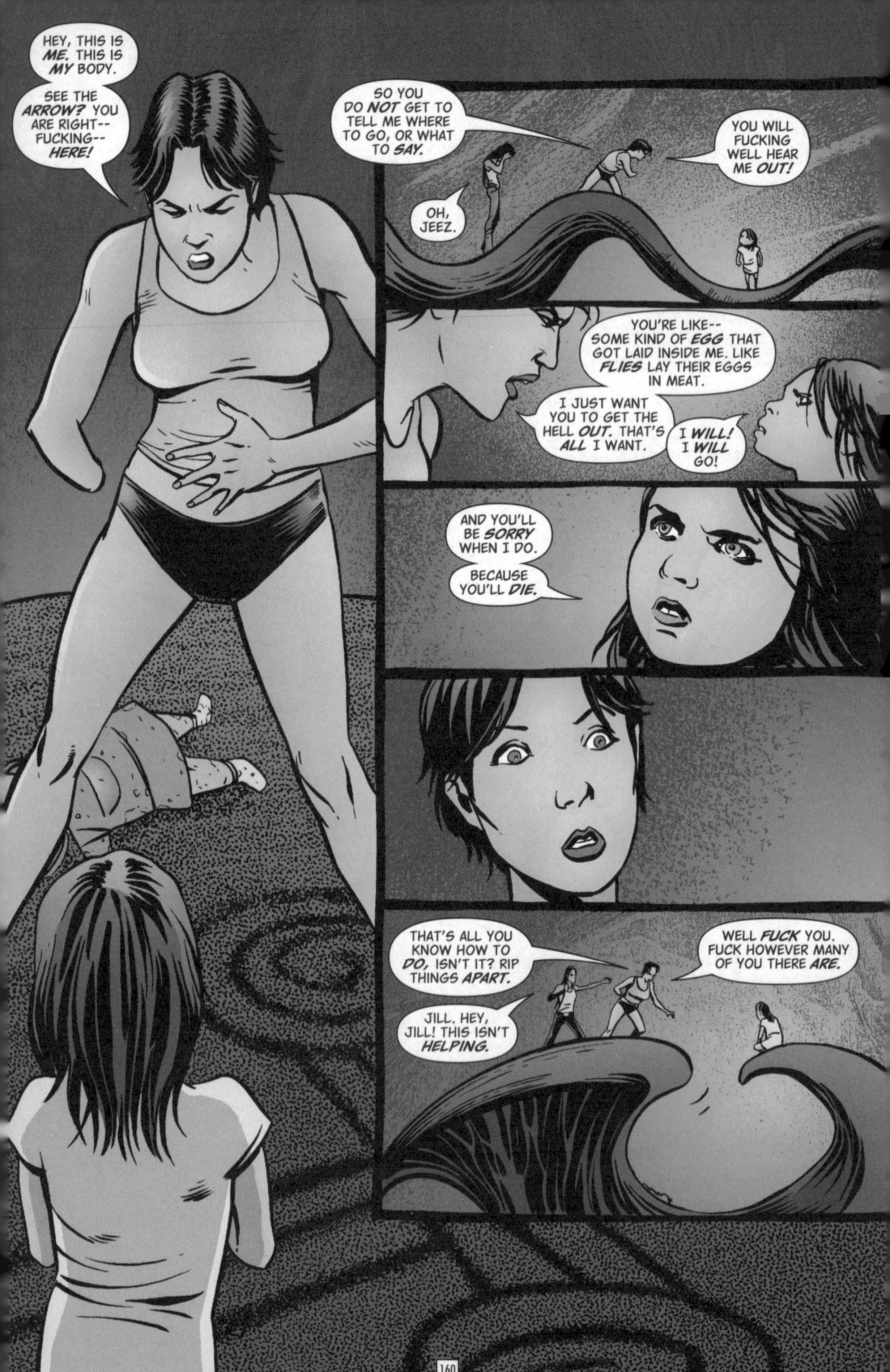
HEY, THIS IS *ME*. THIS IS *MY* BODY.
SEE THE *ARROW?* YOU ARE RIGHT-- FUCKING-- *HERE!*
SO YOU DO *NOT* GET TO TELL ME WHERE TO GO, OR WHAT TO *SAY*.
YOU WILL FUCKING WELL HEAR ME *OUT!*
OH, JEEZ.
YOU'RE LIKE-- SOME KIND OF *EGG* THAT GOT LAID INSIDE ME. LIKE *FLIES* LAY THEIR EGGS IN MEAT.
I JUST WANT YOU TO GET THE HELL *OUT*. THAT'S *ALL* I WANT.
I *WILL!* I *WILL* GO!
AND YOU'LL BE *SORRY* WHEN I DO.
BECAUSE YOU'LL *DIE*.
THAT'S ALL YOU KNOW HOW TO *DO*, ISN'T IT? RIP THINGS *APART*.
WELL *FUCK* YOU. FUCK HOWEVER MANY OF YOU THERE *ARE*.
JILL. HEY, JILL! THIS ISN'T *HELPING*.

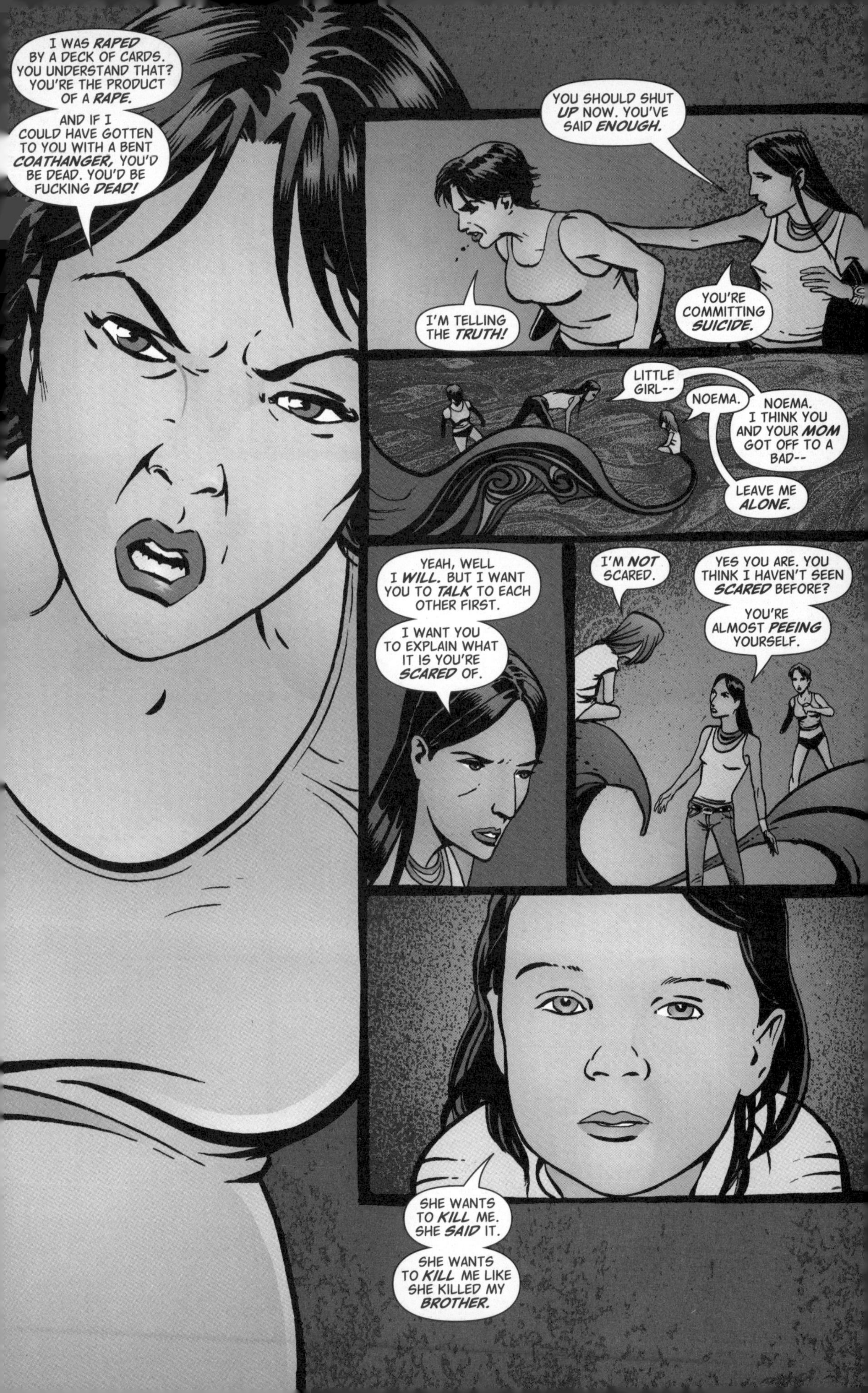
I WAS RAPED BY A DECK OF CARDS. YOU UNDERSTAND THAT? YOU'RE THE PRODUCT OF A RAPE.
AND IF I COULD HAVE GOTTEN TO YOU WITH A BENT COATHANGER, YOU'D BE DEAD. YOU'D BE FUCKING DEAD!
YOU SHOULD SHUT UP NOW. YOU'VE SAID ENOUGH.
I'M TELLING THE TRUTH!
YOU'RE COMMITTING SUICIDE.
LITTLE GIRL--
NOEMA.
NOEMA. I THINK YOU AND YOUR MOM GOT OFF TO A BAD--
LEAVE ME ALONE.
YEAH, WELL I WILL. BUT I WANT YOU TO TALK TO EACH OTHER FIRST.
I WANT YOU TO EXPLAIN WHAT IT IS YOU'RE SCARED OF.
I'M NOT SCARED.
YES YOU ARE. YOU THINK I HAVEN'T SEEN SCARED BEFORE?
YOU'RE ALMOST PEEING YOURSELF.
SHE WANTS TO KILL ME. SHE SAID IT.
SHE WANTS TO KILL ME LIKE SHE KILLED MY BROTHER.

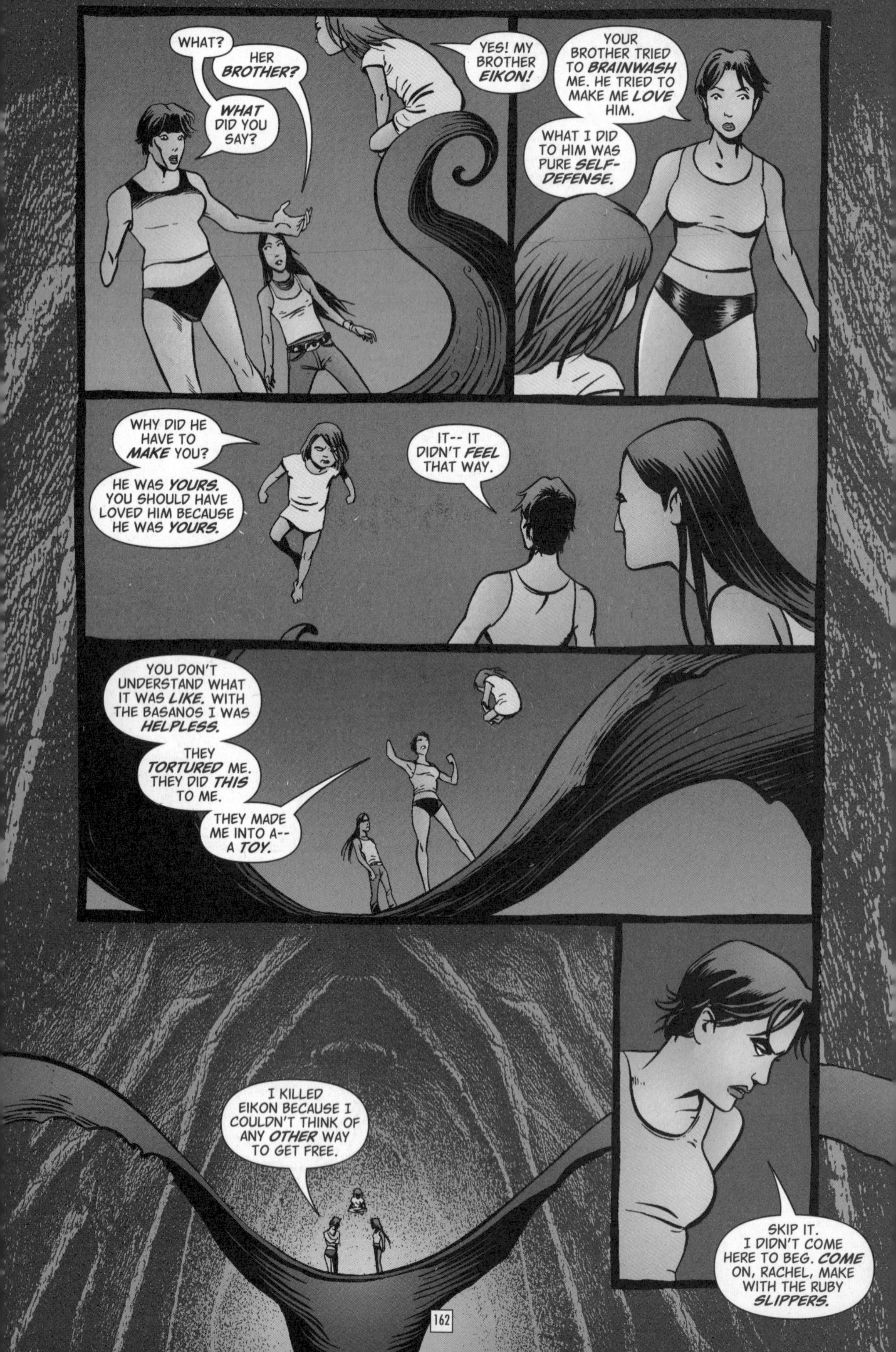
WHAT?
HER BROTHER?
WHAT DID YOU SAY?
YES! MY BROTHER EIKON!
YOUR BROTHER TRIED TO BRAINWASH ME. HE TRIED TO MAKE ME LOVE HIM.
WHAT I DID TO HIM WAS PURE SELF-DEFENSE.
WHY DID HE HAVE TO MAKE YOU?
HE WAS YOURS. YOU SHOULD HAVE LOVED HIM BECAUSE HE WAS YOURS.
IT-- IT DIDN'T FEEL THAT WAY.
YOU DON'T UNDERSTAND WHAT IT WAS LIKE. WITH THE BASANOS I WAS HELPLESS.
THEY TORTURED ME. THEY DID THIS TO ME.
THEY MADE ME INTO A-- A TOY.
I KILLED EIKON BECAUSE I COULDN'T THINK OF ANY OTHER WAY TO GET FREE.
SKIP IT. I DIDN'T COME HERE TO BEG. COME ON, RACHEL, MAKE WITH THE RUBY SLIPPERS.

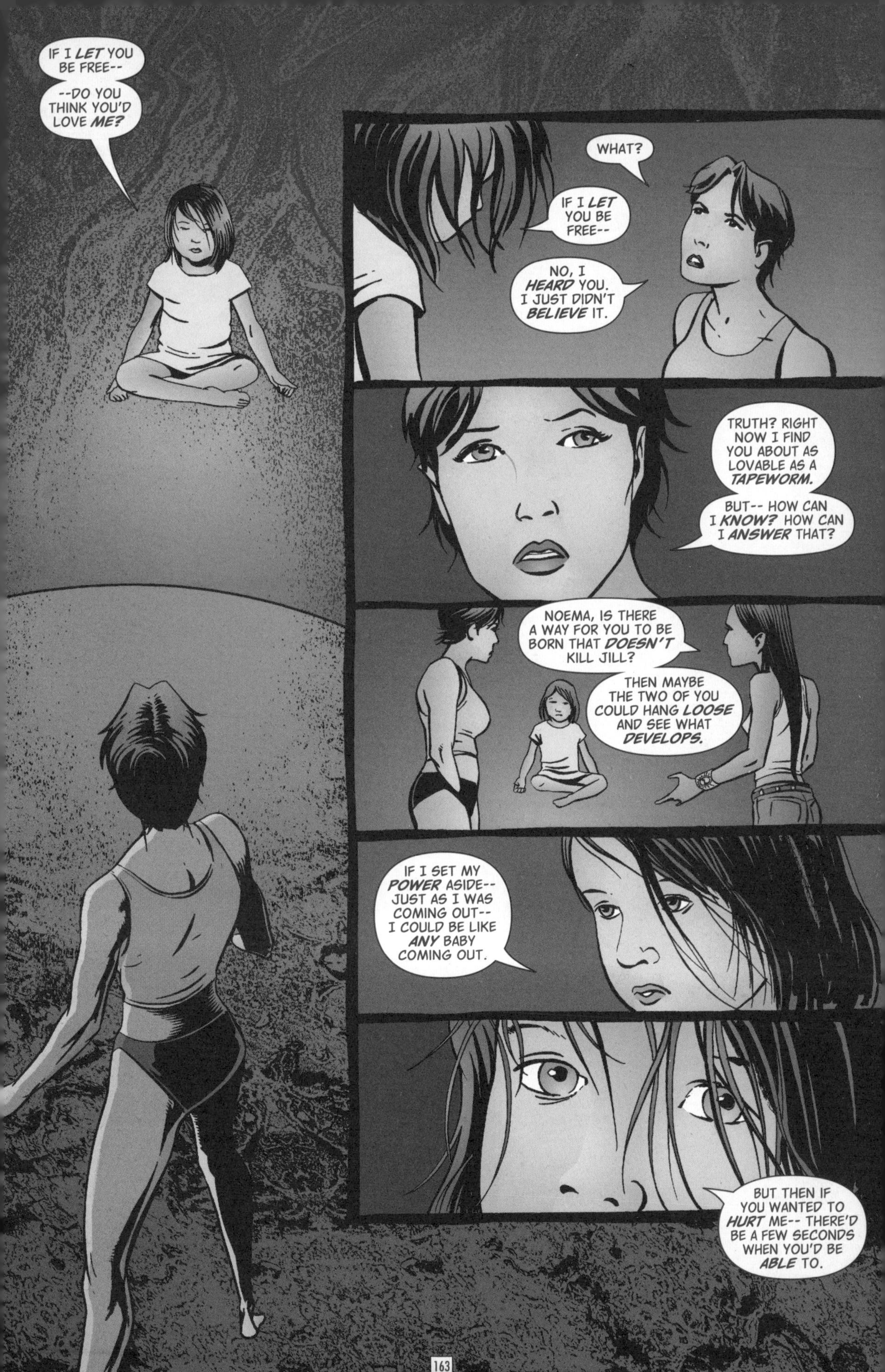
IF I LET YOU BE FREE--
--DO YOU THINK YOU'D LOVE ME?
WHAT?
IF I LET YOU BE FREE--
NO, I HEARD YOU. I JUST DIDN'T BELIEVE IT.
TRUTH? RIGHT NOW I FIND YOU ABOUT AS LOVABLE AS A TAPEWORM.
BUT-- HOW CAN I KNOW? HOW CAN I ANSWER THAT?
NOEMA, IS THERE A WAY FOR YOU TO BE BORN THAT DOESN'T KILL JILL?
THEN MAYBE THE TWO OF YOU COULD HANG LOOSE AND SEE WHAT DEVELOPS.
IF I SET MY POWER ASIDE-- JUST AS I WAS COMING OUT-- I COULD BE LIKE ANY BABY COMING OUT.
BUT THEN IF YOU WANTED TO HURT ME-- THERE'D BE A FEW SECONDS WHEN YOU'D BE ABLE TO.

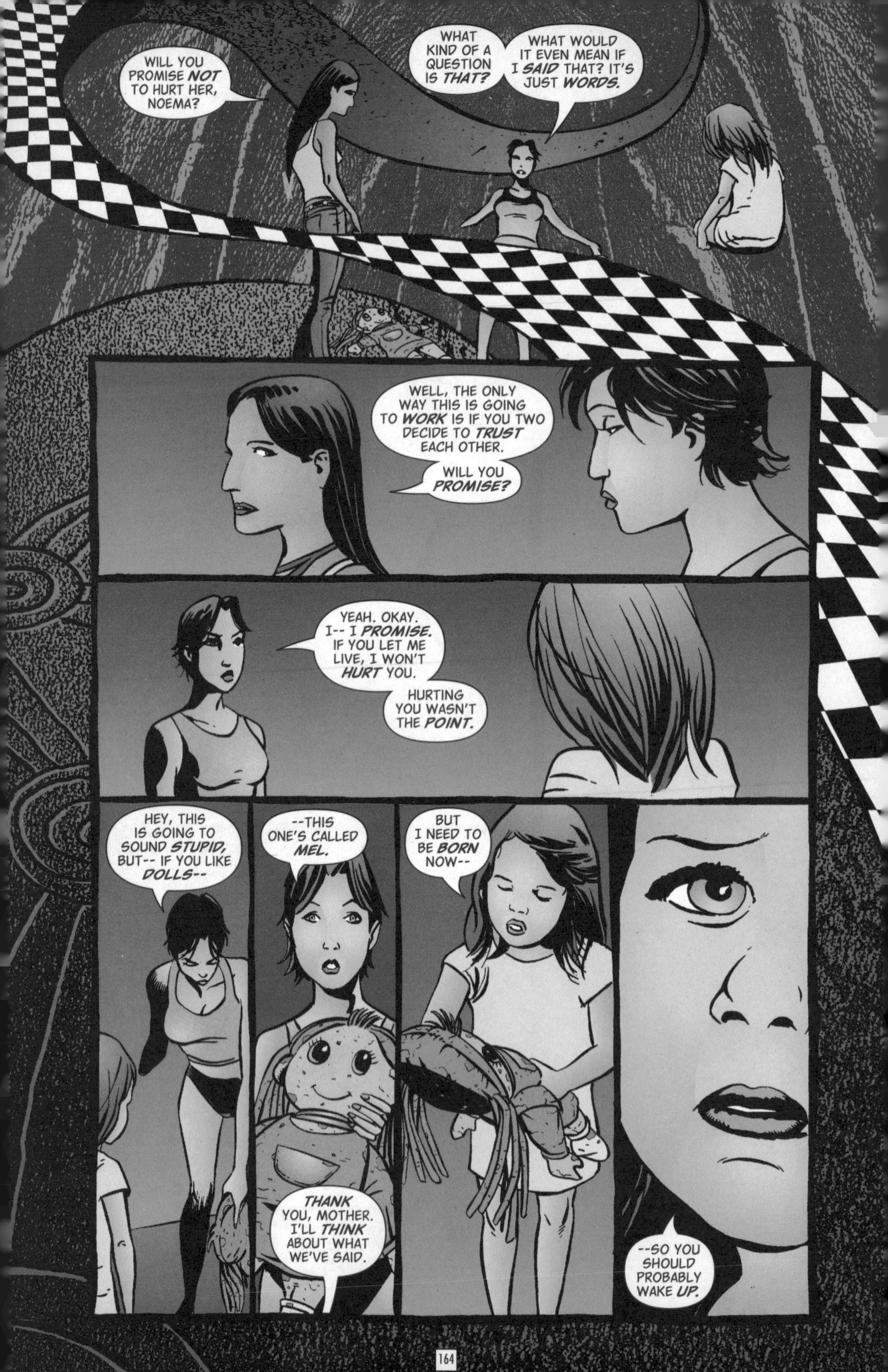

WILL YOU PROMISE NOT TO HURT HER, NOEMA?
WHAT KIND OF A QUESTION IS THAT?
WHAT WOULD IT EVEN MEAN IF I SAID THAT? IT'S JUST WORDS.
WELL, THE ONLY WAY THIS IS GOING TO WORK IS IF YOU TWO DECIDE TO TRUST EACH OTHER.
WILL YOU PROMISE?
YEAH. OKAY. I-- I PROMISE. IF YOU LET ME LIVE, I WON'T HURT YOU.
HURTING YOU WASN'T THE POINT.
HEY, THIS IS GOING TO SOUND STUPID, BUT-- IF YOU LIKE DOLLS--
--THIS ONE'S CALLED MEL.
THANK YOU, MOTHER. I'LL THINK ABOUT WHAT WE'VE SAID.
BUT I NEED TO BE BORN NOW--
--SO YOU SHOULD PROBABLY WAKE UP.

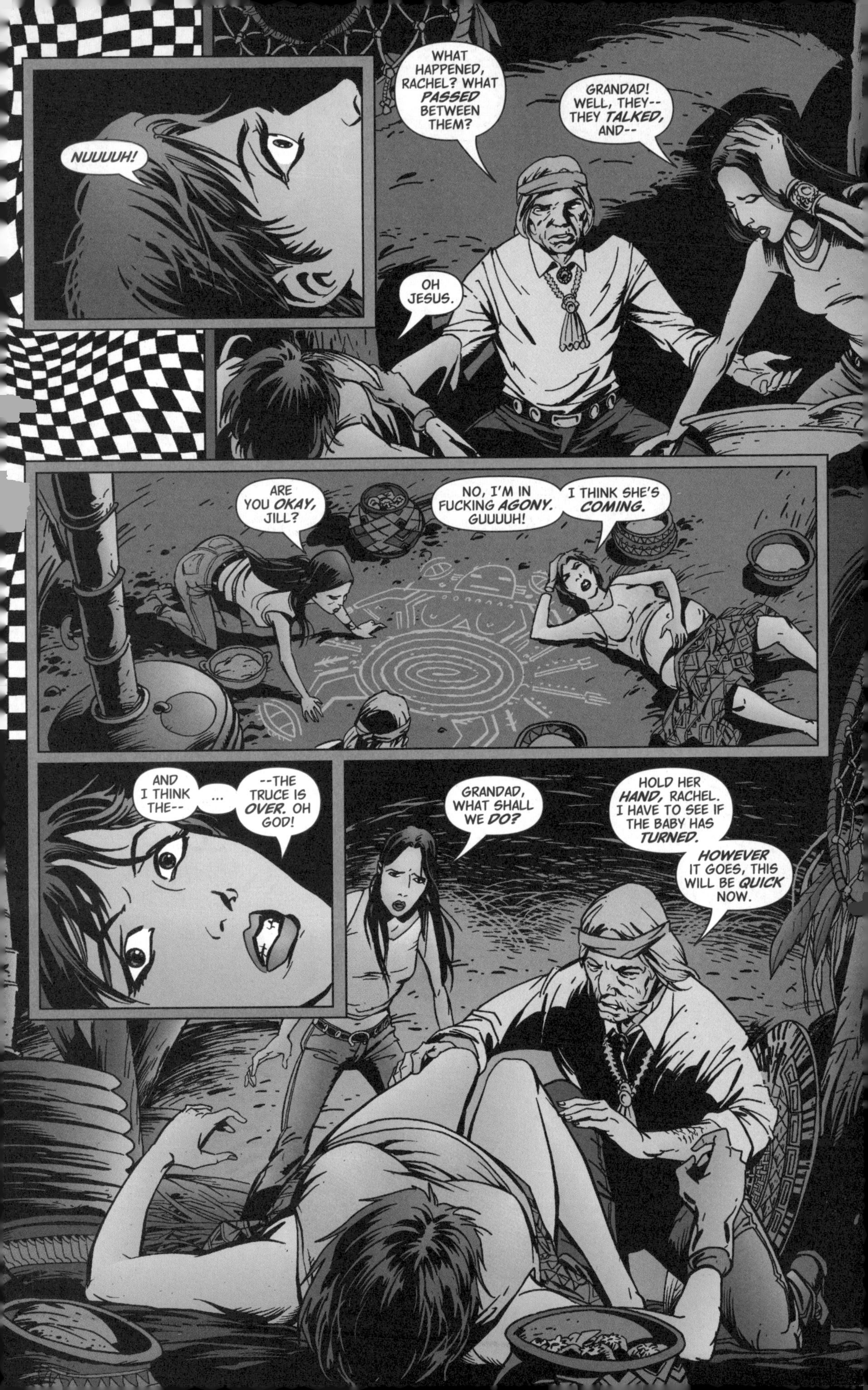
NUUUUH!
WHAT HAPPENED, RACHEL? WHAT PASSED BETWEEN THEM?
GRANDAD! WELL, THEY-- THEY TALKED, AND--
OH JESUS.
ARE YOU OKAY, JILL?
NO, I'M IN FUCKING AGONY. GUUUUH!
I THINK SHE'S COMING.
AND I THINK THE--
...
--THE TRUCE IS OVER. OH GOD!
GRANDAD, WHAT SHALL WE DO?
HOLD HER HAND, RACHEL. I HAVE TO SEE IF THE BABY HAS TURNED.
HOWEVER IT GOES, THIS WILL BE QUICK NOW.

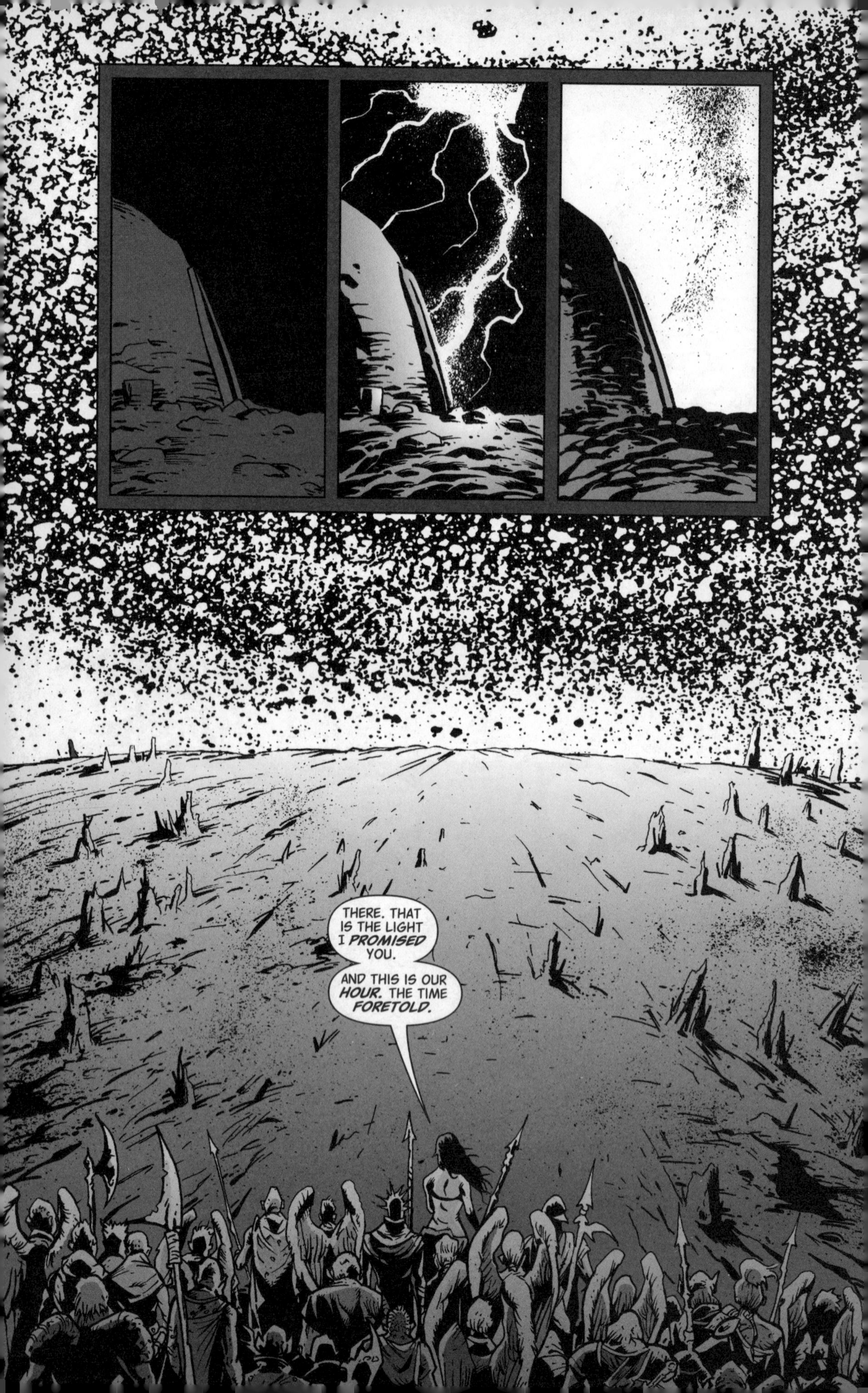
THERE. THAT IS THE LIGHT I *PROMISED* YOU.
AND THIS IS OUR *HOUR*. THE TIME *FORETOLD*.

WALKING OUT OF HELL (AND OUT OF THE PAGES OF **THE SANDMAN**), AN AMBITIOUS LUCIFER MORNINGSTAR CREATES A NEW COSMOS MODELLED AFTER HIS OWN IMAGE IN THESE COLLECTIONS FROM WRITER MIKE CAREY AND VERTIGO:

VOLUME 1: DEVIL IN THE GATEWAY

ALSO AVAILABLE:
VOL. 2: CHILDREN AND MONSTERS
VOL. 3: A DALLIANCE WITH THE DAMNED
VOL. 4: THE DIVINE COMEDY
VOL. 5: INFERNO
VOL. 6: MANSIONS OF THE SILENCE
VOL. 7: EXODUS
VOL. 8: THE WOLF BENEATH THE TREE
VOL. 9: CRUX

"THE BEST FANTASY COMIC AROUND."
— *COMICS INTERNATIONAL*

"AN ORIGINAL TAKE ON THE FORCES OF GOOD, EVIL AND BEYOND EVIL."
— *PUBLISHERS WEEKLY*

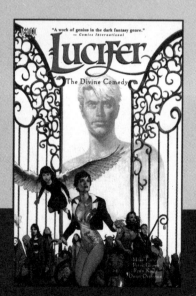

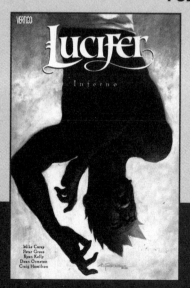

ALL TITLES ARE SUGGESTED FOR MATURE READERS.

SEARCH THE GRAPHIC NOVELS SECTION OF

www.VERTIGOCOMICS.com

FOR ART AND INFORMATION ON ALL OF OUR BOOKS!

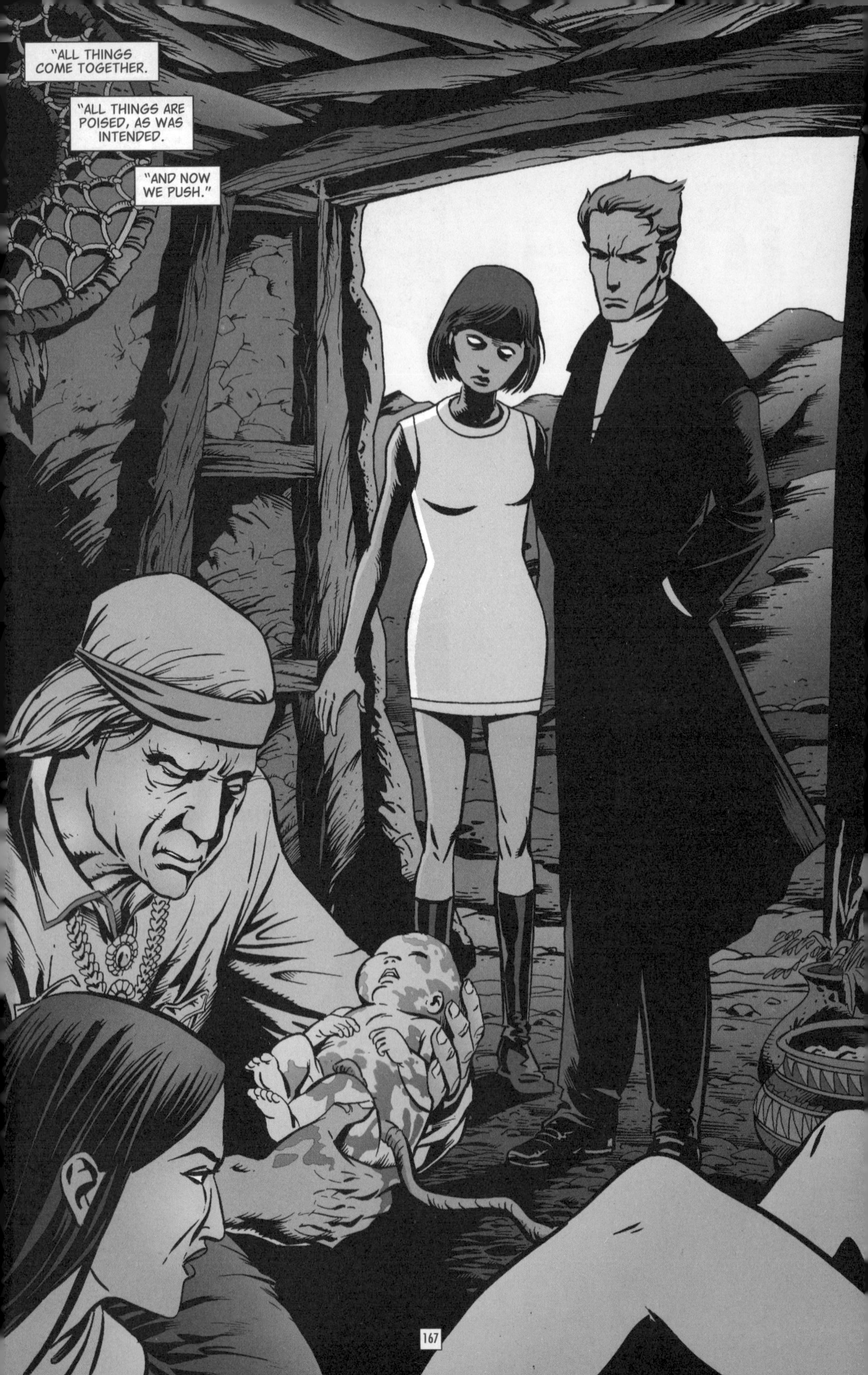
"ALL THINGS COME TOGETHER.
"ALL THINGS ARE POISED, AS WAS INTENDED.
"AND NOW WE PUSH."